POLICING and POLITICS in LATIN AMERICA

POLICING and POLITICS in LATIN AMERICA

When Law Enforcement Breaks the Law

Diego Esparza

LYNNE
RIENNER
PUBLISHERS

BOULDER
LONDON

Published in the United States of America in 2022 by
Lynne Rienner Publishers, Inc.
1800 30th Street, Suite 314, Boulder, Colorado 80301
www.rienner.com

and in the United Kingdom by
Lynne Rienner Publishers, Inc.
Gray's Inn House, 127 Clerkenwell Road, London EC1 5DB
www.eurospanbookstore.com/rienner

Library of Congress Cataloging-in-Publication Data
Names: Esparza, Diego, author.
Title: Policing and politics in Latin America : when law enforcement breaks
    the law / by Diego Esparza.
Description: Boulder, Colorado : Lynne Rienner Publishers, Inc., [2022] |
    Includes bibliographical references and index. | Summary: "Challenging
    fundamental assumptions about the virtues of local control, considers
    why some Latin American countries' police forces are more corrupt than
    others—and what policy initiatives can turn an abusive police force into
    one that works for its citizens" —Provided by publisher.
Identifiers: LCCN 2022004051 (print) | LCCN 2022004052 (ebook) | ISBN
    9781955055505 (hardback ; alk. paper) | ISBN 9781955055628 (ebook)
Subjects: LCSH: Police—Latin America. | Police misconduct—Latin America.
    | Police corruption—Latin America. | Latin America—Politics and
    government—1980-
Classification: LCC HV8160.5.A2 E87 2022 (print) | LCC HV8160.5.A2
    (ebook) | DDC 363.2098—dc23/eng/20220329
LC record available at https://lccn.loc.gov/2022004051
LC ebook record available at https://lccn.loc.gov/2022004052

British Cataloguing in Publication Data
A Cataloguing in Publication record for this book
is available from the British Library.

Printed and bound in the United States of America

5 4 3 2 1

Contents

Tables and Figures

Tables

Figures

Acknowledgments

Several people helped with the creation of this book. I am indebted to my academic training at the University of California Riverside. My professors there, including Ben Bishin, Marissa Brookes, Martin Johnson, Yuhki Tajima, and Will Barndt, made me the scholar I am today. I am especially appreciative of my mentor David Pion-Berlin, one of the most brilliant minds in the field and a great friend. Maiah Jaskoski and Harold Trinkunas played a significant role as outside mentors, and they merit a standing ovation for their willingness to always help others. I acknowledge the various friends who supported me while I wrote the book: Dino Bozonelos, Sean Brown, Steven Cauchon, James Cemo, Allan Colbern, Leslie Cox, Cale Crammer, Andrew Flores, Collin Grimes, Masa Omae, Kevin Sitz, Carrie Skulley, Antonio Ugues, and Tommy Wong. I could not have completed this work without the friendship of Nicholas Roy and Kevin Nasseri. I extend my gratitude to my colleagues at the University of North Texas, who helped me navigate the book publication process: Matthew Eshbaugh-Soha, Jim Meernik, Valerie Martinez-Ebers, Lee Walker, Jackie Walker, and John Ishiyama. I acknowledge Lynne Rienner, who is a fantastic publisher. She and her staff have greatly influenced the shape of the book for the better. Furthermore, Lynne has provided me with the best experience with a press yet. I am proud to work with her. Allie Schellong managed the production process, and Christina Palaia provided a thorough copyedit that only strengthened the book; I appreciate their help.

This book was made possible by funding from the Institute on Global Conflict and Cooperation at the University of California San Diego through the Herbert K. York Fellowship conferral. The Creative and Research Enhancement Activity Time for Engagement (CREATE) program at the University of North Texas allowed me to spend time working on book revisions, submission, and editing. My work in Chile greatly benefited from the support of the Instituto Nacional de Asuntos Públicos de la Universidad de Chile and Jaime Baeza. Furthermore, Marcos Robledo and Ale Mohor were critical in helping me to gain access to various elite interviews. In Colombia, Estella Baracaldo, Yed Milton López, Yesenia Mahecha, and Juan Aparicio provided interviews, support, and connections to many high-level contacts. I would be remiss if I did not acknowledge the wonderful García and Tamayo families that helped me with my research in Medellín. In Mexico, Georgina Rojas, David Crow, Juan Salgado, Carlos Flores, Ernesto López-Portillo Vargas, and María Eugenia Suárez de Garay were instrumental in shaping my understanding of the Mexican case.

I am grateful to my family. I honor my parents, Altagracia and Salvador, who brought me into this world. I am especially appreciative of my sister Fabiola, who has been my biggest supporter. She housed, fed, comforted, and prayed for me when I needed someone's help. I am proud to follow in your footsteps. Esperanza and Luisa, you have been great friends to me, and I will never forget all the hugs, phone calls, and cherished memories we have formed together. I am grateful to the rest of my siblings for wonderful experiences that are too abundant to mention but are nevertheless greatly appreciated. Thank you Adan, Eva, and Benito. To my wife, Andrea, you are my best friend. We have made a household full of support, love, laughter, fun, and comfort together. I can't wait for the many years to come. I love you. Lastly, we have not picked your name yet, and I haven't officially met you, but to our growing baby, I dedicate this book to you.

1

The Problem of
Police Misconduct

> *Eventually, our cities may find it necessary to reorganize their police on
> the pattern of the state police. But this will never happen while political
> organizations retain the slightest power to reward or to punish.*
> —John Steinbeck, *Travels with Charley* (1962)

Democracy and security are intimately linked. As Guillermo O'Donnell
has argued: "The rule of law is among the essential pillars upon which any
high-quality democracy rests" (O'Donnell 2004). This implies that democracy can only be as healthy as its ability to provide security. At the same
time, democratic states cannot cross into the realm of authoritarianism in
their quest for security, lest authoritarianism undermine the civil rights and
liberties that make popular rule possible (Frühling, Tulchin, and Golding
2003). This delicate balancing act is proving to be a challenge for developing democracies transitioning from authoritarian rule. A central challenge for
these democracies is that the law enforcement institutions that are supposed
to address insecurity are instead a significant source of insecurity.

When police engage in misconduct, they inspire mistrust among citizens,
and this in turn has a wide-ranging impact on trust in political institutions
(Theobald and Haider-Markel 2009; Kaariainen 2007; Finocchiaro Castro
and Guccio 2020; Tankebe 2013; Tyler and Huo 2002; Tyler 2003; Buvinic,
Morrison, and Shifter 1999). Several scholars have noted that trust in local
government and trust in police are intimately linked (Sun, Hu, and Wu 2012;
Silva et al. 2020; Silva and Esparza 2021; Liebertz 2020). In democratic societies, experiences with police abuse decrease feelings of political efficacy and
change voting behavior (Kirk and Matsuda 2011). The crux of this problem

1

often rests with the draconian practices that police import into a present democracy from their own authoritarian past. As such, the problem of reducing police misconduct stands squarely in the center of the quest for democracy itself (Berkley 1969; Wiatrowski and Goldstone 2010). For Gerber and Mendelson (2008; 1), misconduct exists where police are "devoted to the personal enrichment and self-preservation of the police themselves." Further, misconduct need not be for strictly personal gain but can also be for the advancement of law enforcement's organizational interests. However, the key differentiating characteristic of misconduct is that it is not just for personal or organizational gain but also to the detriment of the public.

Given the important role of police misconduct in shaping the experience and practice of democracy, I decided to focus my energy on advancing our understanding of when and why police break the law for personal gain. From my analysis, I have derived five key insights about police misconduct. First, centralizing control reduces the frequency of aggregate misconduct because it reduces local political influence. Second, professionalization of police further reduces the likelihood of police abuse of power because it changes the incentive structure for individual officers. Third, the institutionalization of professionalism across a nation's police system often requires some degree of centralization, and in this sense, centralization and professionalization work together to lower police misconduct. Fourth, militarization of police can act as a catalyst for centralization and professionalization. Fifth, in terms of regime types, during periods of authoritarianism or when authoritarian personalities are in control of a democracy, there is an increased likelihood of police misconduct irrespective of police structure or professionalization. Furthermore, having a consolidated democracy does not necessarily reduce misconduct, although it opens the door for mechanisms of reducing police abuse not present in authoritarian periods.

These insights emerged from extensive fieldwork I conducted in multiple locations in Latin America. My research focuses specifically on uniformed preventative police services that patrol the streets providing emergency services or stopping crimes in progress. I do not focus on investigative police forces, who do not wear uniforms and who focus on gathering evidence for the purposes of indicting and convicting criminals.

The next section discusses the major theoretical findings in this book. I then explain why comparing Chile, Colombia, and Mexico makes sense for understanding police misconduct, and I close this chapter with a thorough road map of subsequent chapters.

Can Police Centralization Reduce Misconduct?

Police institutions can be differentiated by the degree to which local (city) authorities have control over police training, promotion, deployment, salary, and benefits. Fully decentralized police bureaucracies emphasize local control by actors such as mayors, city councils, and city managers, who control all aspects of policing. Police are more centralized but still locally based when county services control policing for multiple cities (as in the United States). Additionally, there are semicentralized police systems that are controlled by subnational entities, such as state/provincial/lander-level entities that are higher order than counties or cities. Here, governors or state ministers control the police, and local actors such as mayors do not (as in Canada, Germany, Argentina, and Brazil).

Conversely, national/centralized police come in two organizational varieties. First, there are police institutions with a single chain of command for enforcing the law and maintaining order throughout an entire country. This type of police is fully centralized because it falls under the control of the national executive through a cabinet ministry, such as a minister of interior, a secretary of defense, or a minister of public security. Although this type of police can cooperate and coordinate with local political leaders, the hierarchical structure places ultimate control and responsibility in the hands of a national entity (as in El Salvador or Sweden). Second, there are police institutions with an autonomous centralized body (such as a national commission) that establishes criteria for benefits, recruitment, training, and oversight of police but devolves powers to local political leaders to fulfill these standards. The devolution of power is neither permanent nor guaranteed, and it can always be withdrawn by the national commission. In these systems, the national commission manages police oversight, but there is some degree of local control (as in the UK and Japan). I consider both to be fully centralized systems because full control is not placed in the hands of local authorities but in some form of subnational or national institution.

The question of whether to centralize or decentralize police touches the core of an ongoing policy debate in Latin America: the neoliberalization of public services. The neoliberal era in Latin America that started in the 1980s and continued through the early 2000s brought a wave of decentralization in the form of giving political, fiscal, and administrative responsibilities to local authorities at the city or provincial level (Montero and Samuels 2004; Tiebout 1956; Oates 2011). Furthermore, many national leaders were happy to shift the economic and legal burdens of public administration to lower levels of government. However, in some cases, the movement toward decentralization resulted in less-effective and more-expensive outcomes. The debate over the process of decentralization continues to drive scholarship in the developing world and is at the center of this analysis.

The push toward decentralizing police is based on three logics: democratic accountability, identifiability, and community ownership. First, some scholars argue that police misconduct arises out of a lack of oversight from democratically elected officials (Greene and Mastrofski 1988; Skolnick and Bayley 1988). As Daniel Sabet (2010) notes, "Executive appointment of police chiefs should make the police more accountable to citizens, and executive discretion should facilitate rapid reform" (266). As Grichawat Lowatcharin and Judith I. Stallmann (2019) highlight, because "local governments are closer to local citizens and possess more information about citizen demands and preferences than higher levels of government, decentralized service provision will likely more closely reflect local preferences, increasing police accountability" (197). Thus, police accountability is augmented if the police service itself is controlled by locally elected officials.

Second, to hold someone accountable, you must be able to identify them (Punch 1989). When police are decentralized, they are often stationed within the city where they live. Hence, they are more easily identified and punished by a society that knows who the perpetrators are. Unlike more centralized police services, local officers do not enjoy the same degree of anonymity. It could be argued that a police officer in a centralized system may engage in abusive activity and be transferred out of the region before he can be prosecuted. Meanwhile, a local police officer cannot be assigned out and will face the consequences dispensed by peers in the community. Further, when misconduct occurs, it is much easier to identify the relevant bodies in charge of police oversight at the local level, such as police chiefs, rather than to deal with a vast bureaucracy located in a faraway capital or major city.

Third, decentralization facilitates stronger community-police relations, whereby police take ownership of their local community. The proximity of decentralized police implies that they have developed deep roots in the community and are therefore more accountable and less likely to engage in misconduct (Ligthart and van Oudheusden 2015; Pollitt 2005). Decentralization allows for a greater emphasis on the "plurality of police functions rather than a single-minded focus on crime control; its prioritized community input and involvement over expertise and technical analysis; locally tailored rather than globally rationalized solutions" (Sklansky 2013, 2). These social interactions integrate police in their local societies, and as such police will hold themselves accountable as protectors of the people they have come to know and accept as their neighbors (Maguire 2003; Skogan 2006; Glebeek 2009).

My analysis is critical of this neoliberal vision of decentralized policing. I do not stand alone in this assessment (Berkley 1970; Soares and Naritomi 2007; De la Torre 2008; Eaton 2008; Pion-Berlin 2010; Pion-Berlin and Trinkunas 2011). For instance, Lawrence W. Sherman (1978, 32) asserts that decentralization is a problem because it facilitates capture by political interest, and this "is the leading explanation of why police" engage in misconduct. Angélica Durán-Martínez (2015) has argued in a similar vein that the variation in levels of violence in cities in Colombia and Mexico can be linked to the level of fragmentation of the security apparatus. The more fragmented the security apparatus, the higher the level of violence. However, the more cohesive the security apparatus, the less violence there is. Diego Esparza and Antonio Ugues (2020) found empirical evidence that national police are trusted at a higher level than local police in Mexico. Furthermore, Diego Esparza and Thomas C. Bruneau (2019) highlight that centralized police are better suited to enhancing national security interests than local ones.

Building on this scholarship, I find that centralization is vital to reducing misconduct because it redefines the relationship between local political actors and the police in several ways. For starters, there is a dangerous tendency for local political actors to utilize the police as a personal political tool. This ends up politicizing the police force. In such a world, police (1) are asked to attack opposition party candidates; (2) are hired on the basis of loyalty, not qualifications; and (3) have political protection, which enables them to engage in nefarious activities. Furthermore, because policing at the local level is often paid for by local funds, there is a high degree of variation in the quality of policing across regions: more impoverished areas cannot afford to train and pay police well, whereas rich areas end up with better police. In this book, centralization is a force that destroys this patrimonial use of police by politicians. The destruction of this pattern alone opens the possibility of a less-malfeasant police by reducing the potential for their politicization (Agboga 2021). However, centralization alone is not sufficient for completely undoing police misconduct. The next section focuses on the second factor that reformers can focus on to reduce criminal policing—professionalization.

Does Professionalization Lower Misconduct?

In addition to centralization, police labor needs to institutionalize as a profession in order to change police misconduct. When I refer to the professionalization of police labor, I am referring to the formal and informal institutional codification of standards that differentiate rationalized from nonrationalized public service labor. The critical distinction is that an institutionally professionalized field of public labor "arises when any trade or occupation transforms itself through the development of formal qualification based upon education, apprenticeship, and examinations, the emergence of regulatory bodies with powers to admit and discipline members, and some degree of monopoly rights" (Bullock and Trombley 1999, 689).

I find that professionalization is the process by which a group of experts can insulate themselves from external political influence. In the same way, police professionalism also means insulation from patrimonial domination. Professionalization is a critical process that allows for the modernization of state institutions and removes patrimonial interests and

replaces them with rational-legal logic of behavior. By advancing professionalization, the lines between what is private and what is public become
more delineated and are better enforced. Three institutional policy areas
advance the professionalization of police: (1) welfare, (2) training, and (3)
oversight. Each of these policy areas has various institutional rules and
components that can be manipulated to decrease misconduct (Price 1979).

First, police welfare implies all the factors that provide police with a
standard of living, including remunerations, pension, and health insurance
(Arteaga Botello and Rivera 2002). Professional labor should be remuner-
ated with at least a middle-class wage, with opportunity for bonuses.
Another demarcation of a professionalized mode of labor is provision of a
pension, in which 75 to 100 percent of the salary is made available to those
with twenty-five to thirty years of service. In addition, this type of labor
should provide medical coverage for the officer and immediate family, life
insurance, education for children, fifteen to thirty days of paid vacation per
year, access to housing, and low-interest loans. In contrast, places that do
not treat police labor as a profession simply do not have the same welfare,
remuneration, and insurance benefits. Instead, these more fragile systems
provide only lower-class wages, less than 50 percent of final salary as a
pension, and no healthcare insurance. They also have limited life insurance
coverage, no child education benefits, limited paid vacation, and no access
to discounted vacation rentals, housing, or low-interest loans (National
Police of Colombia 2013c).

The next aspect of professionalizing labor has to do with recruitment
and training. Healthy development systems that aim to build a professional
police force must have high entrance standards that include completion of
high school education, physical fitness tests, high scores on standardized
tests, psychological tests, and thorough background checks of the applicant and family members. These recruitment standards help increase the
number of women in the police force and restrict entrance of individuals
with criminal connections, which taken together reduce police misconduct
(Riccucci et al. 2014; Barnes et al. 2016; Quah 2006; Sherman 1978;
Arrigo and Claussen 2003; Champion 2001; Sellbom, Fischler, and Ben-
Porath 2007; Jenkins 2021; Hassell 2016).

The basic training for a position in a professional field should consti-
tute nine months or more for enlisted-level ranks and three to four years for
commissioned officer ranks. The training itself ought to be physically and
mentally demanding and have reliable academic components. Conversely,
weak development regimes deemphasize professional labor models and
have few or nonexistent entrance standards for education, physical fitness,
and psychological exams. Nonprofessionalized police labor forces have low
education requirements of one to six years of education, and there are no
criminal background checks or committee interviews. The training is short,

from three to six months (less than three months for the enlisted level and less than one year for the officer track), is generally not physically challenging, and is mostly carried out as on-the-job training. Options for additional or continuing training are limited. (Haarr 2001; Eitle, D'Alessio, and Stolzenberg 2014; Getty, Worrall, and Morris 2016; Skogan, Van Craen, and Hennessy 2015; White and Escobar 2008; MacVean and Cox 2012; Hilal, Densley, and Zhao 2013).

Oversight mechanisms are the formal methods of monitoring, investigating, punishing, and prosecuting officers who deviate from institutional norms. Professionalization of labor requires a robust hierarchical system of control that emphasizes subordination to the commander's orders and disciplinary measures from command to enlisted ranks as per the law. This system includes a swift mechanism for the investigation of suspected criminal behavior and the removal of those who are found guilty. Professional labor is also under external oversight that ensures the necessary redundancy, such as a public prosecutor's office, a government accountability organization, or a citizen review board that has auditing power over the police (Prenzler and Ronken 2001). An external societal mechanism might include social movements, private sector activism, or the judicial system (Moncada 2009; González 2020; Peruzzotti and Smulovitz 2006). However, where police forces are not structured according to professional standards, weak oversight systems lack adequate control mechanisms—no external organizations of control exist that can investigate the police. Internal bodies may exist, such as penal police justice, but these interior groups cover both regulatory infractions and criminal behavior. This type of system has a weak emphasis on hierarchy and discipline, providing enlisted police officers with more autonomy in practice. Police forces that lack oversight also make it challenging for top-ranked officers to remove police on suspicion of criminal behavior. Weak oversight mechanisms lack internal investigation ability, lack discretionary powers, and have inadequate or nonexistent external control methods (Mawby and Wright 2012; Pogarsky and Piquero 2004; Prenzler and Ronken 2001).

Professionalism as I have sketched it out has had its share of detractors, especially in police scholarship focused on the United States (Sklansky 2011, 2013; Potts 1982). In the 1980s, community-oriented policing (COP) arose as a rejection of police professionalism that instead "prioritized community input and involvement over expertise and technical analysis" (Sklansky 2013, 2). Some scholars emphasize policing not as a profession but as an occupation that stresses apprenticeship, a generalist approach to policing, a lack of deference to authority, and oral tradition rather than written documentation (Crank 1990, 333). Furthermore, police labor models that deemphasize professionalism instead promote the idea that training should be "undertaken by experienced officers in a master/apprentice

arrangement" (Murray 2005, 352). Some scholars suggest that the consequences of treating policing more like a profession will be reduced accountability and reduced public trust (Bayley and Shearing 2000; Heslop 2011).
Other scholars have suggested that professionalization would reduce civic
engagement (Van de Ven 2007). According to Martha K. Huggins (1998),
"professionalism has been used to disguise police violence."

Given these detractors, why does professionalization matter? The
advancement of recruitment, training, welfare, and oversight matter because
they are the carrots and sticks that work together to shape behavior. Police
choose whether to engage in misconduct on the basis of the structure of
incentives. Like all rational actors, they must ask, "How do I benefit?"
"What is the likelihood that I will get caught?" "Will I even be punished?"
and "What will I lose if I am caught?" There is also the perverse possibility
that police are required to engage in misconduct through pressure or orders
from superiors or elected leaders. This is also a rational choice: "I do not
want to fleece citizens, but my commander/mayor forces me to do that. If I
do not do this, I will receive worse assignments or get fired." In short, police
agents are rational actors who choose, on the basis of incentive structures,
when to engage in misconduct (Becker 1968).

How does professionalization structure institutions differently to
change police behavior? Professionalization of a field of labor like policing
brings with it intense recruitment and training, robust benefits packages,
and efficient oversight mechanisms that work together to reduce the likelihood of corruption in a wholistic way. First, welfare benefits draw in more
and better candidates. Second, better candidates have fewer corrupt pro-
clivities at the individual level and are more amenable to the training they
receive. Third, higher remuneration and prestige make the potential loss of
the job more significant, because the standard of living will drop dramati-
cally for fired officers. This, in turn, provides the institution with a stronger
ability to meaningfully sanction and threaten officers who skirt the line
between legal and illegal activities.

To avoid confusion, I want to make clear that police misconduct is not
just unprofessional conduct but also a specific type of behavior that an
institutionally privileged person uses knowingly—and to the detriment of
their clients—for personal gain. Further, we must think of professionalization as an institutional process and misconduct as a behavioral process. In
short, professionalization is about changing the rules of the policing game
on the front end of the equation, whereas levels of misconduct are the
behaviors of players on the outcome end of the equation. Although rules
are intended to shape behavior, the rules of the game and player behavior
are not one and the same in a tautological sense. Thus, professionalizing
institutions is about the replacement of the old patrimonial game with the
new rational-legal game (Weber 2019). This is not to imply that because

officers are operating in a labor field that has been professionalized they will all act professionally. What it does imply is that officers have more to lose if they are caught, and they are more likely to be caught if they engage in misconduct, and these two factors shape the aggregate level of police abuse of power.

Linking Centralization and Professionalization

Centralized and decentralized police systems have different capabilities for professionalizing policing. The most basic problem is that decentralized policing systems must rely on their local governments for resources; wealthier locations can gather enough funds to provide excellent benefits and salaries to police, but smaller and poorer police forces cannot. In contrast, centralized police forces have more collective resources and financial leverage to provide such benefits as medical insurance, life insurance, and pensions to all police in a country. This ensures that police throughout a country, whether stationed in a poor town or a rich neighborhood, are provided with the resources they need to provide security equally throughout the nation.

Because of the various ways in which wealth is distributed, recruitment in decentralized police systems is more likely to rely on patronage or political clientelism rather than objective standards. Local systems usually draw recruits from within the community they serve, which means that recruits may have connections to local criminal actors. Further, some poor municipalities will rarely have the resources to conduct background checks on applicants, thus inviting in a criminal element. In contrast, national systems have more resources to establish and enforce strong recruitment standards. Centralized systems also recruit from a national application pool. Once trained, these officers are deployed not in their own communities but throughout the territory, which precludes the development of connections to criminal elements in localities.

Regarding personnel development in decentralized police systems, training is done on the job or in seasonal police academies. There are no nationwide training standards, and in many cases the police may not receive any training at all because of a locality's lack of resources. Conversely, centralized police have a unified system of academies or a central college to train all police agents under the same standards as prescribed by the current policy. Training for enlisted persons may vary from six months to a year, whereas training available for officer-level agents is more advanced and can extend from two to four years.

There is also a critical difference in oversight mechanisms between centralized and decentralized policing systems. In decentralized systems, the many smaller police institutions have fewer resources for establishing internal review offices, and when these departments do exist the internal review officers may have a more difficult time being objective because they likely know the officer under investigation. Additionally, decentralized systems tend to develop ad hoc committees to investigate alleged police misconduct rather than to hand cases over to a standing oversight body. Conversely, national police function as one large organization and therefore must develop institutions to coordinate activities and guarantee bureaucratic consistency. Administratively, centralized police systems rely on standard operating procedures that are codified in documents and published in training manuals (as the military does). A chain of command structure and oversight mechanisms ensure consistent behavior. In national policing systems, control mechanisms are developed to ensure that police do not waiver from the standards set forth by the force's top leadership. Oversight controls include a powerful office for internal affairs that can function objectively precisely because the size of the institution all but guarantees that internal affairs officers will not have personal relationships with those they investigate.

Considering these distinctions, I argue that locally controlled and weakly professionalized police forces create conditions for patrimonial logics of public service to arise. It is this patrimonialism that is the driving force of misconduct. Here public servants are allowed and encouraged to augment their wealth through the process of benefice. That is, rather than relying on salary as the basis of their income as public servants, these actors can augment their earnings through the abuse of their office. The cases I include demonstrate that a police system's move from a local and less-professional to a centralized and highly professional model undermines the patrimonialism that undergirds misconduct. I further develop the notion that professionalization is likely to arise when police are centralized rather than when they are decentralized. Bringing these notions together, for structural changes to have the maximum impact on misconduct, reformers ought to couple centralization *and* professionalization. Analysis shows that it is unlikely reformers can professionalize police without some degree of centralizing control at a national level. Table 1.1 illustrates how centralized and decentralized police systems vary in terms of welfare, personnel development, and oversight.

Police Militarization, Democracy, and Misconduct

Militarization of the police is viewed as increasing misconduct (Zaverucha 2000; Friesendorf and Krempel 2011; Hill and Beger 2009; Hill, Beger, and Zanetti 2007). Hugo Frühling, Joseph S. Tulchin, and Heather A. Golding contend that "militarization has unquestionably had an impact on the excessive use of force by the police, which in the case of Latin Amer-

Table 1.1   Comparing Welfare, Development, and Oversight

	Centralized Structure	Decentralized Structure
Welfare	Resources tied to national tax base	Resources tied to local tax base
	Higher salary	Lower salary
	Merit-based rewards	Spoils-based rewards
	Hearty pension plans	Thin pension plans
	Extensive perquisites	Limited perquisites
	National talent pool for recruitment	No rotation
Personnel development	National talent pool for recruitment	Local talent pool for recruitment
	National rotation	No rotation
	Objective standards of selection	Politicized officer selection
	Longer training periods	Short training periods
	Continual training	No continual training
	Meritocratic advancement	No meritocratic advancement
Oversight	National jurisdiction	Local jurisdiction
	National internal affairs department	Local internal affairs department
	Preventative investigation	Ad hoc investigation
	Vigorous prosecution	Weak prosecution

ica means a high number of citizen deaths, along with other human rights violations" (2003, 19). However, I found that police mimicry of military organizational structure can facilitate centralization and professionalization and is not necessarily antithetical to democratic governance. The institutional isomorphism of police as a more centralized and professional body akin to the military produced the desired outcome of less-malfeasant police. Outside the facts presented here, there are multiple paths to centralization and professionalization, and police militarization is but one. These findings reinforce the validity of arguments for police militarization as way of addressing threats from increasingly sophisticated criminal groups (Lutterbeck 2005; Beede 2008; Gobinet 2008).

The final key finding in this book focuses on the role of regime in shaping police behavior. On one side of the coin, policing under authoritarian systems—irrespective of structural configurations or professional institutionalization—increases the likelihood of police misconduct. On the other side of the coin, democratization does not necessarily produce less-malfeasant police. In Brazil and Argentina, transitions took place in the 1980s, yet these nations still suffer high levels of police misconduct. As such, democracy may or may not improve the way police behave. An important factor here, then, is not just the regime type but also the kind of actors who oversee the police. Although this book is about institutional and structural aspects of policing, the leadership qualities of political actors in charge of police forces also matter. Thus, while this book highlights the importance of structural-institutional factors, individual leadership, even in democracies, does impact police behavior.

In short, centralization, professionalization, militarization, and regime structure are fundamental to understanding police misbehavior because they promote a process by which the Weberian rational-legal bureaucratic organization of police replaces the patrimonial order that has come to define Latin American politics and public security (Weber 2019). These findings are consistent throughout the historical analysis and through the comparative analysis presented in this book. I also address the debates about how levels of crime, cultural contexts, colonial origins, and religious foundations relate to police misconduct discussed in the literature review.

Plan of the Book

In this book, I analyze the cases of Chile, Colombia, and Mexico. I chose these cases methodically in the following way: by focusing on the Western Hemisphere with the idea that this would facilitate controlled comparisons and because it is my region of interest. I took four factors into consideration to narrow the scope of cases: patterns of colonization, religion, international pressures, and regime type (Williams 2002).

Several scholars have noted that imperial legacies determine the patterns of policing and misconduct in colonized countries (Hadden 2001; Hansen 2012; Boateng and Darko 2016; Steinmetz, Schaefer, and Henderson 2017; Blanchard 2014; Becker et al. 2014). For instance, Daniel Treisman (2000) notes that having Spanish colonial heritage increases the likelihood of corruption, whereas British heritage reduces it. This has to do with the fact that Spanish rule in the Americas came to an abrupt and revolutionary end, leading to power vacuums where a caudillo (strongman) was the primary method of providing security. These patrimonial practices endured in the long run. In contrast, not only did British colonialism impart democratic institutions and common-law traditions but also the British transitioned peacefully out of politics in most locales. Thus, the insecurity gap was not as prominent in postcolonial British territories as it was in Spanish colonies. I therefore rejected the cases of the United States, Canada, Belize, Suriname, the Commonwealth Caribbean, and Guyana because they have British heritage. I eliminated Haiti because it is the only country in the Western Hemisphere with French colonization. The other French colonial holdings in the Caribbean are politically part of France. Similarly, Dutch colonies continue to be a part of the Kingdom of the Netherlands. Finally, I ruled out Brazil because of its Portuguese colonial heritage.

By selecting former Spanish colonies, I also controlled for a different argument: religion (McFadyen and Prideaux 2014; McNamara and Tempenis 1999). Treisman (2000) found that religion was a significant predictor of corruption; Protestant countries had lower levels of police corruption. Conversely, countries with Catholic majorities tended to have higher levels of police corruption.

Another virtue of studying Spanish America is that it controls for another argument related to the role of international influences. The internationalist perspective is that training by foreign hegemonic forces has a significant impact on the practices of domestic security forces (Carothers 2011; Renda 2001; Müller 2018; Bayley 2005; Sinclair and Williams 2007; Pérez Ricart 2020). For example, US training pressured the Brazilian police forces in the 1970s and 1980s to embrace a national security doctrine that rendered them institutionally abusive to this day (Huggins 1998). Similarly, Spanish American cases show significant influence of US police training and its attendant issues with police misconduct (Huggins 1987). Today, the United States continues to play an important role in training Spanish American police through the International Law Enforcement Academies located in El Salvador and New Mexico (International Law Enforcement Agency 2021). As such, the available cases that allow for control of colonial heritage, religion, and international influence include Argentina, Bolivia, Chile, Colombia, Costa Rica, Cuba, the Dominican Republic, Ecuador, El Salvador, Honduras, Mexico, Nicaragua, Panama, Paraguay, Peru, Uruguay, and Venezuela.

Beyond international influences, many scholars have studied the link between regime type and police misconduct. Here the argument is that democracies tend to improve police behavior. Treisman (2000, 404) notes that police will be less likely to engage in misconduct in democratic societies because the risk of getting caught is higher in "open political systems" where "freedom of association and the press engender public interest groups and reporters with a mission and the right to expose abuses." Some scholars have found that the regime type does matter for police behavior (Cao, Lai, and Zhao 2012; Karstedt 2012), but others note that democratization does not adequately change police misconduct (Arias and Ungar 2009; Cruz 2011; González 2020; Bailey and Dammert 2006). Nevertheless, regime type must be controlled for in this analysis. For this reason, I eliminated Cuba and Venezuela because they are not contemporary democracies. Therefore, the standing universe of cases is as follows: Argentina, Bolivia, Chile, Colombia, Costa Rica, the Dominican Republic, Ecuador, El Salvador, Honduras, Mexico, Nicaragua, Panama, Paraguay, Peru, and Uruguay.

Next, I selected three countries for valid comparison from these fifteen possible cases. I first chose the cases to maximize variation in the misconduct. Measures of police misconduct are difficult to approximate because of a lack of data. However, the level of citizen trust in the police can be used as a proxy for police misconduct. This is a reasonable assumption given that several scholars have found a high correlation between the level of confidence in the police and police corruption or police effectiveness (Morris 2011; Morris and Klesner 2010; Sabet 2010; Tankebe 2010). Using Latinobarómetro data from 1995 to 2017, I aggregated the overall levels of citizen trust and found that Chile, Uruguay, and Colombia had the highest levels of confidence in the police, then assumed that police misconduct was lowest in these cases. Meanwhile, Guatemala, Mexico, and Bolivia had the lowest levels of trust, and hence might have the highest levels of police misconduct. Figure 1.1 illustrates the variation in citizen trust in the police.

To select the best cases for comparison among the six cases of Chile, Uruguay, Colombia, Guatemala, Mexico, and Bolivia, I relied further on the literature. Specifically, I considered the following factors of police misconduct: violent criminal environments, cultures of corruption, weak states, and weak rule of law.

Some scholars find that violent environments create conditions that promote police misconduct in two ways. First, violent criminal environments create spheres of permissibility for police to engage in misconduct (Klinger 2004). The main driving force is that violent criminal contexts create heightened fear in citizens, who ask for police to engage in hardline tactics against criminals (Tankebe 2009; Cruz 2015). Hence, violent contexts are correlated with police misconduct (Kane 2005; Caldeira 2002; Cardia 1997). Second, a sort of isomorphism arises between violent criminals and violent police.

Figure 1.1   Average Citizen Trust in Latin American Police, 1995–2017

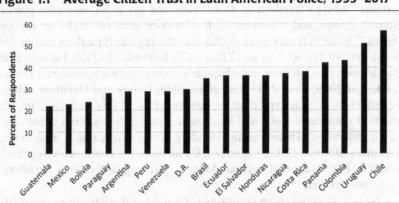

Source: Latinobarómetro datasets 1995–2017. Tabulation by author.

Here, police rationalize that the only way to counter criminal violence is with state violence (Eitle, D'Alessio, and Stolzenberg 2014; Lauchs, Keast, and Yousefpour 2011; Gutierrez-Garcia and Rodríguez 2016).

In terms of the impact of corrupt societies, the basic argument is that police engage in misconduct because the society around them condones it (Wolfe and Piquero 2011; Paoline, Terrill, and Rossler 2015; Fuentes 2005). Sherman (1978) declares that "community tolerance, or even support, for police corruption can facilitate a department's becoming corrupt" (32). Mercedes Hinton (2006) notes that police misconduct is "shaped by cultural toleration for corruption in public office," where there is an "an enormous window of opportunity for all players to exploit an already weakened concept of public good" (192). Here, the media landscape is quite important in shaping citizens' acceptance of police misconduct (Roich 2017; Bonner 2013; Bonner et al. 2018).

There are also arguments about how state strength influences police misconduct (Dinnen, McLeod, and Peake 2006). These arguments are largely rooted in the notion that state weakness implies resource limitations, which in turn limit the capacity for police to be effective in their daily work (Goldsmith 2010; Kakachia and O'Shea 2012; Costa 2011; Wolf 2009, Müller 2012; Mwangi 2017; Marcella, Pérez, and Fonseca 2021). This ineffectiveness and lack of resources might compel officers to engage in misconduct to increase their effectiveness by skirting civil liberties and to engage in corruption to enhance their resources. However, other scholars have noted that changes in state capacity are not always "sufficient to improve police performance" (Taylor 2011, 16).

Finally, scholars have noted that misconduct arises in contexts where there is a weak rule of law. When the rule of law is weak, judges, prosecutors, politicians, and the business world ignore the law and thus stand above it. In these contexts, police rationalize their misconduct as normal and a social good (Davis 2006; Uildriks 2010). In a more refined argument, Daniel M. Brinks (2007) found that Brazilian police in Rio de Janeiro and São Paolo engaged in misconduct because it was tolerated by other public officials in the judiciary and state governments.

Given the major arguments in the literature, I selected the cases of Chile, Colombia, and Mexico from the list of possible cases because they allow for controlled comparison along the dimensions of violent environments, societal corruption, state strength, and rule of law. In addition, these three cases have extreme variation in misconduct: Chile with low misconduct, and Mexico and Colombia with high levels of misconduct. However, Chile stands out as having a less violent environment, a less corrupt society, a stronger state, and a stronger rule of law. Colombia and Mexico, in contrast, have violent environments, more corrupt societies, weaker states, and weaker rule of law. The three cases together allowed me to learn a great deal about how centralization and professionalization influence police misconduct even in the face of these alternative arguments. To build these cases, I describe each individually and in relation to one another for the sake of comparison, beginning with the case of Colombia.

Colombia stands out as a policy-relevant case, with its high levels of citizen trust in the police despite the violent context, rampant political corruption, historically weak state, and attendant weaker rule of law. Colombia is a country of forty-eight million people spread out over one million kilometers of land along the Andean Mountains. It spans from the Pacific Ocean to the Caribbean Sea and shares borders with Peru, Ecuador, Brazil, Venezuela, and Panama. Colombia has a GDP of $314 billion and an economy based on mining, oil production, and agricultural goods. The nation has experienced internal turmoil since its founding in 1830. Civil wars between Liberal and Conservative Party members dominate much of Colombia's history until 1953, when a military coup brought order and stability to the two-party system.

Except for the 1953–1958 dictatorship of General Gustavo Rojas Pinilla, Colombia has had a functioning political democracy throughout its history. A political pact between the rival Liberal and Conservative Parties ended the period of La Violencia and opened a new era for Colombia. However, drug trafficking and internal insurgencies arose during this time, which initiated a new set of violent crises throughout the 1980s (Martin 2012). The constitutional reform of 1991 provided rights and guarantees to marginalized groups and produced a new era of political and security improvements. Although peace accords with various armed groups were discussed, and some were achieved, violence persisted through the 1990s. By the year 2000, the Medellín and Cali cartels had been defeated, and the administration of Álvaro Uribe, with the help of the United States, implemented Plan de Seguridad Nacional, which strengthened the state and weakened the guerrilla movements. This period also saw the demobilization of various paramilitary groups. Ultimately, the Revolutionary Armed Forces of Colombia (FARC) was forced to the negotiating table, and in 2015 a new peace process was initiated that saw the demobilization of these armed combatants. However, Colombia still faces internal threats from other guerrilla groups, such as the National Liberation Army (ELN) and criminal entities such as the Clan de Golfo. Given this history of extreme volatility, it is surprising that Colombia's police force has fared well in terms of public opinion polling. For these reasons, Colombia presents a critical case in developing an understanding of police misconduct.

In Colombia, national police handle all preventative activities and assume investigative law enforcement responsibilities, while the Instituto Nacional Penitenciario (INPE) handles jail security. As of 2012, an estimated 134,241 officers and civilians are in the National Police of Colombia, which is spread throughout Colombia in rural areas and major cities alike. They are under the direct control of the Ministry of Defense of Colombia. In cities, mayors can ask the police for assistance, can coordinate with them on public security policies, and can request support in enforcing regulations. Municipal police agencies also exist; however, they are mostly in charge of traffic and parking regulations. Local political actors have no direct control over police.

For effective comparison, I picked the next case because it has a similar security context to Colombia but differs in terms of the level of trust in the police. Because Colombia has a history of insurgency, drug trafficking, paramilitaries, criminal violence, weak governmental institutions, and Iberian cultural heritage, it was ideal to select a case that was similar in these regards but different in terms of perceived police behaviors. To that end, Mexico provides the most similar case of the low-trust cases.

Mexico is a country of 125 million people spread out over two million square kilometers of land located in North America. It shares borders with the United States, Belize, and Guatemala. Historically, Mexico has had to face similar internal crises as Colombia, ones that pitted Liberal Party members against Conservative Party members for much of the nineteenth century. After Mexico gained independence in 1821, it became an empire from 1821 to 1826, then a dictatorship from 1826 to 1834, then a democratic republic from 1840 to 1850, then an empire again from 1850 to 1860, a democratic republic from 1860 to 1870, a personalist dictatorship from 1870 to 1910, and experienced a revolution from 1910 to 1920. Mexico gained political stability vis-à-vis the authoritarian party regime of the Institutional Revolutionary Party (PRI) that controlled Mexico from 1927 to 2000. Beginning in the 1980s, Mexico began to experience increased drug trafficking and cartel violence, rivaled only by Colombia. Mexico became a democracy in the year 2000 when the rival National Action Party won the presidential election for the first time in its history.

Mexico has a total of 430,000 police with about 40,000 federal, 227,000 state, and 164,000 municipal police forces (Expansion 2010). This provides two points of interests. First, the Mexican police system is federalized. This means that it has centralized police at the federal level, a semicentralized force at the subnational state level, and a completely decentralized force at the city/township level. Second, I consider the Mexican police system to generally be heavily decentralized, given that most policing at the time of this research was in the hands of local, not state or national, police.

There were over 2,457 municipal police in Mexico in 2014. As of 2018, 1,757 municipal police have come under the control of state police, and 700 municipal police departments continue to operate independently of state or federal control. These municipal police report directly to the mayor and council. The governor of the state controls the state police. On the national level, the Guardia Nacional enforces federal law across the country and is under the control of the office of the president. In addition, there are civilian judicial police at the municipal and state level who help the public minister or public prosecutor's office. Again, this study focuses only on the uniformed preventative police forces. Although Mexico has historically had weak security, some attempts were made to provide a more centralized police apparatus during the Porfiriato through the Rurales period, roughly from 1861 to 1914 (Vanderwood 1970). However, since the Mexican Revolution, Mexico has had a decentralized police system. Local mayors have direct control over police appointments, and there is no national body developed for funding, oversight, or recruitment. This decentralized system, although locally controlled, is ultimately beholden to the hegemonic power of the PRI.

Despite slight differences in the trajectories of their political regimes, Colombia and Mexico today are very similar in terms of their levels of insecurity. For instance, both have the presence of drug trafficking organizations. Bender and Rosen (2014) state, "Between December 2006 and November 2012, 102,696 homicides took place in Mexico, of which 70% were drug-related." Colombia's homicide rate is 30.8 per 100,000 people, and Mexico's is 21.5 per 100,000 (United Nations Office on Drugs and Crime 2010–2013). The US Department of State Bureau of Diplomatic Security warns that both Mexico and Colombia have a high degree of terrorism, crime, and political violence (US Department of State 2015).

Both Colombia and Mexico have corrupt cultures, where paying off government officials is a regular and anticipated practice. As such, Colombia scored a 37 and Mexico a 35 (where 1 is the highest level of corruption) on the Transparency International (2013) Corruption Perceptions Index. Colombia and Mexico share similar levels of state fragility, scoring 75.7 and 69.7, according to the Fund for Peace (2019) Fragile State Index (scores range from high state fragility of 113 to low state fragility of 16.9). Bertelsmann governance index (2018a, 2018b) gives Colombia and Mexico each the same score, 7.3 out of 10, on the state's index (the closer to 10, the stronger the state).

Also, Bertelsmann (2018a, 2018b) gives Colombia a score of 6.75 and Mexico a similar score of 6.1 on the level of democracy. Lastly, the World Justice Project (2019) gives Colombia a score of .5 and Mexico a score of .45 on its rule-of-law index (scores range from 0 to 1, with 1 indicating the most robust adherence to the rule of law). Thus, in terms of security contexts, corruption, state strength, and the rule of law, Colombia and Mexico are very similar cases.

To add more analytical leverage, I have employed the logic of most-different systems design. I selected a third case that has high levels of trust but does not have the same security context as Colombia. The case needed a lack of insurgencies, drug cartels, criminal violence, and paramilitary groups and would have low levels of governmental corruption. Chile fits as an appropriate comparison. Chile is an Andean country of 18 million people spread out over 750 thousand square kilometers in the Southern Cone of South America. It shares borders with Argentina, Bolivia, and Peru. Chile gained independence from Spain in 1821 but faced similar issues to both Colombia and Mexico concerning Liberal and Conservative Party competition. All three countries experienced a power vacuum in the early years of independence that gave rise to insecurity and cultures of caudillismo. Notwithstanding the sometimes-violent partisan political competition and banditry, Chile eventually developed a legacy of republicanism that would form part of the cultural fabric of the nation.

Nevertheless, in the twentieth century, Chile was still susceptible to authoritarian rule. In 1927, General Carlos Ibáñez del Campo took over the political regime of the nation, and again in 1973, the military took control of the government and stayed in power until 1990. Aside from its authoritarian legacy, Chile has been able to develop the most trusted and least malfeasant police force in Latin America.

Law enforcement in Chile is divided among three national-level institutions. First, the Policía de Investigacion is civilian-oriented and primarily in charge of the investigation of crimes. Second, the Gendermería de Chile is responsible for providing security and bailiff duties in courts as well as in prisons. Finally, the Carabineros de Chile are the uniformed preventative police in charge of patrolling the streets as well as providing public security, anti-riot policing, and occasional investigative work. This book is primarily concerned with the third type of policing, and hence we will be looking specifically at the Carabineros de Chile. The Carabineros de Chile has an estimated 52,795 uniformed officers and is controlled by the Interior Ministry of Chile. The police can cooperate with local political officials, but they are not under the direct control of said officials.

In comparing the security contexts of Chile and Colombia, no two cases could be further apart under my scope conditions. Although the Colombian government dismantled the Medellín and Cali cartels in the 1990s, these groups simply fragmented and reared their heads in new forms, now called Bandas Criminales (BACRIMS). In contrast, Chile does not have a similar criminal situation. Although criminal gangs in marginalized communities engage in micro drug-trafficking, the level of organized crime pales in comparison to Colombia. Furthermore, Chile has not faced the same problems with internally displaced populations, leftist guerrillas, or paramilitary groups. Thus, Chile overall has a lower level of crime and violence than Colombia. The homicide rate in Chile is only at 3.1 per 100,000 people, whereas in Colombia it is at 30.8 per 100,000 (United Nations Office on Drugs and Crime 2010–2013). Whereas the US Department of State Bureau of Diplomatic Security rates Chile as generally safe, it considers Colombia to be dangerous (US Department of State 2015). Thus, the problems that police face in these countries are different.

Another point of difference is that Chile does not have a very corrupt culture, but Colombia does. According to Transparency International, Chile scores 73 on its Corruption Perceptions Index, while Colombia is much worse at 37 (the closer to 1, the more corrupt the country). Colombia scores 75.7 regarding state fragility, and Chile, with a much stronger state, comes in at 38.9. Bertelsmann Stiftung (2018a, 2018c) gives Colombia a score of 7.3, but it provides a much better score to Chile, 9.8 (the closer to 10, the stronger the state).

Further, Bertelsmann (2018a, 2018c) gives Colombia an index score of 6.75 and Chile a much better score of 9.2 on the level of democracy. Lastly, the World Justice Project gives Colombia a score of .5 and Chile a better count of .68 on its rule-of-law index. Thus, in terms of a security context, corruption, state strength, and the rule of law, Chile and Colombia are very different. Chile is a valuable case because it represents the extreme levels of misconduct in the region but is able to maintain different values in these contextual security conditions. Together, these three cases provide a well-balanced set that can elucidate the driving factors of police misconduct. Table 1.2 summarizes all of these indicators.

Table 1.2   Summary of Arguments

	Chile	Colombia	Mexico
	Alternative Arguments		
Violent environment (United Nations Office on Drugs and Crime 2010–2013)	Low	High	High
Corrupt environment (Transparency International 2013)	Low corrupt	High corrupt	High corrupt
State strength (Fund for Peace 2019)	Strong	Fragile	Fragile
State strength (Bertelsmann 2022)	Strong	Weak	Weak
Rule of law (World Justice Project 2019)	High	Medium	Medium
	My Arguments		
Structure	Centralized	Centralized	Centralized
Development	Professional	Professional	Nonprofessional
Training	Professional	Professional	Nonprofessional
Oversight	Professional	Professional	Nonprofessional

Conclusion

With this case configuration in mind, I conducted field research in each location. I performed interviews with political elites, nongovernmental organizations, police elites, and government officials. I also utilized original document analyses, secondary sources, and electronic correspondences with pertinent officials in each country.

In Chapter 2, I discuss the Chilean police, the Carabineros, which are the best police force in Latin America. However, they were not always that way. How did they become the least corrupt and most trusted police force in Latin America? I trace six significant police reform periods that changed the structure and labor model of Chilean policing, and I assess the impact these reforms had on police behavior. Over time, the Chilean police service was centralized, and by the end of the twentieth century it had become a professional police service—supporting my argument through a historical lens. This chapter also includes a thorough analysis of the various policy reforms enacted by the left-wing parties that took over after the return to democratic control in 1990. The key findings here are that the early model of decentralized policing elicited high levels of police corruption. When more centralized, professional, and militarized models were introduced in 1896, these models outperformed their decentralized counterparts. When the Chilean Carabineros came about in 1927 as a national, professional, and militarized police, they provided effective police services and had low levels of police misconduct. The authoritarian regime of Augusto Pinochet undermined the professionalism of the police by cutting their budget all while using the police to repress political dissent. In this period, the police were highly malfeasant. The return of democracy in Chile meant the return of bigger budgets and better administration of the police, which returned this force to professional status, producing the current era of police in Chile. Note that although centralization and professionalization greatly reduced misconduct in Chile, these reforms are not a panacea. In the case of the Carabineros, some factors still produce abuse and corruption, which, although present, are nevertheless more muted than in Chile's Latin American counterparts.

In Chapter 3, I analyze Colombian policing during seven periods from 1846 to 2013. The chapter traces how police in Colombia evolved, starting out as decentralized and unprofessional police from independence in the 1830s until 1953. During this period, the police were intimately and heavily involved in partisan violence, corruption, and abuse of power. In 1953, a military coup began the process of centralization and professionalization that improved police behavior and reduced factional infighting. The exigencies of the civil war and combating drug trafficking led to the reduction of budgets for the police, which reduced their professional capacities and opened them up for misconduct. In the 1990s, the presidential administration of César Gaviria invested more in funding and expanding professional institutions, which helped to decrease police abuse of authority and to increase citizen trust. These structural and institutional changes have led to an improvement in police service in Colombia. Yet again, centralization, professionalized institutions, and militarization improved police performance.

Chapter 4 compares city police, state police, and national police forces in Mexico in 2013. By looking at the three institutional arrangements, this chapter supports the argument that a nationally organized (or even provincially organized) police force with high professionalization is far preferable to the reliance on municipal police. The chapter illustrates that the decentralized and occupational municipal police in Mexico are engaged the most in misconduct and engender the lowest levels of trust. The state police are semicentralized and semiprofessionalized and induce higher levels of trust than their municipal counterparts. The federal police are the most centralized and most professional, and they exhibit the lowest level of misconduct of the three levels of police.

Chapter 5 summarizes the case analysis and findings and then provides a brief discussion of how the results help us understand policing in the United States. I close the chapter with a set of policy recommendations that make the case for more federal or state oversight of standards, recruitment, and investigation of misconduct. I also argue that the money to protect pensions and other benefits for local police should be funded by state or federal government.

Furthermore, direct control of police by the mayor should be eliminated. Local police chiefs should not be under the control of local mayors but instead under the control of a police board that manages and ensures the qualification of all candidates at that level. However, local co-responsibility for public security is imperative. Councils of local citizens overseeing police should be a part of every city. Mayoral powers should allow for the continuation of strategic development to counter public security issues that are relevant in the mayor's area of operations. It should be the duty of the commander in charge of local police departments to work with, but not for, local authorities to address crimes and other public security issues in the locality.

2

Chile:
A Model for Latin America?

> *Do not ever make the error of attempting to bribe the police, whose
> reputation for institutional integrity is high.*
> —Lonely Planet Guide Book on Chile

Tourists to Mexico are all too familiar with the corrupt practices of the
police. What they might not know is that the problem of police corruption
extends from Mexico's southern border to the tip of Patagonia in the Southern Cone, and it is often more sinister than petty bribery. For instance, on
August 10, 2016, the body of Lucas Muñoz, a Rio Negro provincial police
officer from Argentina, was found near the border of Chile (LaSusa 2016).
Muñoz was killed by his fellow police officers, who were engaged in drug
trafficking activities and who feared he was going expose them. This is part
of a more significant trend of police corruption in Argentina that has been
a continuous issue since the return to democracy in the 1980s. The root of
the problem is that Argentina has a federal system, with police at the federal and provincial levels and traffic police at the city level. Beyond the
decentralized nature of the police system, Argentina has not institutionalized police work as a profession. The depth of the problem for Argentina
is that society has come to accept police misconduct as a normal part of
life. However, a tourist would be mistaken in thinking that all Latin American police are the same.

Looking westward, beyond the Andes and into Chile, travelers are confronted with a different reality. Every year, tourists entering Chile by over-
land routes from Argentina, Bolivia, and Peru are faced with imposing signs
at the border stipulating: "Do not attempt to bribe the Carabineros, you will

be taken to jail." And it is a fair warning. Chile has built a reputation as having an effective, efficient, and corruption-resistant (but not corruption-free) police force. The case of Chile is critical in making the argument that a less-malfeasant police force is within reach of other Latin American nations. Latin American nations can overcome political, historical, cultural, and societal predispositions toward corruption with the right institutional framework.

I will make the case that a significant source of the Chilean police system's resistance to misconduct is related to its structural and institutional configuration. The pattern I identify in this chapter provides evidence for my argument that centralization and professionalization are significant components of developing less-malfeasant police. The evidence is historical. Although, as mentioned in Chapter 1, polling on these sorts of questions only started in the 1990s; nevertheless, I have drawn on archives, books, reports, newspaper articles, and interviews to construct an assessment of the relative level of criminal behavior in police forces. This imperfect measure seems to be the best way to approach such a complicated question. It enabled me to categorize various police forces as having high levels, medium levels, or low levels of misconduct on the basis of the research evidence.

High levels of misconduct exist when the data shows that most police appear to be engaged in corrupt behavior. Intermediate levels of misconduct appear when corruption and abuse exist at high levels of the police force, but not all cops are engaging in these activities. For example, the data shows scenarios when it appears that corruption and abuse, although occurring at high levels, do not define the entire police force; in other words, there is gross abuse of power but also tales of heroic policing. Low levels of abuse and corruption exist when narratives discussing these types of behavior emphasize that cases are isolated, rare, or infrequent. To confirm this classification, I asked interviewees to describe the current relative levels of abuse and corruption compared to other periods. From this rough estimate, I obtained a crude measure of how centralization and professionalization tracked with changes in police behavior over time. In this chapter, I analyze six periods in Chilean policing spanning 1833–2014. I begin by discussing the era of postindependence in Chile.

Chile gained independence in 1817 and inherited a part-time law enforcement apparatus called the Serrano-Vigilante system, wherein lamplighters doubled as law enforcement officers. In 1833, Chile began to develop a centralized, albeit nonprofessional, police force. From 1891 to 1896, the police system became decentralized as a result of the central state's weak finances. This communal police era would prove to be a disaster. In its wake, police reformers scrambled to provide the nation with security, eventually settling on three concurrent systems of police, which operated from 1896 to 1927. This period offers a miniature comparison of various styles of policing. The local city police that were dependent on local revenues fared the worst in terms of misconduct; the centralized but civilian models fared a little better. Still, it was the centralized and professional militarized police that ultimately did much better than the other two. As a result, in 1927, the militarized model was adopted for the whole country. Thus, the Carabineros were born.

From 1927 to 1973, the Carabineros continued to increase their professionalism. Although I lack statistics in terms of police behavior, high-ranking police officers I interviewed, as well as civilian leaders, all agreed that this was the golden period of the Carabinero. They engendered high levels of trust in and proximity to the community. But all of this came crashing down with the military regime that took power in 1973 through 1990, and the police engaged in massive abuse. From 1990 to present, we have a story of a broken police force that is bolstered by new democratic leaders who take it upon themselves to help resuscitate police professionalism.

The analysis of the last three decades results in the key findings of this chapter. First, decentralized police are historically linked to eras of poor police performance and high corruption. Centralization made a difference in terms of police performance and behavior, but when it was coupled with professionalized institutions, police services fared better. Second, militarization was the critical mechanism that brought about centralization. Last, when the regime changed to a militarized one, this change nullified the virtues of centralization and professionalization. In my interpretation, centralization and professionalization can provide their bounty only in the context of democracy. In the context of authoritarianism, it does not matter how police are organized: centralized, militarized, or professionalized, they will be used to repress political opposition and will engage in abuse. Thus, centralization, professionalization, and democratization often work together for better policing.

Origins of Policing in Postindependence Chile

After Chile gained independence, its first organized security service was founded in the capital city of Santiago. This was primarily made up of gas lamplighters known as Los Serenos, who would patrol at night, keep an eye out for fires, call out the time, stop thieves, try to assist anyone in need of help, and extinguish the gas lamps in the morning. However, there was not a comparable service for the daytime until 1830, when the interior minister Diego Portales created the Vigilantes de Policía, made up of ninety men on foot and horseback whose job it was to deter crime, help victims, apprehend criminals, assist courts, and patrol the city during the day (Carabineros de Chile 2012).

Other municipalities, with the help of the central government, also developed a similar style of policing: with Serenos and Vigilantes. These police forces were poorly paid and lacked any training (Miranda 1997, 97). The new police forces were primarily seen as inept and abusive. For instance, the daily *El Araucano*, no. 88, published an article simply titled "The Police" on May 19, 1832, that criticized the police and noted "that the police lacked the necessary resources and workforce. Without resolving the funding question, the poor police service would continue to plague the city [of Santiago] and, indeed, other cities in the country." However, the police service in Chile would not be reformed until 1850, when the police forces of Serenos and Vigilantes of Santiago were unified to form the Brigada de Policía de Santiago, with 470 personnel (Carabineros de Chile 2012). The rest of the country followed suit and developed twenty-four-hour police services in major urban centers, including Cauquenes, Los Angeles, Copiapó, Vicuña, San Felipe, and La Serena (Miranda 1997, 139). Funding for local police varied greatly between large cities and smaller ones. The capital of Santiago and the port city of Valparaíso, for instance, received large enough budgets to sustain their police forces (*La Estrella de Valparaíso* 1922). However, in smaller towns like Copiapó and Concepción, citizens collected donations to hire more needed police personnel (Miranda 1997, 139).

As Chile advanced socially, politically, and economically, its police force remained mostly unchanged and underfunded, and it provided poor service. The lack of necessary funding for the police, resulting in poor pay, made recruitment of quality candidates difficult. For example, on one occasion in 1872, the mayor of Santiago, Benjamin McKenna, was walking down the street when he saw a familiar face wearing a police officer's uniform. Upon closer inspection, McKenna realized that this man was a former convicted felon. Experiences like this led McKenna to write one of the earliest critical accounts of police work in Chile. He observes that the poor quality of police service gave rise to "a general sentiment amongst the people that the police and their agents were repulsive . . . their actions of harassment had angered citizens." Given all the abusive practices, McKenna notes that he himself knew a "thousand Santiaguinos who would rather give the police a foot in the posterior" rather than a helping hand (Vicuña Mackenna 1875, 3).

If police garnered this hatred by being abusive, then what is the source of their violent nature? Again, McKenna notes that people came to the recruitment office daily, remarking that joining the police was their "last recourse from misery, after having exhausted all other means of earning an honorable living." Indeed, the individuals in Chilean society looked at the occupation of "police officer" as a curse or a kind of mange (Vicuña Mackenna 1875, 23). Recruitment was poor, and weak local oversight produced the abhorrent police behavior, which subsequently created animosity from society.

Overall, the postindependence period of policing was rife with problems. The central issue was the lack of necessary funding for professional policing to cover benefits, welfare, and oversight. This brief background of postindependence police development in Chile sets the foundation for the analysis to follow. Given the growing population, with its attendant rise in criminality, the Chilean people will demand more public security. However, this early period reveals problems with policing that existed in every postindependence country in Latin America as new nations began to develop their state apparatus with limited funding.

The Radical Decentralization of 1891–1896

After independence, the Chilean central government tried to help develop police forces for each major city in its territory. However, the new police format was not well-funded and resulted in problems in police service. Given these early setbacks to police development, Chilean leaders looked for alternative ways of improving the police force. The Chilean legislator Manuel José Irarrázaval y Larraín sought to create a decentralized police system. Irarrázaval argued that local control would bring the police closer to the citizens, which would inspire better policing. On December 22, 1891, Irarrázaval shepherded Ley de Comuna Autónoma (Law of Autonomous Communities, or LAC) through Congress. The law divided the country into 267 autonomous municipalities that could elect their mayors, could raise private funds, and were required to provide public services (Biblioteca Nacional de Chile 2014). In effect, the mayors chose political allies as police chiefs. LAC did not regulate who was nominated as police commanders, how they were trained, or how they were paid. The decentralization of police services, accompanied by the devolution of the managing elections, proved a volatile mix in Chile as it would in Colombia and Mexico. This dual decentralization "resulted in complete failure, whose negative effects were particularly felt in the scope of police functions. The police throughout the country were now controlled by municipalities who . . . have made these bodies a powerful instrument at the service of political interests" (Miranda 1997, 185). In every municipal election, mayors would replace police chiefs and all other police personnel with those who were loyal to their interests (Vera 1899). These police forces were often used for the sitting mayor's personal benefit, not for the general good. Police were used to harass figures who challenged the local mayors.

However, decentralization also meant that poorer municipalities with few resources could not, in many cases, afford to develop police forces at all or could recruit only very low-quality candidates. Recruitment was a constant challenge. Where police forces were able to be formed, they tended to be understaffed, lacked efficiency, and were poorly funded, poorly trained, and inadequately paid (Prieto 1996, 5). On February 5, 1896, a government commission presented the Chilean Congress with a report that noted that a significant problem plagued all police in Chile: a lack of funds (Miranda 1997, 190). Because the police were poorly funded, they were unable to fulfill arrest warrants or help judicial authorities collect evidence accurately.

In many cases, the Chilean Congress willfully chose to ignore those requests for funds. In short, the inability of the decentralized police system to address violent security threats "forced the government to mobilize army troops to fulfill the duties that police would not" or could not undertake (Miranda 1997, 190). In Chile, the purely decentralized model evolved over time into a centralized and more professional model. Given the problems of policing under the early decentralized model, Chilean leaders looked for alternative and more centralized models as the solution for the weak policing and increased public insecurity after the Chilean civil war of 1891.

Three Models of Policing, 1896–1927

The civil war in Chile in 1891 produced significant challenges to security in the nation. The demobilized and defeated soldiers took to the countryside to become bandits, using their military knowledge to overpower and overwhelm small police forces or villages without police. Thus, Chile experienced a period when armed groups were not only a significant threat but also the policing system was weak. Crime and banditry in the countryside, especially in the southern regions, were on the rise. Roads that connected significant cities were always under attack.

In the following pages, I present three parallel storylines spanning 1891–1927. First, I discuss the communal police, which represent the decentralized police in smaller cities. Second, I turn to the fiscal police, a police force that was regulated and controlled by the national congress and that provided police services to the major cities. Third, I discuss the Carabinero Regiment and colonial gendarmería, which provided militarized, centralized, and professional policing for rural areas in the extreme south and north of Chile. Think of this synchronous comparison as a natural experiment. The country of Chile had three types of police forces operating simultaneously during this period. Which model, given the controlled context of working in similar environments, would prove best? The decentralized and nonprofessionalized models, or the more centralized and more professionalized ones? This is the puzzle that I try to unravel in the next three subsections.

Muddling Through with Communal Policing

The problems with the communal police force started at its birth under the Ley de Comuna Autónoma in 1891 (Republic of Chile 1891). Robustiano Vera (1899, 29), who chronicled the police service at the time, noted that the president had given control over the police to municipal mayors, and very quickly it became evident how dangerous this arrangement was, as mayors used the police for their partisan purposes. Because of the political nature of policing at the municipal level, there was no emphasis on professionalism. As a result, the police service was filled with illiterate individuals who lacked any training or experience. Vera (1899, 14) notes that it was common for communal police institutions to "bring in the first people they see on the street to apply for the police and make them into police." It was also common for individuals who "before had not belonged to any police and did not have any preparation for the charge they were exercising" to practically overnight be promoted to "chiefs and officers" (Vera 1899, 14). Not only was recruitment deficient, but the police work offered minimal material benefits or oversight. By 1899, it became clear that the communal police were failing at providing security. They were often abusive and "discourteous and disrespectful with the public," which gave rise to a hatred of the police (Vera 1899, 14). It was common for police to be drunk on duty, to abuse "their service weapons and beating defenseless people, and protecting criminals, and asking for bribes" and to be arbitrary in their actions (Vera 1899, 19).

The 1896 decision of the central government to fund police in the capital and larger cities, but not in smaller areas, resulted in an asymmetrical situation in which substantially more and better-funded police existed in larger cities than in more impoverished smaller towns and rural areas. For instance, from 1900 to 1902, Santiago had 2,213 police officers, who were funded and controlled by the central government—by far the largest police force in Chile. The second-largest was the Valparaíso police, with 826 police personnel (Prieto 1996, 5). Prieto (1996) estimates that in 1900, there was a total of 5,814 police officers in the whole of Chile, which means approximately 52 percent of all police officers in the country were concentrated in just two cities, Valparaíso and Santiago.

What did police forces look like in the rest of the country? Two examples demonstrate the context of policing at this time: the cases of La Granja and Tarapaca. From 1912 to 1913, La Granja, a small city outside Santiago, did not receive any money from the central government to fund its police department. It was a typical autonomous city. In 1912, 73 percent of La Granja's taxes went to fund the police force of twenty men (Memoria Nortina 1912, 4). The following year, in 1913, police expenditures represented 66 percent of the city's annual budget (Memoria de la Granja 1914, 6). To put this into perspective, the city of La Granja spent only about 2 percent of its resources on public roads and only 1 percent on public education (Memoria de la Granja 1914, 6). Instead of providing money for essential public services, this small community had to spend most of its money on the police force. Even then, the sum proved insufficient to create a professional body.

For this reason, the community had trouble keeping police in service. From 1912 to 1913, the police force experienced a total of fifty-three personnel changes, which means that fifty-three people quit and were replaced by equally inept individuals in one year. In La Granja during this period, on average, a police officer would last only six months on the job (Memoria de la Granja 1914, 7).

The other illustrative example is the community of Tarapaca, a region in northern Chile bordering Bolivia, where security was a significant problem in the early 1900s. In July 1907, the province of Tarapaca had 1 prefect (police chief), 2 subcommissioners, 5 inspectors, 16 subinspectors, and 254 guardians, 166 of whom lived in the barracks and 88 of whom worked in the countryside. Most of them had no uniforms, only forty-four had guns, and their police training was deficient (Memoria Nortina 1907). In 1907, the prefect complained to the mayor that the appointment of police officers through political "recommendations" did not provide competent "police personnel to provide for good service and instead led to the denigration of the institution with the added threat that those same officials, because of ignorance, fall into illegal activities" (Memoria Nortina 2013). This reinforces the argument that communal police were not only subject to political whims but also inclined to abuse power for their criminal benefit. At the beginning of 1907, the newspaper *El Tarapaca* featured an article titled "The Dangers in Tarapaca" that expressed the fear of the people in the province. The lack of security was aggravated by the malfeasant behavior of the police, the proliferation of crimes, and the arrival of anarchists in the region. The writer noted that "Tarapaca is a time bomb, a territory where, if nobody does anything, can be the source of a revolution that the country would regret" (Memoria Nortina 2013).

Many communal police like those in Tarapaca and La Granja "were not able to maintain security in the countryside, and military entities were created that were tasked with addressing the increasing problem of banditry at the end of the 19th century" (Tamayo Cabello 2012, 129–130). Moreover, the nature of the communal police "had fragmented the power of the state throughout the country and thus damaged national security" (Tuozzo 1999, 33). The use of the local police as a mechanism of electoral intervention, corruption, and irregularities in the electoral process continued throughout Chile well into the 1920s.

The problems associated with communal police at this time prompted the central government to launch an investigative inquiry that assessed the performance of the municipal police. Each public official surveyed agreed that policing had become worse since the implementation of the Law of Autonomous Communities. In most cases, local authorities paid little attention to the police, which resulted in the frequent use of police officers in areas of work unrelated to those assigned to them by law, including political repression in which they abused their power and weapons for personal gain (Ríos 1914, 27).

Four primary reasons for police misconduct in that era reinforce my argument. The first reason is that the constant fluctuation of police personnel endangers the service (Ríos 1914, 28). By linking police budgets to the local municipal tax bases, which fluctuated from year to year, booms and busts in police personnel from year to year can be observed. This pattern promoted work instability, which made the job of police officer undesirable and the last resort for many.

Second, police recruitment was deficient. It was typical that "new police chiefs and officers who have never had any police experience, and who have not received any preparation except for their connection to an influential political caudillo, are suddenly made into police" (Ríos 1914, 28). Because the police were under the control of local political bosses, their selection was based on loyalty rather than objective qualifications. This also implies a lack of oversight from the top down because neither commanders nor enlisted were trained in essential military discipline and hierarchical command, which would have provided at least a modicum of monitoring that was just not present in communal police at this time.

Late in 1922, an article in the *El Mercurio* newspaper stipulated that the communal police did not "serve their purpose, as they were infected by the village politics . . . enough statistics have already found that these policemen are useless to fight crime: and in practice, the police have become the criminals" (*El Mercurio* 1922). In smaller towns, communal police were "disorganized and undisciplined, and they only have a vague appearance of police and instead pose a danger to the public" (*La Estrella de Valparaíso* 1922).

The overall qualitative data in this subsection reveals that the communal police era promoted higher misconduct than the previous period as manifested by daily abuses, political corruption, links to criminal activity, and susceptibility to bribes. This system also supported security gaps that gave criminals room to maneuver and escape, much like what is happening in Mexico today. Banditry plagued rural areas and was a severe problem for commerce in cities. The communal police "saw themselves unable to stop communal crimes" (Navarrete 2000, 106).

A third reason for police misconduct was the "poor salary." Police work was not rewarded well compared to other professional fields. Men had better prospects for a livelihood working in a factory or as a rural laborer. Finally, the fourth reason was a lack of social benefits for police officers. This reduced the incentives to become a police officer and hampered recruitment. As Ríos (1914, 31) notes, few individuals would place their lives in danger knowing "that if they die in their post, the state will not even bother to provide a small pension to help out their family." This is related to the minuscule or complete lack of police welfare to protect them in the short and long term. At the time, police were provided with no medical coverage, received little in terms of pensions, and accessed practically no other fringe benefits. Again, this is all linked to the fact that local governments could not afford to build police benefit systems on their own. They scarcely had enough to give the police a meager salary.

The experiment of a purely decentralized police system in Chile lasted from 1891 to 1896—a total of only five years. After enduring this system, Chileans demanded professional protection. From 1896 forward, the communal police continued to operate, but they did so alongside a more militarized, professionalized, and centralized police institution of the *gendarmerie* and a centralized and civilian institution of the fiscal police. Chileans hoped these other systems would bolster security. And they did. This increase in security theoretically provided municipal police with space to breathe as well as room to grow and develop. However, the examination of the span from 1891 to 1927 reveals that in thirty-six years, police misconduct across the communal police system remained high.

Centralizing Control over Urban Centers

In 1891, the Santiago Police Department (SPD) was the only police force funded with national government resources, and all others were financed by local funds as per the Law of Autonomous Communities. That changed in 1896 when Chile's major cities saw their police forces come under the control and funding of the central government. Thereafter, police were referred to as the fiscal police. The fiscal police get their name from the fact that they were funded by the central government treasury, which in Spanish is *El Fiscal* or in other countries the *Hacienda*. The SPD was an extreme case of the fiscal police structure. The Santiago police were poorly paid, poorly trained, and poorly resourced to carry out their police function. Even still, the SPD was considered the best police force in Chile, which says more about the dire situation of policing in the country than of the quality of the capital's police force. When the national government began taking over policing in larger cities, the police were still locally controlled but were funded by national funds and organized their police labor with the same logic as the SPD. For this reason, an analysis of the SPD highlights not only its early challenges but also the corollary challenges that minor cities also faced at this time.

In 1891, the SPD had 900 police personnel on paper, although in practice this number was lower and fluctuated (Miranda 1997, 185). The variation in number of police personnel resulted from a lack of interest in these jobs, as well as a lack of funding (186). The urgent need for police compelled commanders to shorten training periods to get more men on the streets faster. As such, recruitment and training were hampered as part of a strategic policy that prioritized quantity over quality of police officers. The lack of training, coupled with poor pay and the lack of long-term job security, led to high levels of turnover and the loss of the institutional memory that is critical for any organization to achieve its objectives efficiently. Every year, changes to the municipal budget led to the cyclical increase or decrease in the number of police positions such that, from year to year, most police officers could find themselves out of work. Few were willing to undertake this dangerous profession without having secure labor conditions.

For instance, in January of 1892, the number of police personnel in Santiago increased by 1,500 but only for the summer months of January, February, and March, when crime traditionally peaks in Santiago. However, for the rest of the year, those 1,500 individuals had to look for jobs elsewhere. Qualified candidates often worked instead in year-round positions rather than become police. Additionally, in 1894, President Manuel Montt temporarily increased the police force in Santiago by 1,500 (Miranda 1997, 186). Again, the fact that the growing capital city of half-a-million people needed more police officers but could not afford them was a problem that not only Santiago but also much of the country faced, especially poorer regions. Santiago was wealthy in resources compared to every other city in Chile, yet problems in funding police plagued even this grand city. In the smaller cities that speckled the length of Chile, the increased financial burdens that the Law of Autonomous Communities of 1891 imposed, and the lack of effective taxation to raise resources, resulted in fiscal shortfalls that municipalities could not fix. By 1896, most municipalities were unable to pay for public goods, including policing.

Financial problems plagued the capital city and smaller cities as well as the medium-sized regional capitals called cabeceras. These far-flung regional capitals were spread throughout Chile's 2,500-mile length and had to be protected and remain connected through active roadways. The problem was that their relative isolation from the nation's capital made them prime targets for banditry, especially roadside hijackings. For trade to take place among various regions and for the government to be able to administer its territory, the rule of law had to be instituted in these capital cities. Thus, the central government on February 12, 1896, issued Law 344, which dictated all police forces in department capitals (cabeceras) would be financed by the national treasury and controlled by the presidentially appointed governors or intendants as authorized by the Interior Ministry. These police would henceforth be referred to as fiscal police. Meanwhile, all other police, under the Law of Autonomous Communities of 1891, would remain under local mayoral control (Ríos 1914, 27). Hereafter, all small-city police will be referred to as communal police to denote their local linkage (Carabineros de Chile 2013, 39–40).

The fiscal police were to be organized and led by the president of the republic following the Santiago Police Organization Regulation (SPOR). The requirements for being admitted as a guardian/police officer were as follows: age between twenty and forty-five years, never been jailed, high moral character, an aptitude for service, good health with a robust constitution, able to read and write, and vaccinated. Hence, recruitment standards were fair albeit not stringent enough.

Article 54 of the SPOR notes that the punishments police could be subjected to depended on the infraction, starting with verbal warning, then arrest and up to a month during which the person would have to remain in the barracks when off duty, withholding salary for up to a month, and ultimately separation and expulsion from the service. Offenses that merited expulsion included drinking on the job, insubordination, cruelty, abandoning his position, not following orders, immoral behavior, and debts that prevented an officer's proper functioning (Honorato and Urzua 1923, 109). These early police forces, though some recruitment standards and oversight were in place, still suffered significant setbacks.

Although the law required there to be 2,197 police personnel for all of Santiago, in June 1896, there were only 1,673, a deficiency of 524 administrative and operational elements (Honorato and Urzua 1923, 275). As Honorato and Urzua note, the lack of funding meant that the contingent of police was always in flux and in deficit. Many good officers would refuse to renew their contracts, which, together with the number of individuals kicked out for bad behavior, made it impossible to reach a full contingent and proper preparation of personnel (275). Importantly, this reveals that there was not high demand for the job of police officer; otherwise, more positions would have been filled and contracts extended. The lack of demand was because of the lack of welfare for police.

These problems persisted from 1896 to 1901, when there were 2,033 police personnel throughout Santiago, with a constant rotation of about 1,800 officers who would enter the force for a short time and then quit (Miranda 1997, 198). One example of how bad the situation was for the police is that close to 70 percent of the lower ranks had a good portion of their salary garnered by the courts (Honorato and Urzua 1923, 275). It turns out that many police agents in the Santiago fiscal police were forced to borrow money to subsidize their income and fell behind on their payments; hence, the court garnered their already low wages. Many of these officers eventually had to take up other jobs, finally leaving police work altogether. This illustrates the importance of welfare benefits such as healthcare, pensions, and loans not only to attract candidates but also to maintain them on the force; this is also critical for any institution that wants to develop an institutional memory. This means creating formal and informal standard operating procedures that help new police become active more quickly. Undoubtedly, many innovations in thinking about police work were lost with each resignation.

Up until this point, each fiscal police force in the largest cities in Chile was funded by the national treasury. Still, they were organized, trained, and recruited based on principles laid out by the local governor, which meant the standards varied from city to city. In response to these issues, the president of Chile, Germán Riesco, issued Supreme Decree 3901 in 1904 to unify the regulations of all fiscal police (Miranda 1997, 197; Republic of Chile 1904). Despite its troubles, the Santiago fiscal police force was the best-organized, best-funded, and largest fiscal police force in the country. Paying keen attention to their level of misconduct during this time provides vital insight into the general standing of the police across Chile. If the Santiago police failed to provide adequate service, it would seem to indicate that similar police services would also have had the same faults elsewhere.

By the 1920s, training for a commissioned officer in the SPD lasted nine months, an improvement of the previous method of appointing officers based on political favors alone. The training was extensive and included self-defense, baton use, weapons use, and legal training. Herein lies the first stage of failure for patrimonialism and the rise of the rational police bureaucracy. By 1923, the police of lower ranks in Santiago were paid six pesos per day (Honorato and Urzua 1923, 286)—lower pay than that of an electric streetcar driver, who earned eight or nine pesos per day. Thus, police jobs attracted only lower-skilled laborers who had trouble finding work elsewhere. For this reason, institutional problems persisted in the Santiago Police Department as well as in departments elsewhere in the country.

The low salary would not have been as much of a problem if the government had mitigated it by providing a social safety net to guarantee labor and economic stability. But the government invested very little in social benefits for police officers. Instead, in 1921 the police hospital was built and funded by public donations and internal fundraising among officers, not by the Chilean National Treasury, and without support from the national administration (Miranda 1997, 195). Furthermore, no governmental life insurance was provided for the police—a basic standard of any professional police force. Instead, the police set up an ad hoc system themselves (Honorato and Urzua 1923, 267). If a police officer was killed, the officers themselves donated fifty cents out of their salary, resulting in a lump payment of 1,350 pesos to the family of the deceased. It's critical to note here that the social safety net was not created by the government; instead, the police officers designed it themselves. The government did set up pensions for incapacitation or for retirement, covered under Law 1840 of February 12, 1906. Article 3 provided that incapacitated police officers would receive 100 percent of their last salary as their pension if they had served ten years or more, and 50 percent if they had served fewer than ten years. Thus, a police officer who had served thirty years would receive 100 percent of his salary (Republic of Chile 1906).

The strategy for developing a nonmalfeasant police force requires not only benefits to attract candidates but also training and selection to weed out weak candidates and instill internal controls; it also requires a robust oversight mechanism that includes a strong hierarchy, internal investigations, and judicial bodies. In the end, the scant benefits and pay made the job of fiscal police undesirable. Hence, the ranks of the SPD were in constant flux because enlisted officers saw no benefit in staying in a police force that paid so poorly. If they were to die, adequate life insurance was not paid to their families. Although the police in Santiago were making some headway in the right direction, their evolution was not fast enough to maintain a well-run and professional force. As a result, both corruption and abuse were still at very high levels in the institution.

As revealed by Honorato and Urzua (1923, 275), the police were not able to purge certain kinds of misconduct from the institution. For instance, in 1912, the Civic Action League was established with the support of all the Santiago newspapers with the aim of eradicating the gambling houses that proliferated under the protection of the police. The press and congressional speeches highlighted severe problems (Prieto 1996, 5; Muñoz Silva 1916). Another illustration of the extent of police corruption is an article in the newspaper *La Opinion* that accused the subprefect of police in Santiago, Eugenio Rodriguez Castro, of working closely with criminal entities and providing them with protection from prosecution and cover for irregularities in the administration of justice (Mario 1917, 25). The newspaper accused Rodriguez Castro of hiring criminals as police officers and using them to extort gambling dens. It was alleged that between 1908 and 1917, Rodriguez Castro had fabricated several dynamite attacks on churches, railways, and private homes and had attributed them to anarchist groups (Mario 1917, 25).

The problems in the Santiago fiscal police were so pronounced that a highly respected retired colonel, Henry Phillips, launched a campaign to reform the police. In an article he wrote in *La Opinion* entitled "Reorganizing the Police," Phillips accuses the Santiago police prefect, Nicholas Yavar, of corruption for employing a former criminal as a police officer (Prieto 1996, 4). In 1915, President-elect Juan Luis Sanfuentes promised to make a judicial inquiry and correct the corruption in the police force, but he was unsuccessful (Prieto 1996, 4). The problems of police corruption were no secret to the public or to the officers within the institution. For instance, police lieutenant Ramón Muñoz Silva (1916, 23) wrote a report that discussed the police scandals in the SPD and attributed them to disorganization and demoralization of police related to inadequate training and salaries.

The problems the SPD experienced during this period were typical of what was happing in other police departments throughout the country. Because of this, citizens and business leaders applied pressure to political leaders to do something about the problems in the police. One policy response appeared to gain support: centralizing the fiscal police of all cabeceras by fusing them into one chain of command with one set of regulations. In 1924, the president and Congress passed Law 4052, which unified the twenty-three fiscal police forces in the General Direction of Police under the Interior Ministry in six different zones (Republic of Chile 1924). The unification allowed the establishment of standardized recruitment and training practices throughout the country, a unified command, and centralized funding for pension benefits.

Although the centralization of the fiscal police at the national level was a step in the right direction, there was still much misconduct. The development, welfare, and oversight regimes were not strong enough to overcome problems of drunkenness on the job, abuse of weapons, and corruption. Misconduct of this kind would disappear only when the police enhanced the professionalism of the job under a model of strict training, discipline, and oversight (Bustamante Bascunan 1918, 53). This finally occurred in 1927 with the introduction of a professional and centralized model of policing, which had also arisen in 1896 and which is the subject of the next section.

The Colonial Gendarmería and the Carabinero Regiment

During the same period that the fiscal police were operating in the cabecera cities (1891–1927), smaller rural communities were facing a severe security crisis. While fiscal police provided some semblance of security in major cities, the countryside was dominated by bandits and highwaymen who took advantage of the power vacuum established by the Municipal Law of 1891. These smaller hamlets and towns had weak police that were quickly overpowered by the roving bandits of the Chilean rural regions. To combat this rising insecurity, in 1896, the central government established a militarized law enforcement body called the colonial gendarmería with a focus on the southern Chilean provinces where banditry was most prevalent (Museo Historico de Carabineros de Chile 2012). Initially quartered in the southern city of Temuco and comprised of one commissioner, two inspectors, four subinspectors, and fifty guardians, the unit provided security in the provinces of Arauco, Malleco, Cautín, Valdivia, and Llanque, where the communal police system was too weak to address banditry.

By 1897, the colonial gendarmería had proven that they "were effective in their work, providing security and peace to the colonists . . . the success of this group led to the increase of this force by the National Congress" (Miranda 1997, 206). Two new companies (or sections) were formed in the region for a total of three companies. Each had a commissioner, two inspectors, four subinspectors, ten guardians first-class, and forty guardians second-class. It should be noted that these police did not provide urban policing but were tasked specifically for rural policing, and they were controlled by the central government through local representatives such as governors or intendants (Miranda 1997, 206). The force of 171 police was lean, but it was effective in providing security in their assigned region.

Given the police's effectiveness in establishing a more secure environment in the far-flung southern region of Chile, the national government reorganized and increased the colonial gendarmería. The base pay for a soldier in the gendarmería was 40 pesos per month, or 1.34 pesos per day, whereas the average agricultural worker earned 1.1 pesos per day (Matus-González 2009, 193). What is important to note about this force is that the pay was only slightly above a rural wage, and the officers received little material benefits early on. What they lacked in material benefits they gained in terms of their militarized leadership (Miranda 1997, 206). Under former army captain Hernán Trizano's leadership, this force established a robust professional character through training, selection, and oversight. In terms of misconduct, the record needs to be assessed in a nuanced way. The group of men were capable, courteous, and did not engage in misconduct. To be sure, they did engage in firefights, but they were allowed to discharge their weapons only in self-defense. This colonial gendarmería lost fifteen men, but they killed fifty-one bandits and arrested many more (Miranda 1997, 206).

Because of the success of the gendarmería in curtailing crime in rural regions, on May 24, 1902, the president of Chile, Germán Riesco, ordered the creation of a separate force called the Gendarmerie Regiment. This was made up of mounted units from the army and was intended to combat banditry in other southern provinces not covered by the colonial gendarmería, which was a separate unit. Receiving 59 pesos per month, or 1.96 pesos per day in 1902, the Gendarmerie Regiment was also relatively better paid than their compatriots in the colonial gendarmería.

Because the primary mission of both the colonial gendarmería and the Gendarmerie Regiment was to repress banditry, civilians in the region came to trust them. In short, colonial gendarmerías were transformed from "simple bandit hunters to true police in rural communities" (Tamayo Cabello 2012, 129–130). Chile's northern region, rich in nitrates, was also experiencing problems with security and banditry during the period from 1906 to 1927. As such, Supreme Decree 113 on February 5, 1906, transformed the Gendarmerie Regiment into the Carabinero Regiment under the leadership of Lieutenant Colonel of the Army Roberto Daila, who mobilized this new unit to the northern parts of Chile (Carabineros de Chile 2012). On February 23, 1907, President Montt signed Supreme Decree 255, approving the Regulatory Framework for the Service of the Carabinero Regiment to provide for a robust oversight system (Carabineros de Chile 2012). This centralized and militarized policing institution was useful not only because of its training and ability to share information across regions, but also because of its structural features, which promoted the quick and effective strengthening of development, welfare, and oversight regulations, all of which were severely lacking in the decentralized civilian communal police system.

In 1907, the Gendarmerie Regiment fused with the Carabinero Regiment and extended their presence throughout the country. In 1909, the regiment's first commander created the first school of the Carabinero Regiment for aspiring officers. The corps could thus create its officers rather than relying on seconding army infantry officers. The recruitment of newly commissioned officers for the school had to be from the ranks of retired army officers.

Law 3547 of September 20, 1919, gave the Carabinero Regiment a legal framework, set the personnel positions, and provided for pensions and retirement benefits. Specifically, Article 1 of Law 3547 stipulated that the "Carabineros Regiment is a military institution. It is responsible for ensuring the maintenance of order throughout the territory of the Republic, and, in the fields and public roads" (Republic of Chile 1919). Article 2 granted ultimate control of the Carabinero Regiment to the Ministry of the Interior or, when the president deemed it appropriate, to the Ministry of War. Article 3 stated that the body of the Carabinero Regiment would remain under the laws, norms, and regulations of the military in regard to discipline, training, rank ascendance, sanctioning of crimes of personnel, organizational rules, and distribution of services. The military disciplinary structure served as an effective oversight mechanism geared toward observing and sanctioning behavior from the top down. Article 4 stated that recruitment of personnel of chiefs and officers would be from (1) among the retired chiefs and officers of the army or navy who had retired with honor; (2) among the sergeants and individuals with high school degrees, with no more than eight years of service, and not older than thirty years of age; (3) among the officers from the military reserves; and (4) among the conscripts of the armed mounted units who had completed their fifth year of education. Under Article 5, the law mandated that enlisted were to be recruited from candidates who had finished their military service with an honorable discharge and those who had not completed their military service. Article 12 stated that Carabineros who had spent twenty years in public service, and ten of those with the Carabineros, had the right to retire. Article 13 provided for full or partial retirement for injuries sustained in the line of duty. As such, a robust system of recruitment was built into this organization (Republic of Chile 1919).

The average salary of an industrial worker in 1918 was 4.20 pesos per day, and in 1919 an agricultural worker could earn up to 2.80 per day. In contrast, the Carabineros paid personnel 3.28 pesos per day for entry ranks, 3.78 per day for second corporals, and 4.27 pesos per day for first corporals (Matus-González 2009). Thus, an entry-level job in the Carabineros at the lower ranks paid above that of an agricultural worker's daily wages but slightly below that of the average industrial wage laborer. Depending on rank, a Carabinero's pay was on par and somewhat above the salary of a blue-collar laborer. But industrial workers did not enjoy the job security and retirement pension benefits that the Carabineros did at the time. Even though the wages at the lower ranks were not stellar, the added benefits of working within the institution made this position an attractive option for individuals.

Decree Law 283 of February 1925 expanded many benefits for the officers and the enlisted (Republic of Chile 1925). To that effect, officers who were qualified but who could not ascend in rank because of a lack of available slots were given bonuses when they received their new rank to make up for the time spent at a lower rank. The second lieutenants received money for clothes, equipment, and other necessary materials. Additionally, a bonus of one month's salary was given to individuals who had to change garrison or station to offset the costs of moving (Miranda 1997, 197). The enlisted ranks who were married or widowed with children and who had more than fifteen years of service without incurring a bad mark on their record had the right to a housing equivalent of 10 percent of their salary. In 1927, Decree Law 283 formed the foundation for the active recruitment, welfare, and oversight system for the Carabinero Regiment as a police force going into the future (Republic of Chile 1925). The decree fixed the conditions for the retirement of both officers and enlisted. Those who provided more than thirty years of public service with at least ten years with the Carabineros were first to have the right of retiring completely. For the enlisted ranks, the right to withdraw was granted at twenty-five years of public service, ten of which had to be spent with the Carabinero Regiment (Miranda 1997, 197). The changes wrought by this decree, along with an improved entrance requirement of being able to read and write, established the foundation for one of the most effective, professional, and uncorrupt police forces in Latin America.

During this period, the Carabinero Regiment was the most competent and efficient preventative policing institution in the country. It was built on a base of strong recruitment standards, military training, strong welfare benefits, and strict hierarchical oversight endowed by its centralized and militarized character. Because of its military nature, the organization "developed the tactical and technical qualities to provide for public order and protect the country's borders; as a police institution, it took responsibility for crime prevention and the safeguarding of the personal security of the citizenry" (Galleguillos 2004, 57–58). Additionally, the Carabinero Regiment "was closer to the average civilian person that was the case with the socially segregated members of the armed forces (army, navy, and air force)" (Galleguillos 2004, 57–58). Even though the Carabinero Regiment was "conceived of as rural police, it saw plenty of action in the cities as it confronted social protests, investigation work, and organizing homeless shelters. This happened, in large part, because the communal police failed to address these problems themselves. As such, the military model was looked upon as more efficient at tackling police duties, and thus, more responsibilities would be loaded on to them" (Tamayo Cabello 2012, 130).

Comparing Local Police, Fiscal Police, and the Carabinero Regiment

Between 1891 and 1896, Chile faced a security crisis of bandits in the countryside and rising crime in growing cities. To address the crisis, the national government experimented with several policing models. The first government response was to allow smaller municipalities to retain their own police forces, as before. The second response was to develop fiscal police that were fiscally linked to the central government. This created a centralized and civilian police institution in major cities. The third undertaking was the development of a centralized and militarized law enforcement institution in the countryside and remote areas of the country to counter the rising bandit threat. As a result, there were three competing models of policing in place from 1896 to 1927: the decentralized municipal-based police institutions, a national civilian police institution, and a national militarized institution.

The communal policing experiment failed, and the fiscal one did not fare much better; however, the militarized model made significant progress. Remember that "one of the main motives for the militarization of the police was the fragile nature of the communal police charged with order and security over the whole past century, which translated into corruption, lack of unity, organization or efficiency throughout the country" (Prieto 1996, 4). Filling this void with more centralized and militarized police worked. The Carabineros of 1919 were not necessarily paid high wages but they were paid an adequate salary and provided with the essential elements of welfare benefits. Because they were initially a part of the military, they had the corollary benefits that came along with the military. This included a healthy (for the time) pension, retirement plans, insurance benefits in case of injury on the job, opportunities to climb in rank, access to the military warehouse, and free housing, all of which gave them long-term security. Because the men were recruited from the military, they already had professional training, and no doubt they were already accustomed to a structured environment in which they would be held accountable for their actions. This training process weeded out weak individuals and maintained the strong ones who could withstand the pressures of the job. The job security and the benefits, as well as the romantic mythology surrounding these gentlemen bandit hunters, made the job attractive and reduced turnover. The selection standards and military training imparted important self-discipline in the ranks, and the military hierarchy imposed strong controls. In addition to being controlled by the hierarchy, the Carabineros were also subject to military justice tribunals, which added a layer of control that did not exist in communal police, who were not prosecuted because local clientelist political systems controlled both the police and the legal proceedings. In the next section, I focus squarely on the Carabineros de Chile and their centralization and professionalization right up to the 1973 military coup.

Early Carabineros Era, 1927–1973

The overall trend in the previous decade of Chilean history leading up to the 1920s was an increased centralization and professionalization of police service. The inertia of the impulse to centralize and professionalize carried it into the 1920s. In a speech given in June 1922, President Arturo Alessandri stated that despite the increases in the Carabineros, "there were still not enough Carabineros to fulfill the daily requests received from various parts of the country, and as soon as the circumstances permitted new squadrons were formed in other provinces [so] that each province would have a police unit that would bring peace to rural areas and maintain order in small towns" (Alessandri 1922).

Instead of merely expanding the size of the Carabinero Regiment, a new plan formed to nationalize all police services. This plan came to fruition on March 30, 1927, when the minister of the interior, Carlos Ibáñez del Campo, gave a speech to the 4th Carabinero Regiment Commissary outlining a plan to unite the police forces of Chile. About a month later, on April 27, Ibáñez del Campo signed the Decree with Force of Law 2484 (Republic of Chile 1927). This fused the services of the communal police, the fiscal police, and the Carabineros, merging their personnel and resources into one single police institution: the Carabineros de Chile. This "19,000 strong national police force, Carabineros de Chile, with its high standards of smartness and discipline, came in time to be seen as the finest in Latin America" (Collier and Sater 2004, 217). However, the early history of the Carabineros de Chile saw the Carabineros engage in repressive practices against extremist parties. As the country industrialized, workers took to the streets to unionize and demand increased wages. This was a catalyst for a series of problems for society, such as work stoppages, strikes, protests, and boycotts.

The 1930s saw severe government repression of Nazi, Anarchist, and Communist organizations. This sort of oppression was not related to the day-to-day activities of the police but to presidential policies of repression. Here is a valuable lesson that I will repeat later: Although the structure and professionalization of the police had improved their efficacy in establishing the rule of law and lessened day-to-day mistreatment of citizens and corruption, it did not mean that police would not use force when directed to do so. This is a slightly different phenomenon related to the state's prerogative to establish a monopoly over the legitimate use of violence to promote order. Although political repression and human rights abuses exist in this early period of Carabinero consolidation, the acts are not malfeasant in the sense that the police did not undertake these activities to benefit their own agenda but were directed to these activities by the civilian leaders at the top of the chain of command. Elected officials and their orders were the sources of the misconduct, not the will of the police alone.

Despite the political problems, the Carabineros continued with their strong system of training and oversight, and this helped them overcome these problems. The military penal system that once acted as oversight for the Carabinero Regiment was largely transplanted into the new Carabineros de Chile, as were the training standards and recruitment practices. What remained weak in the early period of professional development of the Carabineros was the reduced benefits they were awarded for their work. This component saw great advancement from 1927 to 1973 and thus is the focus of this section.

In terms of health care, the Carabinero Regiment started to develop a health system for police in 1927. It annexed twenty beds and two private rooms in the Salvador Hospital in Santiago for the specific use of Carabineros staff seeking to recuperate from injuries or to be treated for other ailments. Then, in 1936, the Carabineros de Chile gained funds and land from the government to build a hospital specifically for Carabineros. The hospital was completed on April 27, 1945, giving the Carabineros access to stable and high-quality health care (Cuerpo de Generales de Carabineros 2016).

In addition to the hospital mandate, other laws were passed to help advance the social well-being of Carabineros. For instance, Supreme Decree 4540 of November 15, 1932, strengthened pensions and bonuses for police. The next year, Law 7260 of September 1, 1942, and subsequently Law 7872 of September 25, 1944, increased salary and bonuses and established living expense subsidies.

Through the decades, Carabineros developed strong selection standards, strength training, and strong oversight. In 1968, Decree with the Force of Law 2 was passed, which was an important law because it not only increased the number of Carabineros in the country but also developed the basis for a strong welfare system comprising salaries, bonuses, and health care. According to Article 46 of DFL 2, Carabineros were to receive raises every five years. The first and second increments (at five and ten years of service) together represented a 30 percent increase in base salary. The third and fourth increments (at fifteen and twenty years of service) gave a 20 percent increase in the already increased wages. The fourth and fifth increases (at twenty-five and thirty years of service) provide for a 15 percent increase in the previous salary. Carabineros who worked in hazardous situations received a 10 percent increase in pay as well as an increase determined by law for being married, having children, or being single but with family duties.

In addition to the salary increases, police injured on duty had all their medical expenses paid by the Carabineros. Article 56 provided police with access to governmental housing paid for by the Carabineros from their salary at a heavily discounted price, which could vary year to year but which was around 10 percent of their monthly salary. Article 94 decreed that pensions were to be calculated based on the last salary level with bonuses. For every one year of service, a Carabinero received one-thirtieth the amount of their last salary. For instance, if an officer received a monthly salary of $100 USD and served for thirty years, the officer received 100 percent ($100 USD) monthly for the rest of his life. If the officer served only fifteen years, he received 50 percent of his last monthly salary ($50 USD) per month, with appropriate taxes and fees taken out. In addition to benefits, DFL 2 also contained stipulations for disciplinary action. For instance, Article 69 mandated officers found guilty of serious offenses by the military justice system to be subject to having their pension removed.

In several interviews with former police generals who had begun their careers in the Carabineros before the military junta, one thing became clear: by the 1950s and 1960s, the police had developed a close relationship with the country's citizens. In rural areas, the Carabineros were the only state representatives that villagers knew. In this sense, the Carabineros were one of the early and few genuinely national institutions. Given their important role in rural communities, they acted as a multifunctional agent that assisted villagers with more than just security, often providing educational opportunities, government information, and conflict mediation. In fact, several police officers that I interviewed noted that they joined the Carabineros precisely because the job of a Carabinero was viewed as a prestigious and admirable position in society. My interviews with academics, politicians, and nongovernmental workers reinforced this idea as part of a narrative that has become clear. The Carabineros during this era of the early 1960s were not engaged in misconduct. I attribute this high level of public trust and low corruption to the centralization and professionalization that had been advanced in the early twentieth century. But during the Cold War, more repressive modalities insinuated their way into the police force that would bankrupt society's level of trust in the police. In practice, the punitive policy and the Mobile Group led to the drastic deterioration of prestige that the Carabineros had built up with the population (Prieto 1996, 19).

Allende, Pinochet, and the Carabineros, 1973–1988

The creation of the Carabineros de Chile significantly improved the security of the country. The Carabineros represented a new police force that had less-corrupt practices compared to previous organizational schemes. Nevertheless, as with any police force, the Carabineros de Chile were not free of damage. Specifically, the Carabineros during 1927–1973 were still utilized politically to repress fringe parties, such as communists and social nationalists, who posed a threat to state security. This politicization of the police was different, however, from the history of mayors using the police for their private political ends.

Nevertheless, during this period welfare benefits for the Carabineros continued to advance and the development and oversight that decreased misconduct strengthened. One recurring theme in my interviews with retired and active Carabinero officers, as well as with politicians and security experts, was a sense that, by 1973, the Carabineros de Chile had developed into a core of professional, well-respected police with low misconduct. However, larger political forces would change this trajectory.

The Cuban Revolution inspired revolutionaries in Latin America to take up arms against their governments. The impact in Chile was pronounced as students and intellectuals took to the streets to demand social equality and socialist-oriented economic policies. The state responded by developing a counterinsurgency doctrine that caused the Carabineros to "become an important component in the fight against real or alleged threats to the social order" (Galleguillos 2004, 58). Specifically, the Carabineros de Chile established the "Grupo Movíl, or Rapid Deployment Special Forces, which became the most visible expression of state repression against rapidly radicalizing sectors of civil society (workers, peasants, students, homeless)" (Galleguillos 2004, 58). In 1969, the Carabineros discovered two guerrilla schools, one in the Maipo Valley and another near Valdivia (Collier and Slater 2004, 324).

On top of the political and security threats to the government from leftist insurgents was the social unrest undermining the presidency of Eduardo Frei. Eduardo Frei, the Christian Democrat, attempted to implement moderate economic changes that he termed the Revolution in Liberty, which sought some minor changes in land reform. However:

> Social discontent with Frei's "Revolution in Liberty" saw the Carabineros police increasingly acting in defense of private property, as numerous rural land seizures by landless peasants were accompanied by a growing number of land seizures by homeless marginal peoples in the country's largest cities, especially Santiago. One event that still stands out, especially in that it highlights the growing alienation of police officers from the popular sectors, was the March 1969 massacre by the police of 12 squatters in the southern city of Puerto Montt. (Galleguillos 2004, 61)

The deaths of these homeless squatters at the hands of the Carabineros of Puerto Montt plunged the Christian Democrats into an internal crisis. This coincided with the rising expectation that Salvador Allende, the Marxist candidate for president running under the left-leaning Patriotic Union Party, was making a strong campaign against Jorge Alessandri and the Christian Democrat candidate Radomiro Tomic. In Chile's constitution, if no candidate received a majority, Parliament would elect the president from the top two vote-getters. Allende narrowly won the vote against Alessandri and took power on November 3, 1970. However, in 1973, the military would take over and derail the Carabineros.

On September 11, 1973, at 10 a.m., Chilean army tanks opened fire on their president, who took shelter at La Moneda, the presidential palace. The Carabineros inside of La Moneda immediately took defensive positions, ready to return fire (*El Mercurio* 2003). This moment was tense because General Pinochet had doubts regarding who the Carabineros would back in this coup (González Camus 1988). However, by 10:15 a.m., news had reached the Carabineros inside defending the palace: the rest of the high command were outside and had joined the coup against Allende. As such, the Carabineros left. The military would later bomb the presidential palace, and Allende was no more.

Following the coup, the Carabineros were incorporated into the new ruling military junta alongside the heads of the army, navy, and air force. Under Decree Law 444 of 1974, the Carabineros were transferred from the Interior Ministry to the Ministry of Defense, now controlled by the military (Republic of Chile 1974). However, problems arose from the military involvement in government that would severely hamper the Carabineros' institutional ability to address crime. In an interview, a retired Carabinero general highlighted that an active attempt to replace the police force with the military was made. In effect, the military regime rationalized that because the army was patrolling the streets, the Carabineros would require less funding and fewer personnel. As such, the military junta period presents a drastic decline in the police forces' resources and professionalism.

The military junta did not continue to use the Carabineros for repression. Nevertheless, Carabinero officers were eager to demonstrate their loyalty to the junta. Consequently, during the junta period, Carabineros ramped up their involvement in the anti-subversive campaign. For instance, in April 1974, the Carabineros launched large-scale anti-guerrilla maneuvers in the central Andean foothills (Latin America Weekly Report 1974). Their activities were not limited to the detention or arrest of suspected Marxists; they also included active participation in torture, abuse, and systematic repression of political parties.

Despite the Carabineros' loyalty to the new regime, the military largely ignored the Carabineros in terms of funding. In an interview, a former subsecretary of the Carabineros noted that the Carabineros were always the "poor relative" of the junta, and their budgets were continuously slashed in comparison to other branches. Not only that, but during the dictatorship, roles the Carabineros once served were assumed by the other armed forces. For example, to control public order, Carabineros no longer patrolled the streets at night, but military personnel did.

From 1973 to 1981, the citizens of Chile were afraid to challenge the junta openly; however, in 1981, under failing economic conditions, people started taking to the streets en masse. But the junta had slashed the budget for the police and for anti-riot equipment, which meant that crowds often overwhelmed the police. It was only after these social protests that the regime started to provide more funds to the police. From 1973 to 1985— twelve years of military rule—the number of personnel in the Carabineros hovered around 23,000, despite an increasing national population. After massive anti-regime mobilizations in the early 1980s, the junta determined the need to invest in hiring 5,000 more police. This increase required that the Carabineros be less selective and train for shorter periods. Despite the increased personnel, the budget for materials and benefits for the police was not increased.

The budget increase in 1983 and personnel increases in 1985 did not translate into a material improvement for the average patrol officer. A retired Carabinero sergeant major with whom I spoke, Carlos Ripetti, noted that "there were no resources for Carabineros. There were Carabinero officers without shirts or with the neck worn out. Patrol cars were missing gas; the same people that went by on the street would donate money for gasoline of the vehicles. Most Carabineros went out on foot . . . with holes in their shoes." Another retired Carabineros, who entered the institution in 1983, talked about the logistical nightmare experienced in the Carabineros during the dictatorship: "With all the washing, cleaning, ironing, our uniform starts to fall apart. And you had to try to buy that, and that came out of my money. How would we do it? If I bought a uniform, that meant that my family and I would not be able to eat for a week."

By 1988, the Carabineros had established a grisly history of repression. The Rettig Report (National Commission for Truth and Reconciliation 1990) estimates that there were 2,279 political deaths during the dictatorship. This number includes the armed forces and politicians who were assassinated during the military regime lasting from 1973 to 1989. Through the Rettig Report, the National Commission for Truth and Reconciliation documented more than 3,000 cases of human rights violations, with 965 disappearances during Pinochet's rule. The Chilean spy agencies (known as *la direcíon de inteligencia nacional* and *centro nacional de inteligencia*) were responsible for 40 percent of all human rights abuses. The Carabineros were the second-most notorious violators, with 23 percent of all violations, and the army was responsible for 15 percent of the deaths. The air force and navy had relatively clean hands with only twenty-nine and eleven disappearances, respectively. The unfortunate reality is that the Carabineros played an integral role in repression, a position that haunts them until this day. Not only did Chile lose citizens to human rights abuses, but the trauma of the dictatorship did lasting damage to the security institutions themselves, and the Carabineros in particular.

From my interviews, I gathered that even though the Carabineros suffered resource shortfalls, they did not engage in corrupt activities, such as asking for bribes. Furthermore, much of the distrust citizens had of the Carabineros was linked to their abusive behavior in their role as repressors and their inability to address the rising crime at that time. In terms of abuse, there existed broad political antagonism toward the undemocratic military regime. The following section speaks to the long and arduous road toward achieving the goal of developing a high-quality police force once again.

The Return of Democracy, 1988–2000

In 1988, General Augusto Pinochet was forced to submit to a referendum on his rule following the 1980 Constitution that his junta had written and approved. The 1988 plebiscite had only one candidate, General Pinochet. A *yes* vote indicated support for Pinochet to continue in power for another eight years. The *no* vote indicated a desire for Pinochet to step down and set up civilian presidential elections. On October 5, 1988, the plebiscite resulted in a 54 percent vote of no (Collier and Sater 2004, 380). Pinochet had to step down and set up civilian elections.

On December 14, 1989, the civilian leader of the Christian Democrats, Patricio Aylwin, was elected president of Chile. He took power in March 1990 (Collier and Sater 2004, 382). The election and administration of Patricio Aylwin played a crucial role in the development of the Carabineros de Chile. However, Pinochet would prove to be a specter that haunted subsequent governments and the Carabineros. Before legally transferring power to a civilian government in 1990, Pinochet made changes to the organic laws of the armed forces, basically guaranteeing high levels of autonomy to the military and the police. The Organic Law of the Carabineros gave them more independence. These types of laws constitutionally require a super majority of 4–7 votes to amend. Because of this, there is little or weak civilian oversight of the Carabineros.

As the first civilian president in decades, Patricio Aylwin had a difficult task at hand. Crime was on the rise, remnants of leftist paramilitary groups were still operating, and the Carabineros were financially and morally depleted. One retired police general I spoke with noted that Aylwin removed the military from street patrols and began providing the police with resources to do their work. President Aylwin's first order of business was to drastically improve police welfare. In his first presidential address to Congress on May 21, 1990, Aylwin highlighted the importance of the Carabineros. He stated that at that time, it was "necessary to strengthen the capacity for action of the Carabineros . . . providing them with the means to fulfill their function" (Aylwin 1990). The impact of these reforms was felt almost immediately as described by a retired Carabineros sergeant major, Carlos Ripetti: "When Aylwin came in, he increased his salary substantially, roughly doubling our income. In the dictatorship, the department stores refused to give us credit in the past because we earned too little. Anyone else, a rural worker, right away they would give them credit because they earned more money than we did. But with the pay increase, they gave us credit" (Ripetti, interview with author, December 2012).

Although the Aylwin administration substantially reformed the welfare of the Carabineros, as well as made internal changes in the force, very little was done to establish external civilian control. For example, the Carabinero director-general, Rodolfo Stange, had been at the head of the Carabineros since 1985. Aylwin was not empowered to remove him or any of the other generals. In 1995, President Eduardo Frei solicited the retirement of General Stange as a result of his involvement in human rights abuses (Jorge Zalaquett, interview with author, December 2012). Stange had to renounce his position after indicating that the presidency was more powerful than the police and, as a result, the institution was suffering (Flisfich and Robledo 2012, 79). After stepping down, Frei named the second-in-line of the Carabineros as the new director general, Fernando Cordero. Also, there was the problem of political representation manifested in four Senate members who were designated by the armed forces and Carabineros de Chile (Flisfich and Robledo 2012, 58). Moreover, Frei also attempted and failed to move the Carabineros out of the Ministry of Defense and into the Ministry of the Interior.

Although reforms to civilian control were not sweeping, the Frei administration did introduce essential reforms to the crime-fighting effectiveness, welfare, training, and image of the police. During Frei's government (1994–2000), a change in rhetoric took place, switching the concept of the police from a national security role to a citizen security role, hoping to foster closer relations between the police and society (Ruz Baeza 2010). In 2012, I interviewed Lucian Fouilloux, who was subsecretary of the Carabineros under Frei during the 1994–2000 administration, and we spoke at length about the reforms made to the Carabineros. In 1995, the Frei administration prioritized investing in vehicles, clothes, and infrastructure for the Carabineros. In addition to funding and improving the police welfare system and logistics, the Frei administration made essential changes to professionalism. Fouilloux explained that Frei introduced an internal framework to incorporate an academic aspect of human rights into all police training. In 1997 and 1998, members of Congress approved new laws sent to them by President Frei, laws that modernized the careers of the police through the Statute of Carabineros Personnel (Flisfich and Robledo 2012, 79). These changes made career advancement possible based on capacity and professionalism, but prohibited officers who had been involved in human rights violations from advancing along their career tracks (Fouilloux, interview with author, November 2012). This was a useful tool that slowly purged the institution of corruption.

As Felipe Harboe, a former subsecretary of Carabineros and parliamentarian, noted in our interview, the period from 1997 to 2000 brought the beginning of the institutionalization of democratic civilian control in terms of citizen security. Civilian leaders realized the importance of public security matters, and the government gained power in this arena. Indicators were created to measure the effectiveness of public security processes. The civilian authority started increasing through budgetary control. Toward the end of Frei's administration, he noted in his final speech to Congress that, in 1999, "the Carabineros will increase their operative force with 4,700 new functionaries, a process that will continue until, in December of 2001, [I will have added] the number of 12,000 new agents, recuperated from administrative function, for police service" (Frei 1999). During the dictatorship, the unfortunate reality was that all armed forces became heavily involved in government and became bureaucratic quagmires. Many police who were trained for law enforcement duties had been relegated to office work. Thus, Frei's reforms reoriented police toward police duties. In their place, civilians were hired to take on those administrative duties, bringing Carabineros into day-to-day contact with civilian professionals. In turn, this increased civilian expertise and experience in public security matters, which was necessary for advancing more civilian control in the future.

The next presidential administration of Ricardo Lagos (2000–2004) sought to build on and advance Frei's police reforms. Patricio Morales Aguirre, subsecretary of the Carabineros under Lagos, shared with me in an interview that it was through the power of the purse strings that civilians got some degree of external control over the Carabineros. Although the subsecretary of the Carabineros did not have any operative control, that office's budgetary control provided it with more oversight. Lagos was able to institutionalize his presidential prerogative to nominate top commanders to the armed forces as the old guard from the dictatorship who once dominated the institution began to retire. This allowed Lagos to promote officers who were more inclined to support democratic civilian control of the police forces. Beyond this, Lagos set aside 70 percent of the Carabineros budget for nondiscretionary spending, such as salaries, vehicle maintenance, building maintenance, and the like, but reserved 30 percent of the budget for the president and subsecretary of Carabineros to utilize at their discretion. This further empowered the president to dictate police strategy.

The presidential administrations of both Michelle Bachelet (2006–2010) and Sebastián Piñera (2010–2014) also advanced the police force (Sergio Aguiló, interview with author, November 2012; Ximena Vidal, interview with author, December 2012). Under Michelle Bachelet, "1,500 new Carabineros entered the police force and from here on after in the years between 2007 and 2010 there would be an additional 6,000" Carabineros on the streets pursuant to Law 20104 (Bachelet 2007). In addition, negotiations began in Bachelet's administration to finally transfer the Carabineros from the Defense Ministry to the Interior Ministry. After negotiations, the Carabineros de Chile was finally transferred to the Ministry of

Interior and Public Security under Law 20502, passed on February 21, 2011, which reformed the Organic Law of Carabineros of March 7, 1990. Today, the Carabineros report to the Ministry of Interior and Public Security (Republic of Chile 2011).

Carabineros in the Twenty-First Century, 2000–2018

By the twenty-first century, the various democratic administrations had undone some but not all the harm that the dictatorship brought onto the Carabineros (Alejandra Mohor, interview with author, October 2012). In this process, each subsequent administration has instituted reforms to the training, recruitment, welfare, and oversight of police (Francisco Ortiz, interview with author, January 2013; Marcos Robledo, interview with author, October 2012). The extensive police professionalization made possible by centralization is at the core of understanding why Chilean police exhibit lower levels of malfeasant police behavior. Here, I summarize some of my findings of Chilean policing in the twenty-first century (Yesenia Mahecha, interview with author, March 2013).

The Carabineros have a strong welfare system, and though there is a low base salary, it includes robust pension plans, health care, vacation, housing, child care, education discounts, loans, and upward mobility. Additionally, bonuses can be earned for hazard pay and years of service. For instance, every three years of service comes with an increase in wage, called a *trienio*. At twenty years of service, Carabineros receive an additional bonus as well, regardless of whether one rises in rank or not (Ramiro F. Larraín Donoso, pers. comm., 2012). Also, when Carabineros marry and have children, their monthly salaries are increased. Thus, for lower ranks, the base pay is US$277, but it can rise to US$860 with bonuses. Entry-level commissioned officers earn a base of US$530, and at the upper end earn US$1467 with bonuses. As a comparison, the average monthly minimum wage in Chile is roughly US$356 (Carabineros de Chile 2014). Although Carabineros earn substantially less than the minimum salary at the outset, increments in salary with time and benefits can offset that. Carabineros also receive childcare benefits, such as free day care, preschool, and kindergarten in the major cities of Santiago, Valparaíso, and Concepción; these cities contain the majority of Carabineros positions in the country (Larraín Donoso, pers. comm., 2012).

After twenty-five years of service, Carabineros can expect to receive 619,530 pesos (US$1,106) per month during their retirement (Gonzalo Huenumil Lezana, pers. comm., 2012). A 2013 report by Radio Chile stated that Carabineros' pensions were six times more than the national average, thus indicating the strength of these welfare benefits as compared to what society at large receives (Huerta 2013).

Besides pay and pension, Carabineros also receive health care for any injuries acquired through the police service, and they have subsidized health care for all sicknesses for them and their families. Their healthcare system is made up of two central hospitals, both located in the capital of Santiago, Hospital Institucional and Hospital de la Dirección de Previsión de Carabineros. The hospitals handle major surgeries or treatments for serious illnesses. For less-urgent care, sixteen consultation clinics are in the principal cities of the provinces. In addition, there are fourteen regional dental centers located in the largest cities in the country.

Furthermore, the Carabineros as an organization has agreements with all the public hospitals, private caregivers, and laboratories throughout the country to provide for discounted care. Carabineros also enjoy deep pharmaceutical discounts of up to 55 percent on generic medications and 25 percent for name-brand medications. The Carabineros provide subsidies for funeral expenses of about US$1,070.

Officers with fewer than fifteen years of service get two weeks of paid vacation per year. Once they serve more than twenty years of service, they receive close to four weeks of paid vacation per year. The Carabineros also have various vacation rentals available to them at a deep discount. Carabineros can enjoy 19 vacation centers, 22 family-sized apartments, 96 hotel rooms, and 168 vacation cabins available throughout the country (Larraín Donoso, pers. comm., 2012).

Most Carabineros ages eighteen to twenty-two do not live outside their commissaries (police stations); rather, they live together in dormitories. In my visit to the 36th Carabinero Regiment Commissary in La Florida, I observed the daily life of these young police persons. Commissaries have on-site cafeterias, shared showers, and barrack-style beds, as well as communal areas in which to watch TV and play pool or cards. When Carabineros start a family or move out of the commissary, government-owned housing is available (Voltaire Opazo Ibáñez, pers. comm., 2012). There are 5,815 discounted family housing units available to Carabineros throughout Chile (Republic of Chile 2012).

Furthermore, Carabineros can apply for various types of loans, ranging from US$1,250 to $12,500, from the Carabineros Credit Union (Mutualidad de Carabineros 2014). First, there are free short-term loans, meaning that the money can be spent on anything the borrower decides. This type of loan has a monthly fixed interest rate of 1.05 percent and an annual interest rate of 13.41 percent, with repayment plans anywhere from three to twenty-four months. Second, there are individual long-term loans for medical expenses, education expenses, vehicle purchases, and home repairs/improvements, with repayment plans ranging from twenty-five to eighty-four months at a monthly fixed interest rate of 0.75 percent and an annual interest rate of 5.95 percent. Finally, loans are available for home purchases with an interest rate at 5.95 percent to help individuals purchase their first home.

Beyond a strong set of incentives to join and stay with the force, the Carabineros de Chile has an extensive police development framework that plays a central role in limiting malfeasant police behavior. The beginning of any substantial development structure has to do with recruitment standards and recruitment processes. The current basic requirements to enter the Carabineros are: be a Chilean between eighteen and twenty-five years old, have a high school education, be single with no kids, and be a minimum of 1.68 meters tall (men) or 1.60 meters tall (women) (Voltaire Opazo Ibáñez, pers. comm., 2012).

Beyond these basic entry requirements, additional recruitment criteria weed out potentially problematic personnel. Individuals who join the Carabineros are looking for a profession, not just a job. Recruits must undergo rigorous entrance exams covering basic knowledge in history, mathematics, and grammar. They also undergo physiological, psychological, and dental health exams. The psychological review helps determine a recruit's tendencies toward crime, violence, schizophrenia, or other mental health problems. The final piece of the stringent recruitment regime that sets Chilean Carabineros recruits apart has to do with the declaration of personal history. Candidates must list all family members, siblings, and other immediate and extended family members and their criminal histories. Then the Carabineros investigate to make sure that a recruit is not involved in drug trafficking or any other crimes. Both the enlisted ranks and the officers have the same requirements, but the exams for officers are much more difficult, like university entrance exams.

In short, the acceptance process for the Carabineros is very selective; only about one in four, or 26 percent of applicants, were accepted to become a part of the force during 2005–2013 (Larraín Donoso, pers. comm., 2012). Being allowed in is only the beginning, because once accepted, the recruits face an arduous process of training, which also forces weaker individuals out of the institution.

Police receive training in two types of schools: one for commissioned officers and one for enlisted. The General Carlos Ibáñez del Campo School is for the exclusive training of future Carabinero officers, or the Superior Commissioned Personnel (Personal de Nombramiento Supremo [PNS]). The PNS are commissioned into service by the president, who must approve their ascension in rank. The period of training at this school is four years. In the third year of education, candidates make the rank of second lieutenant. In the fourth year, candidates begin practicing in police units and work on a graduation thesis, after which they receive a degree in public security administration. From there, the ranks increase in the following order: second lieutenant, first lieutenant, captain, major, lieutenant colonel, colonel, and general.

The second type of school is the Personal de Nombramiento Institucional (PNI), or institutionally named personnel, formation schools. There are various schools for enlisted Carabineros trainees in Santiago, Arica, Antofagasta, Concepción, Ancud, and Punta Arenas. The trainees are hired as Carabineros students, and after one year of training, they enter the Carabineros to work in a commissary. Referred to as *la tropa*, these trainees are the equivalent of enlisted ranks in the military, and they engage in general policing duties, such as transit, patrol, and security detail. Their career begins with the rank of Carabinero and can climb to corporal second-class and then corporal first-class. Enlisted ranks can also, after fifteen years of service, apply for noncommissioned officer training of one to two years and receive ranks of sergeant second, sergeant first, subofficer, and subofficer major (Carabineros de Chile 2009b).

Carabinero officers receive excellent theoretical training from well-known teachers from the Supreme Court and the public prosecutor's office and other civilian experts. As mentioned earlier, a remarkable improvement came from the Frei and Lagos administrations when the topic of human rights emerged as an essential requirement to include in the education of Carabineros. One former Carabinero I interviewed noted that "the training was brutally difficult . . . many said that the Carabineros had more exhaustive training than the military." The real difference between enlisted ranks training in the Carabineros and military training is length of training: military training is only twelve to eighteen weeks for army soldiers and enlisted personnel; in contrast, Carabineros enlisted training lasts for nine to twelve months. Their professionalized training inculcates the importance of hierarchy in the minds of the Carabineros. The hierarchical system functions as a continuous form of internal oversight at both individual and group levels. At the individual level, Carabineros know that there are superior officers above them who are watching their behavior. Individuals internalize the power of the hierarchy, knowing that any misstep is not only likely to be discovered but also punished.

Internal hierarchical control is essential, but it also functions at the group level. Lower-rank officers who see a fellow officer doing something wrong are more likely to step in to stop that behavior or report it, lest they also get punished. A Chilean journalist I interviewed in 2013 affirmed the "system functions so that commanders watch over their people constantly. Commanders are going to constantly be on top of their people in a way that the lower ranks do not feel free to act in whatever way they want." A former Carabineros and practicing lawyer with expertise on Carabineros laws, norms, and regulations, commented that "the officers can apply various administrative sanctions like demerits in the personnel file and days of arrest and or denial of payment. When a Carabinero on the street hits someone on the head, he gets taken out immediately. The accused are first removed from duty by commanders, and then there is an investigation into their actions." Indeed, it may be considered unjust and extreme. Still, it is remarkably effective and immediate—in short, the strong hierarchy is a powerful mechanism to deter behavior and may be necessary for the proper functioning of a less-malfeasant police force (Carabineros de Chile 2009a). The hierarchy is a constant force in the lives of Carabineros that shapes behavior. Higher-ranking officers dole out discipline and punishment to lower ranks for acting out of order. They sanction very hard. When an officer steps out of line, a sheet is added to their "Hoja de Vida" folder. This carries a sense of being stigmatized because these sheets can affect career advancement.

Within the disciplinary regulations of the Carabineros are several violations that, depending on severity, require disciplinary actions. Title V of the Carabineros Disciplinary Regulation 11 notes the various offenses related to the moral integrity of the police function subject to disciplinary actions. Various sanctions can be applied to Carabineros. These include written warnings, written reprimands, days of arrest, disponibility, suspension, mark on qualifications, and ultimately a call for voluntary retirement or forced retirement (Carabineros de Chile 2009a). Days of arrest can range from one to thirty days, wherein the sanctioned Carabinero is not allowed to leave the barracks except to conduct their patrol functions (Carabineros de Chile 2009a). Disponibility, a type of sanction, is when the Carabineros is required to work in areas outside their patrol functions, such as in administrative tasks, for a day to three months. During a suspension, the Carabinero receives only basic pay and is not allowed to work for up to two months (Carabineros de Chile 2009a).

Qualification of service means that the person did not receive an adequate score on his or her annual review and will be called upon to submit retirement paperwork (Carabineros de Chile 2009a). This punishment is less severe than forced separation. The difference is that retirement looks better than forced separation to future employers—it is akin to the difference between honorable and dishonorable discharges. These mechanisms are the hierarchy's tools to maintain discipline in the ranks, and they are effectively used to lower instances of and control malfeasant behavior.

Beyond the disciplinary controls, the Carabineros also have internal controls. First, each commissary guards office (police station) conducts administrative investigations to handle complaints and investigate police accused of wrongdoing (Jaime Jorquera, interview with author, December 2012). These investigations are done in-house at the police-station level. If evidence is found to substantiate a claim, the case is taken to the military penal courts.

Second, there is a Directorate of Police Intelligence (DIPORCAL). DIPORCAL offices can be found in every prefecture of the Carabineros

(Daniel Soto, interview with author, December 2012). These offices function as an early warning system, providing the hierarchy with information regarding suspicious behavior or activities that need monitoring. The personnel at DIPORCAL act independently of the hierarchical administration (Opazo Ibáñez 2012; Zuñiga 2012).

Third, in the case of abuse of force, the next chief must confirm or strike down the allegation. When allegations are founded, the chief enacts disciplinary measures and contacts the military tribunal (Opazo Ibáñez, pers. comm., 2012). The person is then court-martialed. However, the military justice system is problematic because it is biased toward the Carabineros, especially in cases of abuse of force. Nevertheless, the presence of a military court is an essential system of control.

The final and most potent internal control mechanism rests in the hands of the director general. The director general has the discretionary power to remove anyone. This means that disciplinary actions for violation of internal rules are not up to local authorities or politicians to decide but are in the hands of the police force's most senior officer, who can fire anybody in the institution right away. Thus, there is no lengthy litigation that keeps potentially offending officers in the institution while the investigation into their behavior is ongoing.

The Carabineros also have a few external controls, including the power of the comptroller, the power of the president, and judicial oversight. Comptrollers ensure that public funds are spent responsibly. For example, if Carabineros stations buy uniforms, then they must use certain norms, they must take public proposals, and they must find the best competitor from which to buy. These safeguards ensure the bidding process is transparent and cost-effective, and purchasers do not unfairly favor one vendor over another.

Furthermore, Chilean presidents have at their discretion the power to remove any director general and need only inform Congress of their decision. This power was granted to the president in 2005 through Constitutional reform Law 20050. This option strengthens civilian control over the top brass of Carabineros, although the removal of other generals is still under the discretion of the Carabineros' director general.

Lastly, civilian courts have controls. In my correspondence with General Voltaire Opazo Ibáñez, he stated, "Acts of corruption are rigorously investigated by the external body of the public prosecutor's office that functions throughout the country's provinces" (Opazo Ibáñez, pers. comm., December 12, 2012). Carabineros engaged in corruption will be prosecuted in civilian courts, and if convicted, the offender will be fired and incarcerated (Opazo Ibáñez, pers. comm., December 12, 2012).

Data I received through a Freedom of Information Act request in Chile reveals that the Carabineros as an institution and its mechanisms of control are functional, and these controls do remove many Carabineros who infringe on institutional norms. From 1990 to 2010, 256 Carabineros on average were fired per year (Transparency Request RSIP No. 18433 2012). The average age of the person discharged from the Carabineros was forty-two. Of the 5,346 Carabineros let go over the past twenty years, 97 percent were male (Republic of Chile 2012). Of those fired, 7 percent were students at the enlisted rank police academies, and 3.5 percent were aspiring cadets at the officer level. Eighty-two percent were active-duty regular enlisted ranks personnel (subofficer major and below), while only 7 percent were from officer ranks. The dismissal of generals, although rare, was handled among themselves, and I was not able to find data on their removal. Most of the time, generals voluntarily retired when faced with potential disciplinary actions (Republic of Chile 2012).

This now raises the question: Why were these people let go? Ultimately, 40 percent were let go for poor conduct, 3.5 percent were discharged for being bad students at the academies, 35 percent were let go because they received poor performance reviews, 20 percent were let go because they violated ethical norms or disciplinary regulations, and 1.5 percent were dismissed as a result of administrative changes (Republic of Chile 2012). Carabineros are frequently removed from office, meaning there are consequences for malfeasant behavior and the regulations are enforced.

When Good Is Not Good Enough, 2018–2021

In 2019, mass disturbances and social movements took place throughout Chile, but they were centered mainly in the capital city of Santiago. The protests, instigated by a price hike at the Santiago Metro, were related to continued and rising inequality that limits the upward mobility and well-being of many Chileans. Of particular importance for this book, the response by the police was abnormally brutal. The high commissioner for human rights in the United Nations has identified that of the 28,000 people arrested in protests, 113 cases of police torture were reported, as well as 23 cases of sexual abuse of women and minors. Meanwhile, 350 people suffered from eye injuries caused by police projectiles (United Nations 2019). Why did this take place despite the centralization and professionalization I have described? Shouldn't the police be less physically abusive overall if my theoretical conditions are met? Although this book is about how institutions structure police behavior in daily interactions with civilians, and not about protest policing, these events provide an opportunity to elucidate the complex realities of police work. I take some time here to explore this reality.

The Carabineros used in protests are not patrol officers but are anti-riot specialists. They are called Fuerzas Especiales de Prefectura, or Prefecture Special Forces. They are easily distinguished from patrol officers because they wear heavy riot gear marked with "FF.EE" and drive anti-riot, lightly armed vehicles, which expel tear gas. These forces specialize in crowd and riot control and are deployed to sporting events as well as to protect the presidential palace. This job is also hazardous. The Carabineros claim that as many as 947 of their officers have received injuries as a result of the 2019 protest cycles alone (Urquieta 2019).

The 28th, 29th, and 40th Commissaries in Santiago house special forces. Thus, these are not standard police officers walking the streets. Patrol officers, although they sometimes wear riot gear, tend to work as backup or traffic control around riots. The abuses perpetrated by these arresting officers and those in the receiving police stations with holding cells are problematic. The degree of violence gives rise to a new puzzle: What explains increases and decreases in police abuse of citizens in protest settings? Although I leave this question to future scholars, I sketch out some impressions here. I think three things drive an increased likelihood of protest policing veering toward abuse: (1) protest conditions and tactics of contention, (2) political leadership qualities and ideologies, and (3) cultural pathologies of the police service as an institution.

First, I want to talk about the 2019 protest conditions. I lived in Santiago de Chile in 2013 at the height of the student protest movement that called for education reforms. I walked in the streets around Plaza Baquedano, or along Avenida Libertador Bernardo O'Higgins, and I saw firsthand the student protests on Avenida Chile in Bogotá in 2014. These experiences gave me a few insights about protest policing that can help frame our understanding of the Chilean demonstrations of 2019.

My experiences in Chile illustrate that there were two types of protests: benign and destructive. Benign protests utilized the standard repertoire of contention, such as marching, speeches, and occupying a space for a rally. I experienced many benign protests, such as a nurses' union march near Cerro Santa Lucía. The response by the police was starkly different from their response to the students. Union protests and marches were less contentious, had no violence, had a predetermined march path, and were met with police accommodation. These protests elicited police cooperation in blocking traffic to facilitate the expression of civil liberties. The special forces were not even mobilized.

However, the student protests played along the more destructive end of the spectrum in expressing contention, and the police treated these protests differently than the more benign ones. Students would not only take over the administration building but would also take to the streets to march without permits. Some students would engage in destructive behavior and directly challenge the police, which in turn was met with violence. The police treated these protests and protesters differently because the style of contention requires a proportional response. My experience was that police treated student protesters from the University of Chile, Universidad Catholica, and Universidad Diego Portales and other universities much harsher than protesters at benign protests. At the same time, these movements had a higher propensity for the destruction of private property and confrontation with police. Student protests were joined by instigators referred to by the media as the "Encapuchados," or the "hooded ones," who took the opportunity of social mobilization to destroy property and attack police; this is part of the repertoire of contention. These situations begin the spiral of attack and counterattack, which gives the police the opening to repress the protests altogether.

Protest policing is inherently contentious as a result of the design of social movements. The likelihood of violent confrontation with police is always higher in mass mobilizations that engage in violent contention. The 2019 protest violence moved beyond simple vandalism (breaking windows and spray-painting) and veered into arson and mass looting. I do not judge the rationale for this, or the justice or injustice of it, but simply observe that some protesters engaged in extreme forms of contention. For instance, in 2019 a total of 667 businesses were looted and burned down and 70 metro stations destroyed, indicating the degree to which protesters engaged in violent practices (La Razon 2019). This degree of unrest and the widespread nature of it, as well as the continuation of it for weeks at a time, stretched the Carabineros special forces so thin that the armed forces also had to be deployed. This is not a normal policing situation. Business owners protecting their businesses were opening fire on looters and killed several. People died in fires set by protesters. Others were killed by the armed forces and the police. Therefore, my assessment is that the higher the degree of violence perpetrated by protesters, the more violent the response of the police force, irrespective of the force's degree of professionalization or centralization.

Second, the abuse conditions are a product of not only extreme mobilization and protester violence but also the permissive environment provided to the police by the presidency, interior ministry, and the general in command of the Carabineros. Chilean president Sebastián Piñera and his minister of the interior defended the police actions in the protests, but they failed to negotiate a more peaceful end to the rising crisis. Further, Piñera had been unable to address a series of mounting crises within the Carabineros from 2017–2020 (González 2019). Instead, Piñera and his administration likely made the crises worse by appointing a newly minted general at the head of the nation's police force "who lacks substantial experience in operational command" and could not "impose his authority on the men of the Special Forces" (González 2019). Piñera and his administration are from the Renovación Nacional coalition, which is a right-wing coalition of political parties. These parties have direct links to the authoritarian era of

General Augusto Pinochet and, as such, promote and maintain ideologies opposed to protester demands for higher taxes on wealthy and better access to more affordable public goods, as well as increased salaries. These political leanings, political miscalculations, and lack of effective control over the police created a more permissive environment in which the police could abuse protesters. It was only after social backlash against Piñera when the degree of abuse was reported that he publicly rebuked officer behavior and called for investigations.

Third, a cultural institutionalist explanation also has currency here. The pathologies of the Pinochet period and its imprint on the Carabineros in terms of institutional legacy cannot be ignored. From 1973 to 1989, leftist officers were purged or left the institution. Those who remained or were recruited were therefore complicit in Pinochet's ideological predisposition. Rooting out moderate officers meant that the institutional culture of the Carabineros evolved to a more conservative view of politics. As such, police viewed the leftists in the streets as subversive Communist enemies of the past. Culturally, the Carabineros were more likely to be abusive in protest scenarios against leftists' uprisings in general. I have not empirically assessed this. However, many of my interviewees made such claims of the protest cycles in 2013. This is an incomplete area of my research beyond the scope of this project. Nevertheless, I am inclined to think that self-selection has taken place and has influenced police perceptions of protesters that further their dehumanization and abuse at the hands of the Carabineros.

Given this reality, I suggest this chapter be interpreted through the following lens. This chapter does not mean to construe the Carabineros as the apotheosis of policing in the world, but Chile indeed has the best police force in Latin America. It is known for its relatively lower levels of misconduct, the evidence of which can be found in various data sources. For instance, in Chile, only 6 percent of respondents in a Transparency International Survey in 2013 reported having paid a bribe to the police. Furthermore, public opinion polling reinforces the high level of trust in the Carabineros. According to José Miguel Cruz (2009), only 3.7 percent of citizens reported being physically or verbally abused by the Carabineros in 2009 as compared to 8.7 percent in Argentina.

However, the Carabineros are not free of misconduct. Even though they, on average, garner the trust of 57 percent of Chilean citizens in the Latinobarómetro surveys, this level of trust does not approach the trust placed in some of the best police forces in the world (e.g., Norwegian, Finnish, and Swedish and police services). According to data from the World Values Survey, between 1981 and 2014, 87 percent of society on average trusted the police in Norway, followed by Finland with 85.2 percent, and Sweden with 76.5 percent (Inglehart et al. 2022). This illustrates that further improvements can and should be made even if the Carabineros are the best police force in Latin America. The case of Chile serves to illustrate that centralization and professionalization lower (but do not eliminate) misconduct. Remaining arguments, such as ideology, leadership, and cultural pathologies, are ripe topics for future research on police misconduct. Further reforms can and should be made to training, and more mechanisms of citizen oversight should be added. These reforms are more feasible within the centralized and professional structure of the Carabineros than in a decentralized structure that lacks professionalization mechanisms.

Conclusion

The construction of the Chilean Carabineros was a process of centralization and professionalization. Specifically, the period of 1896 to 1927 that pitted three institutional models of policing against one another shows that the centralized and professional model used by the gendarmería and then the Carabineros was far superior to the decentralized and demilitarized model. The purely communal police system of 1891 to 1896 in Chile provided little in terms of professionalism, precisely because of the obstacles that decentralization presents. Indeed, it was not possible and was very costly for poor rural communities to have police at all. The evidence was provided was La Granja's budget: roughly 70 percent of its local taxes went to their police, and this was not enough to provide an adequate salary, let alone to offer proper training, oversight, and benefits. The early period of police decentralization, especially under the Law of Autonomous Communities in the 1890s, reveals the depth of the problems that decentralized systems pose. From 1900 to 1920, it became increasingly apparent that police at the municipal level were facing severe difficulties with misconduct, and the process of police centralization ensued. Hence, the decentralized system proved ineffective and increased police misconduct. Thus, the data rejects this hypothetical argument.

National control of police alone would not suffice, as exhibited by the police development era of 1833–1891, as well as the case of the fiscal police in 1896–1927. Centralization without professionalization does not reduce misconduct in the same way that centralization and professionalization do together. Therefore, in the case of Chile, the occupational models of municipal police fell victim to vice and patrimonial relationships. As police in larger cities were centralized under national control, they were also professionalized. The gendarmería units also became more professional, with benefits, development, and an oversight structure, and hence performed better than local police. From 1890 to 1927, local police had high levels of misconduct. During this same time period, the more professionalized and centralized Policías Fiscales, Gendarmerie Regiment, and Carabineros had lower levels of misconduct.

In terms of militarization, the pure demilitarized system implemented from 1891 to 1896 was associated with poor policing because it created security gaps that allowed bandits to dominate the countryside. Evidence shows that the communal police were abusive, drunk, involved in criminal enterprises, and helped local political leaders manipulate electoral outcomes. When Chile put a militarized model in place in 1896 with the rural gendarmería units and later the Carabineros, insecurity decreased. These police forces, in narratives and interviews, were considered less malfeasant than the simple communal system. Militarization brought a professional model of work to the police. Sometimes professionalization is a by-product of importing military institutions that are beneficial for controlling deviant police behavior.

Blaming malfeasant police behavior on the criminal contexts does not work in the Chilean analysis. It is the other way around: banditry arose in Chile because the police were so weak. When the government in 1896 created the gendarmería, it sent centralized and militarized police with professionalized institutions against the bandits. To be sure, the Chile of the 1990s and 2000s does not compare to Colombia around that same time. However, the comparison is fair when we consider Chile in the nineteenth and early twentieth centuries, with bandits roving the countryside, threatening the state. It may be an important argument, but this analysis illustrates that a more substantial explanation of police misconduct is linked to the structure of the police and the professionalizing institutions that were copied from the military.

Other arguments presented in the literature do find currency here. There is a clear difference between police in authoritarian regimes and police in democratic ones. Thus, I cannot refute that regime type is an important factor. The scope of my model covers only free periods. Thus, centralization and professionalization curtail corruption but do not address the abuse of citizens. Because Chile is a former Spanish colony and mostly Catholic, we can control for these hypotheses in this case and reveal that, despite these antecedents, Chile can develop a high-quality police force.

In the next chapter, I look at the historical development of policing in Colombia. What will become apparent is that despite different historical contexts, both Chile and Colombia share a similar historical evolution of police. They both developed centralized and professionalized police, and this is what explains their status at the top of public opinion surveys on police behavior.

3

Colombia:
Policing in Times of
Civil Conflict

In 1993, Colombian homicide rates peaked at 70 homicides per 100,000 people (Medicina Legal 2012). Leftist revolutionary groups roamed the countryside pursued by conservative paramilitary groups, with citizens caught in the middle. During this time, the Cali and Medellín drug cartels were at the peak of their power. During the early 1990s, only 23 percent of respondents polled in Colombia reported any trust in their police (CIMA 1993). Then, there was a dramatic reversal. By 2013, the homicide rate had dipped to 33.2 per 100,000 (Medicina Legal 2012), the government had disbanded the Cali and Medellín drug cartels, paramilitary groups were outlawed, and leftist guerrillas were pushed back. From 2000 to 2013, 68.5 percent of Colombians came to trust the police (Gallup Colombia LTDA 2007)—a stunning volte-face for Colombia. What explains this remarkable turnaround? This chapter answers the question by engaging in a historical analysis of the evolution of law enforcement in Colombia. The findings point toward a process of centralization and professionalization as critical changes in reforming the police and increasing security and order in Colombia.

I employ an analysis of Colombian policing in seven periods: 1846–1885, 1885–1953, 1953–1962, 1962–1985, 1985–1993, 1993–1997, and 1997–present. From 1846 to 1885, the Liberal Party dominated the political system and set forth a Confederal constitution that gave different departments (states) the right to have standing military and police. This decentralization was challenged in 1885 when the Conservative Party took over and created a unitary government. The Conservative Party created the National Police of Colombia (PNC) with the intent of centralizing all municipal police under its authority. This reform attempt did not materialize, and

63

instead, the PNC had jurisdiction only in the capital city of Bogotá. Alongside the PNC, each department (state) and municipality had its local police. As my theory predicted, police in local regions came to be dominated by local political party elites, who used them to attack opposition party members, thereby increasing violence in Colombia.

The assassination of Jorge Eliécer Gaitán in 1948 led to an insecurity spiral throughout the country. Liberals and conservatives used their local police forces to kill and attack each other. The violence reached such high levels that, in 1953, moderate Liberal and Conservative Party leaders called on the military to intervene. In 1953, General Gustavo Rojas Pinilla's military dictatorship set about restoring order to society, and police misconduct decreased considerably. Police were by and large honest and effective in their jobs through the 1960s. The real problems with misconduct came in 1980, with the rise of narco-trafficking. In 1993, the PNC appeared on the verge of collapse. The mounting security crises led society and politicians to mobilize and fully professionalize the police. The police were given better salaries, received extended training, and were provided with more robust oversight mechanisms. These changes helped mitigate the influence of drug trafficking, and police misconduct decreased once more.

These empirical findings confirmed that the centralization of police worked to decrease police misconduct. In 1953, the military regime initiated a process of centralization and professionalization. Centralization was so critical because it removed local patrimonial control over the police. Although centralization removed patrimonial relations, it did not adequately address the problem of police professionalization. In 1993, Colombian political leaders decided to deepen their commitment to professionalizing the police by increasing welfare, development, and oversight regimes. Following these dramatic developments, the police not only engaged in less misconduct but also started to win back the trust of society. Thus, the historical findings in Colombia support the professionalization hypothesis as well. The following section discusses the historical political and policing background of Colombia over two centuries. One thing is clear: In the case of Colombia, centralization and professionalization helped reduce misconduct.

Origins of Policing in Postindependence Colombia

In the period following independence, Colombian cities developed the Serenos system of public security, which was identical to Chile's. Establishing these new police forces, according to Law 8 of 1821, was the responsibility of the respective administrative authorities in the departments, provinces, and cantons of the republic. Furthermore, Law 11 of 1825 obligated governors and mayors to provide general tranquility and order, the security of persons and property, the execution of laws or the executive power, and everything having to do with policing in their political units. According to Dayanna Becerra (2010, 153), "The multiplicity of assigned functions given to governors and mayors resulted in the existence of different bodies of police throughout the country." Meanwhile, Decree 2 of 1827 authorized the president to directly name the police chief of the capital of Colombia in Bogotá. In 1831, political infighting led to the dissolution of the Republic of Colombia into three countries: New Granada (present-day Colombia and Panama), Venezuela, and Ecuador.

From 1832 to 1858, the country of New Granada centralized its political system controlled by the president and his intendentes (mayors assigned rather than elected) in subnational units. During this period, the congress of New Granada promulgated Law 8 of 1841, which created a dual policing platform: one under national control, and the other under a regional authority. This structural formulation, coupled with two polarized parties, would prove a volatile mix, as it did in the previous chapter on Chile. The Conservative Party favored a stable centralized government, a role for the Catholic Church in society, and the protection of land. In contrast, the Liberal Party endorsed a federal form of government, a decentralized security apparatus, the separation of church and state, and the redistribution of land.

In 1853, Liberal elites took control of the political system and adopted a federal constitution that provided more regional autonomy, giving birth to the Granadine Confederation (1858–1863). This new system of government was less centralized, and it promoted an extreme form of federalism. During this period, both local and regional communities had more power than the central government, and this allowed for the creation of provincial armies by both parties while restricting the federal government's ability to intervene in departmental conflicts (Mazzuca and Robinson 2009, 287). This partisan bickering led to the politicization of security forces that would dominate the political landscape for much of Colombia's history. The Liberal form of government also separated the church and state by nationalizing church-owned lands and wealth and barring clergy from their traditional role as educators. Such extreme policies drew an exaggerated response from the Conservatives. When the Conservatives won the presidency from 1858 through 1862, they tried to reverse these changes, which then spurred hatred from the Liberals, who rose in armed rebellion to halt the reversals.

A civil war ensued from 1860 to 1862 between Liberals and Conservatives over the divisive issues and ended with Conservative defeat in 1863. The Granadine Confederation dissolved, making way for a more robust federalist United States of Colombia (1863–1886), which divided the country into nine autonomous states and which reserved more power for the central government than it had in the previous confederation (Delpar 1994). During this period, known as the Olimpo Radical, Liberals dominated the presidency from 1863 to 1885.

Despite the various changes in political leadership, policing remained mainly under local control and was a poorly funded, disparaged institution. For instance, Decree 819 of 1885, Article 4, prescribed that police officers at all levels had to be chosen "amongst the most respected residents of the city from landowners, businessmen, professors, scientists, and artisans" (Republic of Colombia 1885). However, the reality was that local municipalities lacked the resources to recruit the elites of society. Instead, because of the low remuneration, the Colombian police hiring pool consisted of vagrants, beggars, drunks, and unemployed persons (Puentes 2013, 314). The police of this era were known for making "arbitrary arrests, womanizing, engaging in street fights, drinking on the job, committing sexual offenses, issuing public threats, abandoning their posts, and [the] loss of police property" (Martinez 2001, 513).

The political competition between Liberals and Conservatives only exacerbated unprofessional policing and subsequent abuse of authority. In 1885, Conservatives gained control over the federal government through elections and built a centralized form of government under the 1886 constitution called the Republic of Colombia. The *Hegemonía Conservadora* (1886–1930) was established, a period when successive Conservative governments controlled the country and reversed the policies that Liberals had implemented during their period of control. Conservatives built a system that centralized power, liquidated regional autonomy, restored and enhanced the powers of the president, returned confiscated property, and reset the educational role of the church. However, the policing system remained decentralized and in the hands of local elites, resulting in continued police misconduct. Many members of the police throughout the country were illiterate, lacked legal knowledge, and did not understand administrative protocols (Martinez 2001, 327).

Partisan Law Enforcement and La Violencia, 1886–1953

Intense political competition between Liberals and Conservatives, coupled with direct control over the police and weak institutionalization of professionalism in police labor, led to high levels of police misconduct (Rincon 2003). Both political parties used police to beat, jail, repress, and murder opposition party members (Hudson 2010, 313). Police work was viewed so poorly by society that often rumors circulated "that the draft into police service would coincide with elections." This rumor dissuaded unenthusiastic voters from showing up at the polls for fear of being forced into the police force (Deas 2002, 25). The administration of Carlos Holguin passed Law 90 in 1888, followed by Decree 1.000 of 1891, which established the

PNC with a working budget and normative framework (Becerra 2011, 255). Although it was called the National Police of Colombia, it only operated in the capital of Bogotá. A French officer, Jean Marie Gilibert, was commissioned to head the new institution, which replaced the old police force in the capital. As General Miguel Antonio Gómez (2009) remarks, Gilibert "would have to confront the first challenge: clientelism," whereby mayors would hire politically loyal personnel. Along with clientelism, Gilibert had to fight the stigma associated with all Colombian police. On top of these issues, the PNC, with only 450 men, did not have enough resources to extend its coverage throughout the country (Hudson 2010, 313). Although the vision was to create a police force that would spread throughout the country, the process was slow. It did not supplant the municipal and departmental police that already existed.

Most of the policing in Colombia outside of Bogotá was done by various municipal, departmental, rural police and gendarmeries under the control of subnational politicians (National Police of Colombia 2013c). These forces also suffered from partisanship, corruption, and misconduct. A lack of resources made it difficult for local municipalities to hire enough local police to ensure public order. As an example, by 1897, the governmental authorities noticed the poor response to police recruitment campaigns due to the poor pay and low benefits offered to police at the time. The government officers had to venture out with a census and arbitrarily draft men to fill the empty spots in the police force. Drafted men would submit written refusals and preferred to pay fines instead of joining. Those who were successfully recruited were disinterested in serving because there was a social stigma against this type of work (Martinez 2001, 325).

The individuals who did apply for subnational police positions arrived with written "recommendations from influential politicians" (Gómez 2009, 56). Politicization, combined with the lack of viable candidates, resulted in a police force filled with generally undesirable agents who were far from meeting the specifications in regulations. As a result, the police forces of Colombia were "full of drunks, laggards, and even criminals" (Gómez 2009, 57).

By 1898, citizens were widely aware that all police recruits and agents were motivated by extreme partisanship and incentivized by superiors to commit electoral fraud (Martinez 2001, 332). This rapid politicization predisposed police toward abuse. Furthermore, Deas (2002, 27) notes, "the local and departmental police [could not] offer any guarantee of neutrality or security." In fact, they were the source of insecurity. Juan Ignacio Gálvez, a Colombian journalist and politician in 1912, writes that "politicians organized police to induce fear and uncertainty for political gain. The abuses were spread throughout the whole institution, and as a result, hate and resentment grew amongst the population towards Director, right down to the least offensive of its agents. We saw police committing voter fraud by having each agent vote two or three times, and what is most wicked is that they flaunted this crime in front of their chiefs" (Gálvez 1912, 5–6).

Beyond the problem of poor policing was the lack of funds to hire, train, retain, and provide for adequate police. As such, police were both poorly funded and highly partisan. Table 3.1 is a snapshot of how many police were stationed in an ordinary municipality from 1917 to 1918.

Ideally, police-to-citizen ratios should be 1:450, according to United Nations standards (Kimani 2009). Although in some cases cities managed to approximate that ratio, most municipalities did not have adequate police services. For example, Girardot, a city of more than 12,000 people, had no police at all. As Gutiérrez (1920) notes, during the 1920s, it was evident that most police lacked resources, such as uniforms and weapons. The lack of police agents resulted in increased banditry throughout the country and insecurity in general. For instance, in 1916, it was reported that 200 bandidos, led by Humberto Gómez, attacked government authorities in Arauca, killed the police commissioner and others, and proclaimed their republic (Acevedo 2000).

By the 1920s, the country was suffering from insecurity, massive corruption in its governmental institutions, and the vast global depression. The elections of 1925 were fraught with significant electoral irregularities, and it was reported that the conservative "police would distribute ballots that were already marked with candidates that were friendly to the [Conservative] government" (Alvarez 2010, 96). As a result, Liberals fomented uprisings. In response, the Conservatives passed Law 18 of 1928, which sent troops to Antioquia, Atlántico, Bolívar, Caldas, Magdalena, and Valle del Cauca because the central government feared the many laborers and Liberals in those areas would shut down Colombia's economy (Becerra 2011, 255).

On December 6, 1928, the Liberal Party led workers to strike against the United Fruit Company, resulting in army troops attacking and massacring an indeterminate number of strikers. This repression led to a national outrage that undermined support for the Conservative Party in power. Furthermore, the poor economic performance of Colombia and the internal party split led to the defeat of the Conservatives in the 1930 presidential election (Hudson 2010, 313).

The election of the Liberal Enrique Olaya Herrera in 1930 coincided with a broader political role for the police. As Vásquez (2014, 265–266) remarks:

> The new Liberal political leaders, aided by the police, retaliated, based on resentments due to excesses committed by the Conservatives during their great prominence in power. There also exists significant documentation of complaints of abuse of authority against the departmental, municipal, and national police as well as civilian leadership. These authorities committed grave violations against the Conservative populations. It is important to note that, for their part, some municipalities

Table 3.1   Distribution, Size, and Types of Police in Colombia, 1917–1919

City	Department	Total Police 1917–1918	Police to Citizen Ratio
Amagá	Antioquia	3	1:3149
Amalfi	Antioquia	9	1:1194
Andes	Antioquia	11	1:2038
Angostura	Antioquia	3	1:2787
Bolívar	Antioquia	4	1:3208
Campamento	Antioquia	1	1:4852
Caramanta	Antioquia	5	1:1132
Carolina	Antioquia	5	1:1361
Concordia	Antioquia	6	1:1850
Copacabana	Antioquia	3	1:2159
Entrerios	Antioquia	2	1:1764
Fredonia	Antioquia	11	1:1849
Ituango	Antioquia	3	1:4172
Jardín	Antioquia	4	1:2360
Jerico	Antioquia	13	1:1449
Puerto Wilches	Antioquia	7	1:465
Remedios	Antioquia	6	1:310
Salgar	Antioquia	3	1:3463
San Andres	Antioquia	2	1:3006
San Roque	Antioquia	3	1:352
Santa Barbara	Antioquia	6	1:2096
Santa Rosa de Osos	Antioquia	10	1:1629
Santo Domingo	Antioquia	9	1:1336
Támesis	Antioquia	9	1:1528
Tiribi	Antioquia	10	1:1352
Valparaíso	Antioquia	3	1:2008
Yarumal	Antioquia	16	1:1245
Yolombo	Antioquia	9	1:1955
Magangué	Bolívar	16	1:879
Anserma	Caldas	8	1:2005
Manizales	Caldas	19	1:356
Riosucio	Caldas	18	1:1016
Girardot	Cundinamarca	0	No police
Armenia	Quindío	20	1:870
Pereira	Risaralda	27	1:873
Santa Rosa de Cabal	Risaralda	14	1:1421
Honda	Tolima	66	1:112
Ibagué	Tolima	88	1:298
Buga	Valle del Cauca	50	1:271
Cali	Valle del Cauca	15	1:1849
Cartago	Valle del Cauca	29	1:740
Palmira	Valle del Cauca	43	1:628
Roldanillo	Valle del Cauca	12	1:766
Tulua	Valle del Cauca	28	1:545
Total		629	1:913

Source: Gutiérrez 1920.

where there were Conservative mayors or judges, the Liberals presented the same complaints. In this manner, police powers were used at the local level to harass political opposition.

The situation of politicized police became such a significant problem that Congress tried to address it by passing Law 72 of 1930, which prohibited all departmental, municipal, and national police, along with all other armed forces, from voting. However, this law was insufficient and did not stop the politicization of law enforcement (Republic of Colombia 1930).

Liberal governments continued to use the police as a vehicle not only to control society but also to diminish the power of the Conservative Party (Becerra 2011, 258). The successive Liberal Party administrations, in power from 1930 to 1946, appointed Liberal Party personnel to the national police as well as to the departmental or municipal police under their control. As a result, collective murders of Conservative partisans occurred on electoral days at the hands of police in areas such as Capitanejo, Molagavita, Guaca, and García Rovira (Becerra 2011, 259). Reprisals from Conservative police against Liberal candidates occurred in other regions. Thus, the police continued to be "the instrument to settle personal vendettas" (Guzmán, Fals, and Umana 1962, 273). Also, at this time, the PNC "maintained within its ranks, officers that leaned towards the Liberal Party that were put in place during Liberal rule from 1930–1946" (Aparicio Barrera 2003, 47). Decentralization opened the door to the increased politicization of the police.

By 1946, the Conservative politician Mariano Ospina Pérez won the controversial presidential election. The Liberals claimed there was electoral fraud, and a new round of conflict, led by police, ensued between the factions. In October 1946, Liberals launched strikes and riots in the capital. Ospina Pérez ordered the director of the PNC to clear the roads, but Liberal Party leaders had ensured that Liberal stalwarts staffed the PNC. Thus, police ignored Ospina Pérez's orders, and police remained inactive and allowed the masses to grow. Because of this inaction, the city quickly fell under the control of Liberal armed groups that destroyed cars and rails and looted stores. Eventually, the multitudes tired out and returned home, but the pattern of police engaging in partisan violence continued. This party loyalty came with privileges, and police would use their offices for personal enrichment. According to James Henderson (1985, 109):

> In [the department of] Santander, the secretary of government Pedro Manuel Arenas searched desperately for true Conservatives willing to enter the departmental corps. Whenever he happened on a likely candidate, he recommended him to the departmental police chief, who was then obliged to hire him. Eight months later, Colonel Blanco (departmental police chief) confronted the secretary of government with . . . documents and accused Arenas of turning the police of Santander into a "clan of

criminals." The man so strongly recommended turned out to be a convicted killer and cattle thief. To further substantiate his claim, Colonel
Blanco produced documents revealing that others [from] the secretary's
"highly recommended" recruits had committed as many as four homicides
as well as a variety of other crimes.

The interparty conflict and abuse of power would reach a critical point
on April 9, 1948, when Jorge Eliécer Gaitán, the popular Liberal mayor of
Bogotá, was assassinated while leaving his office. In response, Liberal partisans took to the streets in Bogotá and other parts of the country in open
revolt against the Conservative government. The ensuing violence destroyed
downtown Bogotá and left between 3,000 and 5,000 people dead, and it initiated an extended period of partisan conflict called La Violencia that would
engulf all of Colombia (Becerra 2011, 265).

Members of the PNC openly aligned themselves with the popular revolt
and took part in "looting, setting fires, and crimes of all degrees" (Foreign
Radio Broadcast 1948b). The Fifth Division of the National Police of Colombia, allied with the Liberal Party, installed a revolutionary council in its
police station with the participation of another fifteen divisions—each with
300 personnel. These police provided members of the Liberal Party with
weapons. In Bogotá, the departmental police known as the Civil Guard of
Cundinamarca had 500 members, who also participated in the riots on the
side of the Liberals (Aparicio 2003, 47). Congressman Roberto Piñeda (1950,
xxiii) reported that although only 20 percent of the police force acted in inap-
propriate ways, the other 80 percent did little to regain control of the masses,
standing by as Bogotá burned. The police's role was undeniable; their actions
and inactions led to the destruction of downtown Bogotá.

Following the political and human disaster of the Bogotazo, as the
destruction of Bogotá came to be called, the government of Ospina Pérez
quickly realized the ineffective nature of the PNC and ordered the PNC's
director general and the government to "terminate all uniformed personnel
of the institution" and to raise a new police force (Aparicio 2003, 48;
Becerra 2011, 266). This wholesale liquidation of the police meant old
agents were asked to leave their positions without anyone to replace them.
It would take three years to train both officers and agents to do the job. The
move by Ospina Pérez was costly in terms of resources and quality of officers. Up until this point, command-level officers, such as colonels and generals, needed approximately fifteen years of experience to be properly
trained, and these officers were now out of work. Agents required at least
three months of training and an additional twenty to thirty months of working on the street to learn the job of policing (Piñeda 1950, xxiii). Consequently, the military was unduly burdened with the task of maintaining law
and order in the capital while these new police ranks were formed.

Following the tumult of the Bogotazo, it took the army three days to regain control of the city and assume policing functions. As Camacho Leyva (n.d., 29) notes, this was military police–imposed order in Bogotá. However, the assassination of Gaitán initiated a significant problem for Colombia beyond the capital. The violence continued elsewhere, and on July 18, 1948, a clash between civilian and departmental police took place in the city of El Carmen, department of Bolívar, resulting in the deaths of seven persons. The Liberal papers blamed the Conservative police for the incident, while the Conservative newspaper *El Siglo* stated that Liberal civilians attacked the police with stones and firearms (Foreign Radio Broadcast 1948a, b).

The military had to be withdrawn to tackle issues in the countryside, where violence was escalating. According to Camacho Leyva (n.d., 29), the withdrawal of the military police from Bogotá led to a drastic situation in which partisan politics could once again infiltrate the capital. After the removal of the Liberals following Bogotazo, Conservatives staffed the PNC. Even so, the lack of professional standards persisted. People who were selected for police service at the agent level were new to police work and received no education or training before taking on their role (Camacho Leyva n.d., 29). Once again, political parties at the municipal and state levels fomented criminality and violence because the police force was focused on political harassment rather than on preventing crimes (Becerra 2011, 264). In the National Police of Colombia, it was a goal of the Conservative police officers to destroy the Liberal political machine (Llorente 1997, 21).

One of the new characteristic components of the PNC was an elite task force called *Los Chulavitas*, or the political police. They were recruited from the Conservative bastions of Boavita in the department of Boyacá (Guzmán, Fals, and Umana 1962, 279). The Conservative government often transferred these police to Liberal-dominated areas and used them as an oppressive force (Aparicio 2003, 49). These individuals had been given job recommendations to become police by Conservative elites, who wanted to use their recruits as vengeance agents. As such, the PNC passed from Liberal to Conservative control, all the while maintaining sectarian political biases rather than professionalizing and focusing on maintaining law and order (Guzmán, Fals, and Umana 1962, 279).

The year 1949 was particularly notable in this regard, as the following incidents illustrate. On January 18, 1949, in Trujillo, department of Caldas, there were reports of "eight persons wounded and one killed in the Department of Caldas as a consequence of a clash between civilians and Municipal Police in Pijao" (Foreign Radio Broadcast 1949b). In August, in the town of Capitanejo, "several members of the departmental police force fired on assembled Liberals, killing the veteran Liberal Party leader Arronago Lozano and a woman. Five other persons were seriously wounded" (Foreign Radio Broadcast 1949b). On September 15, 1949, local "police razed the town of La Raya, where, according to reports, more than 100 persons were killed" (Foreign Radio Broadcast 1949a). In October 1949, in Cali in the Valle del Cauca, police entered the Liberal headquarters "and assassinated in cold blood all twenty-four people present. . . . That year in Colombia, there were 18,500 victims of the political struggle, [many of whom were killed by law enforcement]. In 1950, the number rose to 50,000" (Paredes 2011, 51). The violence would continue, not just in the countryside but also in the capital of Bogotá. On September 6, 1952, the Conservative Party provoked public riots. Under this cover, *Los Chulavitas* dressed in civilian clothing and attacked the Liberal newspapers *El Tiempo* and *El Espectador*, the homes of Liberal Party leaders, and the Liberal Party headquarters.

Up until this point, the police system had been decentralized, although the national police was slowly established in other regions. By 1950, the National Police of Colombia had taken over some departments, such as Antioquia. The Conservative government promoted this move toward centralization. According to Christopher Michael Cardona (2008, 179):

> This reform had a modest but notable impact on the composition and professionalism of the police corps. . . . What immediately stands out in comparing service records is that after nationalization, much fewer agents exited the service due to discipline problems. The proportion dropped from one-half to one-third. Dismissals for drunkenness were cut in half after the reform, and firings for lack of discipline also fell.

However, the country remained mostly decentralized with the national police, the fifteen departmental police, tax police, various municipal police, rural gendarmeries, and intelligence police throughout the country—all under the control of Conservative or Liberal local party leaders (Guzmán, Fals, and Umana 1962, 278). Brigadier General Fabio Arturo Londoño served in the National Police of Colombia at this time as a young lieutenant. In an interview, he recalled the following:

> The decentralized system was perverse because the municipal police and departmental police would completely change each election. If the new governor were Conservative, he would name Conservative police as commander and replace all the ranks downward to Conservatives. If he were Liberal, he would change the chief and all the police personnel as well. They did not receive any training because [of a] lack of resources, and there was also lacking a system of organizing the police. Here it was not organized at all. You would get elected mayor today, and tomorrow your friend became chief of police . . . no training or anything. (April 4, 2013).

As noted by Guzmán et al. (1962, 288), the misconduct of the police in the decentralized period engendered hatred from society toward the police, a hate that became deeply rooted, "implicating a problem that would hamper the recuperation of this institution, which would become a titanic project for the commanders that were to follow." This national crisis of La Violencia would be solved only through military intervention.

Military Dictatorship and the Frente Nacional, 1953–1970

Colombia had been experiencing a mounting crisis since the murder of Jorge Eliécer Gaitán in 1948. Murder rates jumped from 39.33 per 100,000 in 1948 to 64.14 per 100,000 in 1953 (Villaveces 2001). La Violencia was made possible by the politicization of the police, who were more interested in doing the bidding of their patrons than fighting crime. Brigadier General Londoño stated:

> Departmental police and municipal police confronted one another. For instance, in Medellín, I saw a municipal policeman was attending a case. The person that was in the police van said these municipal police were beating him. A departmental police officer showed up and began questioning the municipal policeman for what he was doing. They began to argue, and they eventually stabbed each other with bayonets. There were many deaths because of that interpolice fighting during this period before police nationalization. (Br. Gen. Fabio Arturo Londoño, interview with author, April 4, 2013)

The continued widespread corruption and government inefficiencies that plagued Colombian society added to the trouble. As per Becerra (2010), the 1940s and 1950s were marred by police succumbing to the vice of pursuing personal benefits at the cost of the public. This phenomenon of corruption reduced the credibility of public institutions, increased the number of guerrillas, and increased public disorder (Becerra 20011).

Eventually, as a result of the Liberal and Conservative fighting, the collapse of public institutions, and the gridlock in government, general disorder throughout the country reached a boiling point in 1953. Both Liberal and Conservative factions, as well as most of society, called for military intervention. On June 13, 1953, with popular support, General Rojas Pinilla launched what was called the "Opinion Coup" against the Conservative presidency of Laureano Gómez. The internal fighting among security forces and police in the prior period forced the military government (1953–1957) to subordinate the national police, departmental police, and municipal police (Llorente 1997, 21). With Articles 2 and 3 of Decree 1814 of 1953, General Rojas Pinilla centralized policing by incorporating police into the structure of the armed forces, which brought the police under the control of the Ministry of War (Republic of Colombia 1953). This essential aspect of the takeover resulted in the positive benefit of centralizing and partially professionalizing the police. In 1953, the creation of the Section of Social Welfare for the Police Forces of Colombia marked a vast improvement in the benefits that municipal and departmental police officers received, as many previously did not have any social benefits. This also led to the construction of schools for primary and secondary education for police officers and their families.

In 1954, the Rojas Pinilla government centralized the command ranks and personnel of the police departments (states) of Boyacá, Cauca, Córdoba, Chocó, and Huila. That same year, the Rojas Pinilla government created the police rotary foundation to sell discounted household products and provide soft credit to members of the PNC. Another welfare program the Rojas Pinilla government initiated was the credit union for military housing, through which after fifteen years police could ask for subsidized credit for a house or materials to build their own home. In February 1955, Rojas Pinilla set up the retirement pension fund for the police. He also created recreational facilities for the police, allowing police to join the military club in Bogotá, and he assigned land in Melgar in 1957 to construct a noncommissioned officers club. In this way, the dictatorship of Rojas Pinilla laid the foundation for the current welfare system.

A fully centralized police system would be implemented in 1962 with Decree 1272, which mandated that Colombia have under its charge the sustainment, funding, and payment of all police in all territories of the republic. The National Police of Colombia incorporated all the uniformed officers who provided services on behalf of departments, so long as they conformed to the physical and educational regulations for entrance into the PNC. Many did not; therefore, the departmental governments retired all municipal or departmental police personnel who did not fulfill the new requirements. Former National Police Brigadier General Londoño, who lived through these changes, explains:

> The PNC from the 1950s was just a small group of police in the capital and the periphery in Leper Colonies of Agua de Dios, Contratación, Canyon del Oro, and mining operations in Barrancabermeja, Istimina, and other gold mines. When the British mission had completed its training of the PNC officer, the government began to send officer commanders to the departmental and municipal police. I was posted to Antioquia by myself in 1953; we only had eighty-six PNC officers throughout the nation, one or two in each department. We began the hard battle for centralization. The enlisted ranks under my command were former departmental or municipal police. But it was a nationalization process that was very mediocre. The National Police directors only named command-level officers. The joint agents were appointed by the mayor or the department, so they were not National Police personnel. In 1962 that ended, and the national government assumed the pension and budget of all the staff. Thus, the beginning of professional development happened as of that point. (Br. Gen. Londoño, interview with author, April 4, 2013)

This period is important because the dictatorship of Rojas Pinilla nationalized the police and increased police professionalism by providing better benefits, training, and vertical oversight. Centralization had an immediate impact on police service in regard to its past pattern of politicization. First, centralizing the PNC removed a stable source of power from local mayors. Second, the police incorporation standards made training more military oriented. Third, it introduced an extensive oversight and sanctioning system for police through the penal military justice system. And fourth, Rojas Pinilla focused on increasing the social benefits for police. All these actions allowed the government to establish a better state presence as well as improved rule of law and civilian oversight of the police in a way that never existed before. It also professionalized, depoliticized, and increased the police's power to institute security.

By 1962, political currents had also changed, with both Liberals and Conservatives united in pressuring Rojas Pinilla and later a military junta that replaced him to return the country to a democratic form of government (Francisco Leal Buitrago, interview with author, March 21, 2013). The agreement between Liberals and Conservatives was that each party would share control of the presidency and other government positions every presidential term for sixteen years. This pacted democracy—called the Frente Nacional—was agreed upon by both Liberals and Conservatives and formed a dual hegemony whereby the Liberals and Conservatives dominated the political landscape and excluded other parties. One consequence of this exclusive pact was that the leftist groups—including communists—formed the Fuerzas Armadas Revolucionarias de Colombia (FARC, or Revolutionary Armed Forces of Colombia) and other guerrilla groups.

In terms of policing, the Frente Nacional precluded the need for police in elections. By 1963, the police were depoliticized. They had also advanced their professionalism in lockstep with centralization thanks to newly created training schools, pensions, healthcare benefits, and the provision of uniforms, equipment, and technology for which they did not have to pay out-of-pocket, as was the norm before centralization. The change was dramatic. As David Laughlin, chief of the US Mission for Police Reform in Colombia 1963, remarked: "There is a good administration of the personnel that contributes to the professionalization of the police officer and the rest of the personnel. Their good loans and programs of social welfare contribute notably to the stability of the personnel to confront low salaries and other difficulties of service" (quoted in Rodriguez Zapata 1971, 303). This stands in stark contrast to the previous system of politicized control in which misconduct ran rampant.

Interparty rivalry, patrimonialism, and decentralized police fomented La Violencia, which increased the homicide rate in Colombia to 50 homicides per 100,000 people from 1948 to 1961. Once the police were fully centralized and professionalized, homicide rates fell to 30 homicides per 100,000 from 1962 to 1984 (Medicina Legal 2012). As Ruiz (2009) states, "Thanks to the pact of the Frente Nacional, the police were able to excel as a new institution away from violent manipulation and the traditional party alliances that had motivated past disturbances." Centralization and professionalization brought about by both the Frente Nacional and the Rojas Pinilla regime helped change the police (Juan Ruiz, interview with author, March 14, 2013).

The Rise of Drug Money, 1970–1990

Although the centralized structures were superior in providing quality policing compared to the previous decentralized and nonprofessionalized period (1830–1953), the PNC still faced significant challenges in its development (Rodriguez 1971). Perhaps the first and foremost challenge was that the welfare, development, and oversight structures became poorly run and underfunded in the 1970s and early 1980s, despite the strong structural foundation. This occurred because leftist revolutionary forces grew into a significant threat to the state, and, as such, police personnel and resources were reoriented toward counterinsurgency campaigns. Mauricio Rubio (1997) confirms this and notes that the excessive spending on the military was to the detriment of the police and impacted their professionalization. The focus on counterinsurgency turned the police away from their civilian role and gave them a military character. This was especially prominent when the military drew individuals away from policing and placed them in combat zones, which increased each police officer's workload even as the benefits did not rise to compensate for the increased stress.

The growing power of leftist guerrillas and the increase in narco-trafficking in the 1970s and 1980s further eroded the PNC. Many units were drawn away from public security as their personnel were co-opted into the military to address national security problems. As demonstrated by the mounting death toll, violence once again grew in Colombia. Therefore, the police developed a profile poorly suited for police work: focusing on national security instead of public security. In Colombia from 1980–1993, the PNC were a force parallel to the military, needed to fight the insurgency more than to provide public safety.

A second complication obstructing national police professionalism was related to the rise of narco-trafficking. Through the 1980s, the public image of the police had been eroding as a result of successive scandals and high levels of corruption. Pablo Escobar's policy of *plata o plomo* corrupted many police with bribes and led to the demise of honest ones. What is not well known is that police were often the ones murdering one another to receive Escobar's payments (Martin 2012, 197). At this point in Colombian history, the decline in funding for the police reduced professionalism and financing for its welfare system. The lack of professionalism made police susceptible to the influence of drug money. Although it is hard to assess how many police were bought off, we do know that Pablo Escobar financed the murder of 400 police officers in 1990 alone (El Universal 2013).

To recap, although centralization in the 1950s depoliticized the police and improved their professionalization, the dual threats of leftist insurgency and narco-trafficking changed the course of this development. With dwindling resources and increased risks, policing once again became a less-than-desirable job. To cope with reduced pay and benefits, many officers turned to working for drug cartels as informants and assassins. As discussed in the next section, essential reforms would be undertaken under the administrations of Virgilio Barco (1986–1990) and César Gaviria (1990–1994). But prior to these two administrations, there was little advancement in police professionalization (Alejo Vargas, interview with author, February 20, 2013). I refer to this as a period of centralization and semiprofessionalization because some standards, albeit low, did exist for recruitment, and the police did receive training. Additionally, although there was vertical oversight, there was neither external oversight nor healthy internal controls, which are essential to ensure a professional force. A critical explanatory factor here is that drug money increased police misconduct. The next section traces the process by which the police force in Colombia was professionalized, and how this contributed to overriding the misconduct that plagued it in the narco era.

Reforms in Welfare, Development, and Oversight, 1990–1997

By 1993, Colombia was suffering the worst homicide rates it had ever experienced, 78 deaths per 100,000 people. The police had also suffered high losses in prestige, professionalism, and personnel. From the 1980s to the 1990s, more than 2,000 police officers had been killed fighting the drug war in Colombia (Gerard 2012, 197). Police work was no longer geared toward public security, police funding was cut, and neither recruitment nor training had improved much. Because of these problems, as well as problems with the arcane criminal justice system and constitution of Colombia, the outgoing administration of President Virgilio Barco Vargas and the incoming administration President César Gaviria set about reforming the constitution, the police, and public security (289).

Additionally, they also worked to dismantle the Medellín cartel, accomplishing that task in 1993, which set the foundation for dismantling the Cali cartel in 1998. The reforms that took place in the 1990s did substantially professionalize the police, transforming them from a stagnant semiprofessionalized institution of the 1960s and 1970s into one of the most modern and professional police forces in Latin America. Note that the collapse of the Medellín and Cali cartels are outcomes, not causes, of the police and public security reforms undertaken across these two administrations.

The Vargas administration set the foundation for the Gaviria administration to implement a series of reforms from 1990 to 1994. As Rafael Pardo, minister of defense from 1990 to 1994, noted, a lot of policy continuity across the administrations allowed the reforms to happen (Rafael Pardo, interview with author, May 17, 2013). This period of change strengthened three areas critical for controlling police misconduct: welfare provision, development procedures, and internal and external controls.

Bringing about a complete reform of the Colombian police was a tough task. The background problem was the lack of civilian trust. Thus, Rafael Pardo, as the first civilian minister of defense under the new 1991 constitution, set out to build on the previous reforms and reduce the high levels of misconduct. As Pardo recounts,

> Initially, I asked the police to propose how to reform themselves, and the proposal was frankly a reform to leave everything the way it was. Then another improvement, and it was the same, another one, and finally, I was not able to get the institution itself to come up with a proposal for reform. But the credibility of the police was zero, very low in polls, one of the most corrupt institutions in the country, and corruption was everywhere. (Rafael Pardo, interview with author, May 17, 2013)

In 1991, Pardo presented a reform package to Congress to overhaul the PNC, but the project gained little traction. Real change finally began to take place after an extremely disheartening case of misconduct. In 1993, a little girl walked into a police station to visit her father, who was a police officer. Her body was later found raped and murdered in that same police station. This incident ignited deep-seated feelings of disgust and anger toward the police. Initially, the father was blamed for the rape of his daughter. But the investigation revealed that it was, in fact, another police officer who had committed that rape and murder. This singular event had a galvanizing impact on reforming the police. Pardo, incensed by the death, decided to act. He explained in an interview with me:

> That day I went to the General Santander Officer Cadet School in Bogotá. I called together all the major officers in the city and the officers there taking courses. I gave them a speech, informing them that we were going to do reform of the police over three months and that there would be an external commission and an internal one made up of all the ranks from the lowest to highest. Those commissions had to provide recommendations in three months, and in three months, I would ask Congress to establish a reform of the police. So, from there, the process began. We had an external commission with academics, members of Congress, [and] ex-police, a

plural commission with political parties, [and] an internal one with agents, and officers being represented. In the end, the presidency used these commission reports to propose a bill that would become Law 62 of 1993. That project was one of the fastest in history. (Rafael Pardo, interview with author, May 27, 2013)

The goal was to enhance the professionalism of the police in the three critical areas of welfare, development, and oversight. First, the minister of defense and the general in charge of the police implemented welfare reforms by changing salaries, facilitating upward mobility, improving pensions, and incorporating managerial models to improve services in health, disability, life insurance, housing benefits, and recreational activities. Second, the administrations significantly improved police development by raising standards for entry into the police, allowing those who had to complete compulsory military service to do so in the PNC, increasing training length, providing police with opportunities to gain university education outside of the academies, and granting university-educated civilians a path into the police. Finally, reforms changed the disciplinary structure of the police to incorporate more forceful methods of prevention of and action against corruption from internal and external entities.

Reforms to Police Welfare Regimes

An essential part of the Colombian police reform process was the procurement of better welfare and social security benefits for the members of the institution. From 1990 to 1997, the government expanded and improved salaries, pensions, health care, housing, vacation benefits, and life and disability insurance. This section explores these changes.

Articles 17–54 of Decree 1213 of 1990 provided for various salary bonuses for police, including a yearly bonus equivalent to half a month's pay and a Christmas bonus equal to one month of salary (Republic of Colombia 1990). However, there was a problem: the old system formed an extremely flat pyramid with three levels, or steps. The first level, making up 90 percent of the pyramid, was police patrol, and it included only one rank: agent. The second level, much smaller and constituting 8 percent of the pyramid, was made up of noncommissioned officers of the following ranks: corporal one, corporal two, second sergeant, vice first sergeant, first sergeant, and sergeant major. Finally, the top 2 percent of the pyramid was made up of officers of the following ranks: first lieutenant, second lieutenant, captain, major, lieutenant colonel, colonel, brigadier general, major general, and general director. The issue with this flat pyramid is that salaries were tied to rank. Any bonuses were also linked to rank. If there was limited upward mobility (the case for the lowest but largest rank level, agent), then there was no path toward increasing salary for time served. In this older system, the officer class benefited the most, but officers made up only a small percentage of the overall police force. Because their rank was higher, they were paid more and they could regularly expect to rise in rank every three to five years. In this system, a person could enter the police force as an agent and remain an agent all his life.

According to former defense minister Rafael Pardo, the reforms were necessary to create a career path with opportunities for upward mobility that rewarded police for time served and merit. Decree 132 of 1995 did away with the middle rank of noncommissioned officers and the lowest agent level and replaced them with an executive-level rank system that allowed for greater and more regular upward mobility. After five to seven years in their current rank, individuals were called to take exams. If they scored very well on the exams and maintained an excellent service history, they were permitted to rise in rank. These mechanisms took into consideration time served as well as merit. So, the rank structure became less "flat" and resembled a true pyramid, with better distribution of ranks and better salaries for police personnel (Rafael Pardo, interview with author, May 17, 2013). Table 3.2 illustrates the salary increases for the basic patrol enlisted rank, by year and percentages, from 1992 to 1998.

The goal of these drastic increases was to attract better candidates to police work while providing a higher quality of life for police. Police at the basic level in 2012 were paid 1,072,887 pesos (Republic of Colombia 2012), which translates to US$560 a month in Colombia, where the monthly minimum wage is US$280. This means that, as of 2012, police salary was double the minimum wage, and this did not include salary bonuses. In addition, police received thirty days of paid vacation every year, half a month's pay bonus every year of active service, and one month's

Table 3.2   Changes in PNC Monthly Salaries, 1992–1998

Year	Salary of Lowest Rank of Police, in Pesos	Exchange Rate, in USD	Percentage Increase in Salary from Previous Year
1992	73,040	146	—
1993	96,250	151	24%
1994	149,000	174	35%
1995	194,000	212	24%
1996	247,711	238	22%
1997	294,462	258	16%
1998	347,360	243	15%

Source: Republic of Colombia 2012.

pay bonus for Christmas. Putting these bonuses together with the thirty days of vacation, Colombian police work eleven months out of the year but earn thirteen months of pay.

However, a stable salary alone is insufficient; it needs to be linked to a quality pension system. The National Police of Colombia historically had access to a retirement fund that they contributed to throughout their career. Article 104 of Decree Law 132 of 1995 stipulated that all police would receive 50 percent of their salary as a pension after fifteen years of service. For every year of service beyond that, the pension would increase by 4 percent. After thirty years of service, police personnel could receive up to 95 percent of their base salary, plus standard bonuses, as a pension (National Police of Colombia 2013a). Police received a 30 percent increase in remuneration to subsidize their family when they married, a 5 percent increase in pay for the first child, a 4 percent increase for a second child, and so forth up to four children. These improvements in salaries and pension packages brought long-term stability. They also were essential to drawing quality applicants to the institution, which improved the pool of applicants.

After 1990, competitive salaries and pensions were not the only enticing benefits to becoming a police officer. Although the government had incorporated a social welfare division into the PNC in 1983, it was poorly funded and ineptly run by police commanders who had no experience in public administration. The health division concentrated on providing services to officers of the larger urban areas and thus did not meet the demands of all national police. To address this problem, Article 93 of Decree 1213 of 1990 stipulated that the government must provide police with medical care, including surgery, dental, and lifetime pharmaceutical care for them and their families until children were twenty-one, when they would stop receiving benefits (Republic of Colombia 1990). Law 62 of 1993 and subsequent reforms sought to improve this inefficient social welfare system, which had not changed substantially since the period of Rojas Pinilla's military rule. The creation of the Institution for Social Security and Welfare of the Police (INSSPONAL) in 1993 as an autonomous agency increased social welfare quality (Republic of Colombia 1993). This new institution extended social benefits to 700,000 active and retired police personnel and their families.

On December 17, 1997, the PNC divided INSSPONAL into separate sections, health and social welfare. To staff these new divisions, PNC recruited professionals with degrees in public administration. A concerted effort was made to attract university graduates, on the one hand, and to train officers in management in the police, on the other. Police have full general health care, maternity care, preventative care, recuperation and rehabilitation, surgery, dentistry, hospital care, and pharmaceutical coverage.

Articles 117– 120 of Decree 1213 of 1990 provide disability insurance and payment based on time served and severity of an injury (Republic of Colombia 1990). It should be noted that total disability provides officers with 100 percent of their base salary plus discounted benefits. Additionally, police are given life insurance equivalent to two years of pay or, if they have served more than fifteen years, the equivalent to a pension. If they die in service or are permanently disabled, the money can be transferred to the primary caregiver, usually a spouse or parents, who also receive funds for funeral services (Republic of Colombia 1990).

Decree 353 of 1994 reformed the military housing promotion fund, which now provides police with homeownership opportunities by providing brokerage, credit, and financial conditions to facilitate house purchases or purchases of materials for construction as well as greater access to quality discount housing (Republic of Colombia 1994; Diana Luengas Díaz, pers. comm., March 10, 2013). In addition to housing benefits, police also receive recreation benefits, which include discounts for vacation resorts and recreational clubs. Private primary and secondary education for children of police is also available. The government committed itself to developing a reliable healthcare system just for the police, with various regional clinics around the country and a central hospital for more complicated procedures (Serrano 1994, 5). These welfare changes were only the beginning in this critical process of reform. Benefits attract pools of high-quality candidates, but selection and training are what makes a police officer a capable provider of public security.

Reforms to the Police Development Regime

Article 9 of Decree 1213 of 1990 required that applicants to the police needed to (1) be a Colombian citizen, (2) be between eighteen and thirty years of age, (3) have finished the second year of high school (tenth grade), (4) have no criminal record, (5) never have participated in politics or be a member of a political party, (6) pass the admission exams, (7) prove that parents and immediate family have not served prison time, and (8) prove their spouse and children are in good health (Republic of Colombia 1990). These standards are similar to those that existed previously, but the significant change was that two more years of education were required. The previous minimum level of education was eighth grade.

Having raised education standards over time, the PNC also began to conduct more vigorous background checks of its candidates in the 1990s. After passing the initial exams and completing the application process, candidates were required to (1) pass a physical aptitude test, (2) pass a psychological test battery, (3) submit to home visits by human resources officers, (4) undergo a thorough background analysis, including review of any criminal records of applicant and family members, (5) have a formal interview with the training school director, and (6) meet with the council of admissions. Requirements for officers were the same, except they needed to score higher on officer aptitude tests, which often necessitated high school completion.

In the early 1990s, Minister of Defense Rafael Pardo implemented another significant change. Colombia has mandatory military conscription for all males. Those who go to college are exempt but must register for service. Those who do not attend college are selected for military service. Recruits can choose between the army, navy, and air force. Pardo decided to allow individuals to do their service in the police force as auxiliaries. His goal was not only to increase the size of the police force but also to bring in people from the outside to learn more about the institution and improve social relations (Rafael Pardo, interview with author, May 17, 2013).

Beyond increasing the types of recruits, this era under Rafael Pardo also saw reforms around personal development. Academies for entry-level rank police provided a broad academic discipline, with an emphasis on human rights, ethical instruction, leadership, and community service (Estela Baracaldo Mendez, interview with author, February 11, 2013). After reforms, higher and middle police ranks would take courses in administration, human rights, ethics, citizen participation, and other themes at the best universities in and outside of the country (Gerard 2012, 326).

Today, as per Article 35 of Decree 1213 of 1990, police agents must have eighteen months of training: twelve months at an academy followed by two months of training after their first year, two months of training after their second year, and a final two-month training course in their third year (Republic of Colombia 1990). Decree 1213 further established that enlisted and commissioned ranks receive promotions based on merit and completion of training courses, which would become increasingly more difficult (Republic of Colombia 1990). As such, this law created a rigorous training regimen focusing on both the theoretical and the practical aspects of police work. As of 2013, police can train in one of twenty-six schools; there are nine specialty schools, fourteen training schools for agents, and three training schools for officers, including a postgraduate school where officers can earn a master's degree (Angel Horacio Rueda Zacipa, pers. comm., March 14, 2013).

The president forced the police to open to lateral incorporation of civilian experts to gain more skilled officers who could better manage the administration of the police force. Individuals with university degrees can enter the police force provided they are thirty years of age or younger, are single or married with no children, and fulfill all the other requirements identified previously. Also, applicants must have a degree in the area of business administration, educational administration, public administration, accounting, law, economics, statistics, physics, industrial engineering, psychology, psychotherapy, or chemistry. These candidates train at the police academy for only one year since they already have a comparable degree.

In 1993, Defense Minister Rafael Pardo allowed officers to take classes in universities and required them to wear their uniforms on campus. This measure was important because it exposed police to society and society to police, which increased mutual understanding. In addition, it also improved the educational attainment of officers (Rafael Pardo, interview with author, May 17, 2013).

Hugo Acero, an expert in Colombian police reform, views the improvements in selection and training, along with the increased police welfare, as significant. When there is a good selection process and a good training process, police service improves. Whereas in the 1990s people came to police work as a last recourse, by 2013 there was substantial demand for that sort of work. The reason for the higher number of applications to join the PNC was related to the social welfare benefits. The security these benefits provided to members of the force were more attractive than those of many other jobs in Colombia (Hugo Acero, interview with author, March 18, 2013).

Given the increased demand for police jobs, there was a related increase in applications to the police. For instance, in 2011, of the 54,191 people who applied, only 17,028 met the requirements and begin the process of incorporation. This means that 17,028 underwent the vetting process of psychological exams, physical exams, background checks, house visits, and interviews. In 2012, there were only 4,408 students training for the basic level patrol agent and 895 officer cadets (National Police of Colombia 2013c). In total, from the 2011 pool of 54,191 applicants, only 5,503 made it to the academy, a 10 percent acceptance rate.

Not only are there more applicants, but also there are better applicants. Results of the survey that I conducted at the National Police of Colombia Postgraduate School (ESPOL) in 2013 attest to the increased quality of police candidates at the officer level: 8.1 percent had a baccalaureate (high school) degree, 10 percent had a technical degree (associate's degree), 67.6 percent had a professional degree (bachelor's degree), and 13.3 percent had a master's degree. Although both recruitment and training have been refined in Colombia, that alone does not suffice to reduce misconduct. Oversight structures need to be robust and effective, and this theme is taken up in the next section.

Reforms to Police Oversight Regimes

Although the militarized police system instituted a secure chain of command of hierarchical vertical oversight, it alone was insufficient to stop corruption in police ranks (López Cabarcas, interview with author, May 9, 2013). Putting in place additional controls was vital. Before the 1991 constitution, police were subject to military courts of justice. When officers' cases went to the military penal court, judges usually dismissed many charges because of a lack of concrete evidence and the propensity of military courts to protect their ranks. While under investigation, police continued to work, on average, for up to five years until they finally went to trial. Thus, the system made it hard to fire police who were known or highly suspected of being involved in corruption or abuse (Clara Cecilia Mosquera, pers. comm., April 1, 2013). Reforms that were implemented by the national government from 1990 to 1997 sought to rectify this by strengthening the internal discipline and internal control mechanisms over police misconduct (Gómez and Baracaldo 2007, 101). As of 1994, there are four basic internal controls: (1) the military penal justice system, (2) the inspector general of the police, (3) the directorate of police intelligence, and (4) the discretionary power of the director general.

However, the constitutional changes of 1991 and subsequent changes to the military penal system changed the old military control system (Lorena Mosquera, interview with author, March 18, 2013; José Poveda Montes, interview with author, March 3, 2013). No longer would this legal system protect officers from the civilian political system. Instead, the military penal system for police would be used primarily to render judgment on violations of institutional norms and regulations, some of which overlap with criminal behavior. For instance, if an officer is on night watch and falls asleep on duty or discharges his weapon while on a mission, the officer would stand trial in a military penal court. As Lt. Col. José López, a judge for the military criminal court in Medellín, explained, the military courts judge violations that arise by nature of one's role as a police officer. The police have since changed the system to now run as an oral and accusatory system, where the judge is a lawyer from the National Police of Colombia who understands military penal law (López Cabarcas, interview with author, May 9, 2013). In contrast to procedures in 1991, defendants today can hire an attorney to represent them. If they cannot afford a defense attorney, a military prosecutor is assigned to serve them. Officers who violate both internal regulations and criminal law face a trial in the military penal court and then face criminal charges. As such, the military penal justice system does work to control officers within the police ranks.

The second layer of control rests with the PNC's inspector general's office, which is charged with preventing and investigating violations of internal norms, regulations, and laws. This office generally investigates infractions by all ranks below brigadier general and metes out punishments, which may include: (1) separation from the institution for life; (2) separation from the institution for ten to twenty years; (3) one month up to 179 days without pay and being barred from working as a police officer; (4) 10 days up to 180 days without pay (they still have to work); (5) a written reprimand; and (6) rebuke by requiring written reports about the importance of discipline related to their particular infraction (Claudia Pulido, interview with author, March 18, 2013). The attorney general of Colombia investigates violations committed by the brigadier generals and above.

The third important oversight mechanism rests with the work of the Police Intelligence Directorate (DIPOL). This group is in charge of gathering intelligence about actors and factors that undermine public security and the security of the country (National Police of Colombia 2019). Major Héctor García notes that DIPOL engages in activities of counterintelligence oriented toward specialized knowledge of the phenomenon that affects the institutional integrity, gathering, processing, analyzing, and publicizing of information (Héctor García, email comm., March 20, 2013). In this sense, DIPOL provides the information required to decide whether internal threats harm the institutional image. Lieutenant-Colonel Claudia Pulido also shared with me that DIPOL conducts plainclothes-officer operations that investigate police corruption within the ranks (Claudia Pulido, interview with author, March 18, 2013). That is, DIPOL agents perform integrity checks by trying to bribe police and seeing whether they accept. Because even this amount of oversight and investigation may not suffice, the government instituted a fourth mechanism during the reform period of 1990–1997.

Law 62 of 1993 granted the director general of police the discretionary power to fire anyone without cause and to issue internal investigations or military penal procedures (Republic of Colombia 1993). Rosso José Serrano, the director general of the police from 1994 to 1999, used these powers to remove 8,500 police personnel (or 12 percent) who were suspected of illegal activities. Importantly, this reform improved on the previous system in which police suspected of corruption or other criminal activities could not be fired. Purging the police of corrupt personnel was fundamental to reestablishing internal discipline (Gerard 2012, 326). Minister of Defense Rafael Pardo described this reform as the most critical measure for establishing oversight of police (Rafael Pardo, interview with author, May 17, 2013).

Thus, both the military penal system and the inspector general of the police have the power to investigate, prosecute, and remove police officers who are engaged in malfeasant behavior. The inspector general keeps records of all police and their infractions and prevents police misconduct by studying indicators and flagging individuals who are at risk for engaging in this behavior. Officers who are flagged can be retrained to preempt abuses of power. Furthermore, if officers are suspected of corruption or abuse of authority, the inspector general can investigate these cases and remove the offending officer if found guilty. The inspector general also can remove officers who have three infractions over five years. For these reasons, the role of the inspector general—a robust control mechanism—provides the National Police of Colombia with an essential tool in limiting misconduct before it happens and for dealing with incidents after they occur.

Centralized and Professionalized Policing Era, 1997–2016

The data from 1990 to 2013 shows evidence of changes in police behavior that correlates with these reforms. Figure 3.1 illustrates that before the reforms of 1993, police were implicated in various assassinations; however, after 1993, police assassinations dropped off (Centro Nacional de Memoria Historica 2015a).

Figure 3.2 provides another view of police corruption. The Centro Nacional de Memoria Histórica in Colombia recorded the number of people who were killed by police in massacres. This revelatory data correlates with the premise that more professionalized police are less abusive. The period from 1983 to 1992 saw the police implicated in many killings. However, after the 1993 reforms, massacres drastically declined.

Beyond the decline of police activities in these sorts of heinous events, citizens' perspectives of police also improved as a result of these changes. Figure 3.3, derived from data provided by Iberobarómetro surveys, indicates that from 1991 to 2010, citizens' trust in police increased by 30 percentage points, from 20 to 50 percent. This highlights the importance of police professionalization as a causal influence in lowering police misconduct.

The improvements in the police force can also be ascertained by observing the demand for Colombian police reform experts abroad. For example, former General Óscar Naranjo of the PNC was hired as an adviser

Figure 3.1   Assassinations Carried Out by Police in Colombia

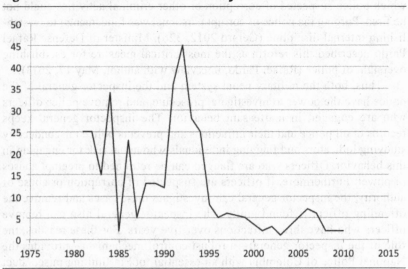

Source: Centro Nacional de Memoria Histórica 2015a.

Figure 3.2   Number of People Killed in Massacres by Colombian Police

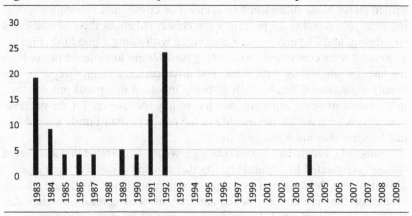

Source: Centro Nacional de Memoria Histórica 2015b.

Figure 3.3   Respondents With Some or a Lot of Trust in Colombian Police

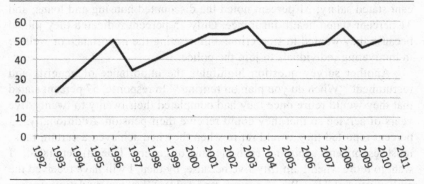

Source: Iberobarómetro 1992–2012.

by Mexican president Enrique Peña Nieto. His advice likely steered Mexico toward developing a more professional and centralized police system, which is still in the process of change. Although this policy of centralization and professionalization, called *mando único* in Mexico, is far from complete, it does illustrate that the general strategy of structural reform that promotes centralization and professionalizatio is perceived as successful. As I discuss in the next chapter, this strategic change is what is required of Mexican police.

The data from 1993 to 2013 shows much evidence of substantial changes in police behavior. In the police survey I conducted at ESPOL in 2013, I asked the following open-ended question: "What concerns do you have of being a police officer?" Of the respondents, 50 percent were concerned about being disciplined or accused of crimes and subsequently losing their job. Another 25 percent were concerned about their security and well-being, and 21 percent were concerned with doing a good job. Finally, 11 percent were concerned about losing their family to violence or not having spent enough time with them. For instance, Lieutenant Gregorio, age twenty-eight, stated that he feared "being involved in a penal process that, independent of being innocent, one has to pay for lawyers for the defense, which represents a cost that nobody in the police or their family should pay just because they are a police officer."

Similarly, Lieutenant Esmeralda, age twenty-five, stated that she feared "being investigated by criminal courts that can end my career aspirations." This manifests the weight of oversight on police activities. Police are acutely aware that they are being watched and they must be careful how they act, lest they are investigated, found guilty, removed from the institution, and lose all their benefits.

In that same survey, 80 percent of police respondents noted that a primary reason they decided to join was the robust pension package; 51 percent stated salary; 31 percent noted the discounted housing and loans; and 31 percent stated health insurance. Only 25 percent indicated they joined because they wanted to stop crime—illustrating the importance of welfare in motivating individuals to join the police.

Another survey question highlights the importance of benefits and recruitment: "When do you plan on retiring?" In response, 57 percent stated that they would retire once they had completed their twenty to twenty-five years of service so that they could receive their pension. Additionally, 33 percent reported they would retire when they had achieved a certain rank; most respondents aspire to reach the rank of general. One officer stated, "I want to retire when I am fifty-five because, by then, I will have received the rank of general." Finally, 14 percent reported that they had no definitive time or plan to retire and that they would retire when the institution decided it was their time to go. Most of the respondents had a long-term career-oriented outlook. Their responses illustrate two points related to my argument. First, the welfare regime is an essential motivator for service, especially the pension. Second, the pension package attracts qualified candidates who have professional career aspirations and plan to rise in rank.

In 2013, I surveyed students at the Police Postgraduate School, and the results confirmed the importance of this new incorporation system. Of the respondents, 32 percent of officers came from blue-collar households, 22 percent came from white-collar households, and 21 percent came from an upper-class background. In terms of obligatory military service, 3 percent came from the air force, 11 percent had done service in the army, and 30 percent had done service with the police. Although the reforms allowed for significant improvements in the professionalization of the police in Colombia, several challenges to continued improvement remain. I briefly sketch out these challenges in the following section.

Post-FARC Colombia and the Policing Crises of 2016–2021

In 2016, a peace agreement between the Colombian government of Juan Manuel Santos and the Revolutionary Armed Forces of Colombia (FARC) was negotiated. A pivotal point of any peace accord is to provide security guarantees to rebels transitioning out of the conflict and back to civilian life. The police, who were heavily involved in the negotiation process, were incorporated as the guarantor of physical security for demobilizing troops. Specifically, the peace accords led to the creation of the Police Unit for the Building of Peace (UNIPEP). This role for the police was welcomed by the FARC themselves, who, according to my interviews with UNIPEP officers and military officials in Colombia in 2018, trusted the police more than the military in providing security.

The groundwork laid by UNIPEP and the National Police of Colombia was built according to elements of the peace accord and strategy set forth by the Santos government. This, like any other peace accord, was viable only if both sides remained committed to implementing the procedures of peace. However, in 2018, Iván Duque (an acolyte of Álvaro Uribe) rode a wave of dissatisfaction among the Colombian electorate, instigated by the way in which the peace accord was rushed. His party, the Centro Democrático, campaigned against the peace accord and promised to renegotiate key aspects. Subsequently, the Duque administration has worked to systematically dismantle the peace accord, by ignoring some provisions and by underfunding key mechanisms. This has affected the police in two key ways. First, the PNC developed strategies and resources with the idea that the peace accords would be implemented. In this way, it was fulfilling its assigned role. However, under Duque, the police have not been adequately deployed in accordance with the peace provisions. This has left former FARC territories open for the taking by other armed groups. Second, Duque's contradictory guidance has made it difficult for specialized units like UNIPEP to implement some of the integration and protection strategies they developed. As of this writing, Duque has been increasingly pressured by the Biden administration to reinforce the peace agreement. The role of the police in the peace process and in subsequent peace agreements that may arise with other armed groups is a pressing challenge for the National Police of Colombia.

Further, it was the hope of the PNC and many policy experts in policing that the peace accords would allow the PNC to transition into a less militarized role. Although militarized organizational schemes and ranks are not necessarily a problem for policing, the military mindset that has increasingly grown in the police remains a major impediment to reducing misconduct. This mindset, along with training and equipment, was critical to reinforcing the police when they became targets of rebel and narco-trafficking groups. However, it is likely that this mindset in the era of peace has outgrown its usefulness. This opens the door to the possibility of a different police doctrine, one that is oriented away from state security and toward citizen security. However, the Duque administration's lack of implementation of the peace accord has already driven members back into fighting, led by FARC commander Ivan Rodríguez. If internal armed conflict remains widespread in Colombia, there will be little incentive to demilitarize the policing doctrine by politicians and the police themselves. This type of reform was likely placed further out of reach by the National Liberation Army of Colombia's car-bombing of the National Police Academy in Bogotá, which killed twenty-two individuals.

If a militarized doctrine remains in place, there will continue to be problems of abuse of force and distance between police and the people they serve. As I mentioned earlier, militarized doctrines are about social control, whereas civilian doctrines are oriented toward human security. The difference is subtle but significant. Although the ranks, hierarchical structure, training, oversight, and remuneration are adequate, the reality is that the doctrine of policing is oriented toward a militarized us-versus-them mindset; this mindset permeates the police force, causing police to see citizens as potential enemies and subjects of state control. Further, social control prioritizes state security over citizen security.

Although I primarily focus on how police as a labor force are organized, I recognize that the intangible aspects of philosophical and doctrinal mental schemata are powerful determinants of police abuse of force, as well. As such, the future of police professionalization in Colombia must undertake an assessment and reform that shifts Colombia away from a social control model of policing to one emphasizing public security. Absent these reforms, police abuse will continue at a significant level.

Thus, it comes as no surprise that in 2019, civilians throughout Colombia mobilized to protest the continued levels of police abuse of force. The crisis arose after the lawyer Javier Ordóñez was killed by excessive use of taser shocks. Like in the United States, the average citizen's increased access to recording apps on cellular phones allowed them to capture the images and disseminate them across social media. These protests touched a nerve and mobilized Colombians who had also been the victims of similar police overreach. The ensuing protests left more than a dozen individuals dead and countless others hospitalized. This violence only reinforced the growing narrative that the National Police of Colombia were an abusive instrument of social control. These social movements have not resulted in the necessary reforms for two reasons. First, Iván Duque, a staunch conservative, reinforces the status quo of the police blindly, even though the police force historically has been amenable to some reforms. Second, the rise of coronavirus and the subsequent role of the police in enforcing lockdowns, as well as people social distancing, likely stifled the momentum for reforms.

In the coming decades, it is likely that the National Police of Colombia will undergo a process of demilitarization of police doctrine and make the following changes. One critical change will be to remove the PNC from the Ministry of Defense and place them in a more civilian ministry, such as the Ministry of the Interior. Two, although the high degree of centralization has some virtues, as the country advances, it should incorporate more mechanisms of decentralization and civilian review bodies into the police system. The police currently coordinate public security with local mayors, but they can still operate largely independent of the mayor. Having a more formalized role for the mayor in directing police activity, without giving the mayor powers of promotion, removal, or selection, is a necessary reform to improve policing. Another task of demilitarization would be to improve the judicial mechanism that oversees, investigates, and punishes police behavior. This would likely require that the police no longer have a separate justice system from the civilian one.

All these changes require constitutional reforms owing to the organic law that establishes the national police. The issue is that the stifling of the reform movement, coupled with a lack of substantial blocks of political actors in office to push through the reforms, will keep Colombia from substantially improving its police force. To be clear, my analysis simply states that the national police, in terms of misconduct, have greatly improved compared to previous regimes of policing. But this should not be read as a vindication of this model. In fact, in my view, centralization and professionalization are starting points that provide a bare minimum of professionalization on which to build a high-quality police force. Further reforms are required, and Colombia is no exception.

It is worth noting that policing does not operate in a vacuum: history, society, institutions, and political economies have implications on the behavior of police. Theoretically, if one were to place the Colombian police structure within a society that was less fractionalized, had a more stable electoral system, and was a social democratic economy, the police would behave more like their Scandinavian counterparts. However, the problem for police in Colombia is that, despite being organized and institutionalized in a functionally efficient way, the police are utilized by political elites to reinforce neoliberal norms and elite privilege and to repress protesters who challenge this status quo. The reason this tends to happen is because the legislative system allows too many parties to operate, which then produces dysfunctional legislatures unable to check the power of the president. In this context, Colombian presidents can use police to protect their own elite faction from the opposition. Thus, presidential politics and leadership styles can shape police behavior.

This by no means absolves the National Police of Colombia of its abusive behavior, but it helps us understand how at this moment, with such extreme upheaval throughout Colombia, this police force, which has made so much progress in reforming itself for the better, still has leagues to go. The greater point is that no amount of reform is enough to overcome the political and economic structures that have historically enabled various elites and dissidents to engage in violence on behalf of and against the state. Police reform is an iterative process that asks police to be a partner in reshaping their institutions of recruitment, training, and oversight, but it should also ask elite leadership to work to address the drivers of poverty, crime, and violence, which are one and the same. If a system of inequality that privileges property over people permeates an elite class that perennially takes control of the mechanisms of power, we can expect that elite class to wield the police force to protect its interests.

The point of this book is not to suggest how a bad police force can, through some changes, improve itself completely, but to highlight that this type of reform is difficult and elusive and takes a long time to achieve. Somewhat uncomfortably, reform arises when elites seek to centralize control over the police for their own ends. Along the way, they inadvertently improve the police structure in a way that is amenable to better policing. Thus, despite the conditions of poverty, authoritarianism, violence, and conflict that permeated places like historical Chile and Colombia, there were also historical moments of centralization and professionalization that improved police and policing in contexts where law enforcement should have simply continued to be corrupt. That did not happen. Instead, despite those conditions, policing was improved. And this book relates the story of what specific rules or features of the policing game have been tweaked to produce a better outcome. This provides some clues and evidence of which factors matter theoretically for improving police at a basic level. At the same time, there is a high degree of historical contingency. It may be the case that both Chile and Colombia experienced police reform because of the extraordinary periods and conditions of their history, which are not easily replicated, and thus police reform of this nature may not appear in the same way again in another country. I recognize these limits but remain hopeful that this blueprint for police reform can facilitate the process of improving policing in developing countries. Indeed, as the next chapter illustrates, political elites have a clear understanding that centralization of policing in Mexico would be beneficial in addressing the cartel violence that occurs there.

Conclusion

This chapter has illustrated that, during the decentralized period of 1886–1953, the police force was used as a partisan tool of patrimonial party leaders, and this led to extreme misconduct. As such, the police were not concerned with security. Instead, they focused on using their power to harass and abuse citizens of the opposite party. In times of crisis, the police either stood by and did nothing or actively participated in the melee. A significant turning point for the National Police of Colombia came in 1953 when the military intervention initiated the centralization and professionalization process. The militarization of the police would prove to be a good thing. The new uniforms came with increased regimentation of recruitment, training, and oversight. It also included a replication of the military benefits and remuneration structure. Because of militarization, the police were not just centralized but also more professionalized. From my interviews, I gathered that this improved police behavior significantly. By 1962, Colombia successfully depoliticized the police and thus removed local patrimonial control over them. Today, police are officially barred from voting and affiliating with a political party. In this sense, the level of police misconduct has lowered significantly. Police were by and large honest and effective at their jobs in the 1960s (Br. Gen. Fabian Londoño Cardenas, interview with author, March 4, 2013).

However, the problems with misconduct arose once more in the 1970s and 1980s with the rise of narco-trafficking, the appropriation of the police for anti-insurgency activities, and the underfunding of police. When the drug trade hit the police and corruption started to rise during the 1980s, part of the problem was that police welfare, development, and oversight could not stand up to the money and threats of cartels. Despite being a democracy, police misconduct existed at high levels. Part of the lesson of this case is that democracy does not automatically equate to better policing. From the cases, I find that policing can improve within a context of democracy when there is some form of centralization and professionalization. Colombia during the 1980s had centralized police, but what it did not have any more was professional police. This came in 1993, when welfare, development, and oversight were significantly improved. These changes helped mitigate the influence of drug trafficking, and misconduct substantially decreased. This can be seen by the drastic changes in citizen trust in the police, which increased from 23 percent in 1993 to close to 50 percent in 2011. It was the transition from a vocational to a more professional model of police that brought about these changes.

The story of Colombia is the story of a state that has invested in its police, and the product has been a strengthened law enforcement institution that can create, implement, and sustain professionalism. However, as is the case in Chile, the National Police of Colombia require further reforms. As of this writing, allegations of police abuse of power continue to animate a population that demands reforms. As this chapter indicates, to better control these cases of abuse, a more robust system of external oversight by autonomous citizen boards that reinforce internal oversight mechanisms needs to be put into place.

Despite recent problems with corruption and abuse, the story of reform of the police presented in this chapter indicates that the Colombian police are imperfect, but they stand on better ground than they did thirty years ago (Jineth Bedoya, interview with author, April 12, 2012). The next chapter analyzes the case of Mexico by studying three levels of policing: the municipal police, the state police, and the federal police. As the systems move from decentralized and less professionalized to more centralized and professionalized, there should be a corollary improvement in welfare, development, and oversight. Simultaneously, there should also be a decrease in police misconduct as we move from municipal (most corrupt) to federal (least corrupt) police. I show that the structural constraints of decentralization condemn Mexico to chronic police misconduct.

4

Mexico:
Reforming Police During
a Drug War

Mexico experienced over 200,000 deaths in 2006–2017, with 30,000 homicides in 2018 alone (Agren 2017). In 2017, there were 25 million victims of crime in a country of about 122 million people (ENVIPE 2018). At the core of Mexico's problem is a failed policing system. Mexican police are infamously corruptible because the country never professionalized law enforcement. Furthermore, the decentralized nature of policing impedes much-needed reforms and facilitates cartel co-optation. Because local police are paid so poorly, they are easily co-opted into becoming allies with cartels; they protect drug traffickers as well as provide intelligence about state and federal police missions that might jeopardize a local drug cartel's operation. Angélica Durán-Martínez (2015, 1377) notes that violence in Mexico is extreme in part because "trafficking organizations compete and the state security apparatus is fragmented." However, police at the state and federal levels have been more impervious to, although not free of, corruption. The case of Mexico lends additional credence to the idea that more professional and centralized bodies offer a better outcome for police misconduct than do local and less professionalized systems. In this chapter, I begin by discussing the historical antecedents of Mexico's modern police system. I then turn to examining the three types of police forces in Mexico and their divergent professionalization. I conclude by discussing the general behavior of and level of trust in each of these forces.

Law Enforcement from the Revolution to the 1980s

After the Mexican Revolution ended in 1920, army generals Plutarco Elías Calles and Álvaro Obregón consolidated their political power through the

97

National Revolutionary Party (PNR) (PNR; 1920–1929). The PNR formed the foundations of the Institutional Revolutionary Party (PRI), which dominated Mexican politics in the twentieth century. The PRI won every presidential election and the congressional majority from 1930 to 1994, over sixty years. The PRI was able to do this through co-optation and repression—the last falling to the police and the military.

The Mexican Constitution under Article 115, Part VII, did not create police institutions at the national or state level, but only at the municipal level. Although "successive laws and constitutional changes continued to acknowledge the free municipality and a federalist system," the PRI would undermine local governments by siphoning funding sources away from them. At the same time, "the national government assumed control even for such local concerns as road maintenance, sewerage, and water provisions," but policing remained a local task (Grindle 2007, 28). Federal and state preventative police would not appear until 1997 and 2004, respectively. There were federal and state highway patrols, but they were not tasked with traditional prevention of crime outside of roads. Hence, local police were the only game in town throughout PRI rule, which lasted from 1920 to 1997.

Under the municipal system, police were poorly paid and received little benefits. Nevertheless, police were rewarded by a parallel set of privileges that made up for these shortcomings. The PRI used the police to maintain power in exchange for allowing the police to behave like a private enterprise. The central police "industries" were extortion, racketeering, and solicitation of bribes. In exchange for these rewards, police were expected to follow all regime orders to repress social and labor protests. Thus, human rights abuses and corruption were the products of the politicization of the police. In Mexico, from their origins, the police were created not to provide public security but to protect the PRI. From 1930 to 1950, police repression was used sparingly, as the regime preferred co-optation as the preferred mechanism of controlling opposition. As the following section discusses, the police in Mexico would become a more repressive and violent force from 1950 to 1980, a tradition they have maintained into the present era.

From 1950 to 1980, the PRI was engaged in a campaign against subversive elements in Mexico. These insurgencies and student-led mobilizations arose from the discontent over the economic situation and elite dominance of the political system, and drew inspiration from the Cuban Revolution. This is referred to as the "dirty war" or low-intensity war. This period was marked by repression, torture, disappearances, executions, and corruption. The police played an active and violent role in suppressing public movements to preserve the PRI, including the 1959 railway workers strike, the 1960 Guerrero student movement, the 1965 doctors movement, the 1966 Michoacan student movement, the 1966 Nuevo León student movement, the 1967 Chihuahua student movement, the 1968 Tabasco student movement, and the 1968 Tlatelolco massacre in Mexico City (Procuraduría General de la Republica 2006). During the eighteen years of the dirty war in Mexico, municipal police were complicit in many of the 645 reported disappearances, 99 extrajudicial executions, and more than 2,000 cases of torture (Procuraduría General de la Republica 2006).

Beyond abuse, there was extensive police corruption. The most important case was related to the presidential administration of José López Portillo. López Portillo had appointed his loyal childhood friend, Arturo Durazo Moreno, to the prominent position of the chief of police of Mexico City for a six-year term spanning 1976–1982. Durazo Moreno became infamous for his audacious use of this office to amass a personal fortune. According to Miguel Cabildo (1984), every three months, each police officer in Mexico City was obligated to collect 4,000 pesos for Durazo Moreno and his staff. To get this money, the officers had to extort the residents of Mexico City. Failure to do so resulted in dismissal. In addition to extortion, Durazo Moreno amassed millions of dollars via international drug trafficking (Gunson 2000). As soon as the López Portillo administration ended, Durazo Moreno fled the country. The US Federal Bureau of Investigation caught him in Costa Rica and returned him to Mexico, where he was sentenced to a sixteen-year prison term for drug trafficking and corruption (Gunson 2000).

The same sort of corruption was found in all municipal police throughout Mexico, as commanders maintained quotas for fines and bribes that the lower ranks had to collect. This activity was so prevalent that it gained the moniker *la mordida,* or "the bite." Citizens came to expect most police interactions to end with *la mordida,* and thus, citizens did their best to avoid any unnecessary police contact. The local PRI mayors allowed this to happen because the police controlled political dissent, and mayors received kickbacks from police graft. Because mayors served only three-year terms and could not be reelected, they had nothing to fear regarding electoral repercussions for this type of behavior.

Beyond social control of opposition forces and extortion, local municipalities also engaged in protection of the drug trafficking trade (Grayson 2009, 29). Extensive cooperation emerged between the municipal police and criminal organizations. By the 1980s, Mexico accounted for 70 percent of the marijuana, 25 percent of the heroin, and 60 percent of the cocaine transported to the United States (Chabat 2002, 136). As the next section discusses, the electoral reforms in the early 1990s disrupted the equilibrium between drug cartels and the PRI Party, injecting new actors and parties into the political system throughout Mexico. Despite these changes, the corrupt and abusive municipal police remained unchanged.

In 1983, President Miguel de la Madrid enacted decentralization reforms at the local level, explicitly amending Article 115 of the Mexican Constitution, which provided local municipalities with increased control over budgeting and appropriations. Also, cities were given authority over levying property taxes. With this increased financial power came increased responsibilities for municipalities in the areas of public utilities and public transportation (Grindle 2007, 29). Second, during this era, calls to reform the electoral system grew as political opposition to the PRI regime strengthened. This produced a different set of problems in the new era.

Democratization and Presidential Police Reforms, 1988–2018

As drug trafficking increased, so did the internal pressure for electoral reforms. In 1988, the PRI splintered into a left-wing faction and a center-right faction. The leftists ran under the banner of the National Democratic Front and countered the PRI candidate, Carlos Salinas de Gortari, with their candidate, Cuauhtémoc Cárdenas. Cárdenas was the son of former President Lázaro Cárdenas, a leftist-populist leader in Mexico. Given his family and personal credentials, Cárdenas appeared poised to win the upcoming election. And indeed, on election night, exit polls pegged him to win the presidency. However, through fraudulent mechanisms, the PRI manipulated the polls, giving Salinas de Gortari the victory. The public outcry at the fraudulent results prompted the Salinas de Gortari administration to concede to some electoral reforms in 1990. Subsequent changes in 1993 and 1994 led to the further opening of the political system to fair competition.

Here is a critical insight regarding my theoretical discussion—Mexican police had been thoroughly corrupted, not by their hand alone but by the political actors that dominated them at the local and national levels. Indeed, power was centralized in the hands of the party led by the sitting president, who used the police to maintain PRI dominance. But local PRI actors still used their local police in a patrimonial fashion to repress and extort citizens. However, the literature argues that a crucial condition that defines the level of police misconduct is the type of regime (Treisman 2000). Is it the authoritarian regime or the structure of police that explains misconduct? So far, we cannot parse out this difference in Mexico, and one would be inclined to blame the PRI rather than the structural problems noted.

One way to make sense of this is by considering Mexico in two periods: the PRI era and the post-PRI era. If the PRI regime was the only causal factor facilitating police misconduct, when the PRI left power, we should have seen a decrease in misconduct; however, this was not the case, as Table 4.1 illustrates.

The logic is that if the PRI created these relationships, then once the PRI is removed, these links would break down. All other things being equal, we would expect local mayors from different political parties to reform their police and make them professional servants of public security. How-

Table 4.1 PRI Era and Post-PRI Era Policing

	PRI Era	Post-PRI Era
Militarized police	No	No
Violent society	Yes	Yes
Corrupt society	Yes	Yes
Regime type	Authoritarian	Democratic
Police system	Decentralized	Decentralized
	Occupational	Occupational
Misconduct	High	High

ever, the mere act of democratization does nothing to change the police behavior, and the depth of the problem with local and occupational police models reveals itself. As Table 4.1 notes, despite having a democratic regime, police misconduct remains unchanged.

The National Action Party (PAN) and the Revolutionary Democratic Party (PRD) started to win local offices in 1994, and going forward they ended up replicating the same schema that the PRI developed during its dictatorship—patrimonial, corrupt, and oppressive policing. After the transition, the police continued to be used by political actors. The new officeholders (from the PAN and PRD) maintained the autonomy of the police and used it for illicit purposes. Thus, in the postelectoral reform era in Mexico, the decentralized police system remained, as did the patrimonial system of misconduct.

In the democratic era, police mostly continued the same behavior they had become notorious for during the authoritarian period. In the next section, the focus turns toward the administration of Ernesto Zedillo, who is significant for being the first president who sought to enact extensive structural reform to the policing system. Before the Zedillo administration, there were few police reform attempts. His policies led to the development of the Federal Preventative Police and further centralization and professionalization efforts in subsequent administrations.

The Zedillo Administration, 1994–2000

Although the electoral reforms passed in 1990 and 1993 ensured that the 1994 presidential elections were free and fair, the PRI candidate, Ernesto Zedillo, won the presidency. However, far from continuing with the same PRI policies, the reform-minded Zedillo administration sought to change public security in Mexico. He put forward two major public safety reforms. First, in 1995, Zedillo created the National System for Public Security with the goal of coordinating local, state, and federal police agencies through an information-sharing network. This represented the first impulse to centralize police work by establishing channels for information sharing throughout the Mexican Republic.

The second broad reform under Zedillo was the creation of the Federal Preventative Police (PFP) in 1999. The Federal Judicial Police—a plain-clothes investigative police service charged with helping federal prosecutors investigate crimes—already existed, as did a federal highway police force, which secured the federal highways. Other than these two limited roles, however, there had thus far been no uniformed national police service tasked with preventing crime or providing day-to-day public security activities in Mexico. The PFP was the first foray into developing a nationally based uniformed police department to help local authorities and to pursue federal crimes (María Eugenia Suárez de Garay, interview with author, September 10, 2014). Initially, the PFP's primary role was to protect highways, arrest criminal offenders violating federal laws, and provide support services to the local municipal police. Specifically, it was tasked with safeguarding borders, government buildings and properties, ports of entry, highways, and national parks.

The Fox Administration, 2000–2006

Vicente Fox (PAN) was the first non-PRI presidential candidate to win an election in Mexico in over seventy years. Regarding public security, Fox proceeded in the same direction as his predecessor. He created a cabinet-level office called the Secretariat of Public Security specifically tasked with overseeing federal public security policy throughout Mexico, and he put it in control of the PFP. During his presidency, the PFP grew to include 12,000 agents (Presidencia de la Republica 2012).

An additional measure that Fox undertook was the development of the Federal Investigation Agency (AGI), modeled after the US Federal Bureau of Investigation (FBI), to support the prosecutor general's job of enforcing federal laws. But under Fox, the AGI would become rife with corruption and would eventually be combined with the PFP. Fox's successor, Felipe Calderón, deepened the centralization and professionalization of both federal and state police.

The Calderón Administration, 2006–2012

Felipe Calderón's (PAN) administration mostly continued the process of consolidation but also enacted two significant public security policies. First, Calderón understood that municipal police were too weak to address the rising problems of drug trafficking and that the PFP lacked enough personnel and resources to match the power of these cartels. Thus, Calderón gained notoriety for militarizing public security using the army and navy in counter-drug-trafficking operations throughout Mexico because they were widely perceived to be less corruptible. However, the militarization of public security did not undermine the growth or importance of the PFP. At the beginning of the Calderón administration in 2006, there were 12,000 PFP agents. By the end of his six-year term in 2012, there were approximately 37,000 PFP personnel (Presidencia de la Republica 2012).

Second, under this administration, state governors started to use federal funds to develop state-level preventative police units, to bolster the public security system in the face of weaker municipal police. At the same time, Calderón proposed the creation of a national police, but the constitutional reforms required for these changes proved challenging to implement through the legislative process. Instead, Calderón proposed an alternative formulation of *mando único* based on the thirty-two police commands, one for each state and the capital city (Ellingwood 2010). As such, there was a noticeable increase in state preventative police throughout the country as governors prepared to make the required changes for the transition, but the system proved difficult to implement owing to the objection of local mayors. However, a compromise was reached among the federal government, state governors, and local politicians. The state preventative police would take over municipal police duties only in places where municipal police departments were not able to meet specific standards set forth by the secretariat of public security. Cities, usually the larger ones that were able to meet to these standards, could maintain control over their police force. To date, this reform was only partially implemented because of pushback, hence many states still do not have state preventative police, and municipal police continue to operate throughout the country (García 2010).

The Peña Nieto Administration, 2012–2018

Recognizing the inefficiencies and incentives for police corruption at the local level, presidential and gubernatorial candidates in the 2012 elections increasingly supported the centralization of public security policy and preventative police to combat the drug cartels more effectively. However, by 2017, Mexico experienced its highest homicide rate since the beginning of its drug war in 2006, with close to 30,000 homicides ("Drug Violence Blamed" 2018). For instance, PAN presidential candidate Josefina Vázquez Mota proposed developing national police, similar to the police in Chile and Colombia, to address the insecurity in Mexico (Reyes 2012). Although the PRI candidate Enrique Peña Nieto defeated her, some of Mota's ideas were adopted by his administration.

The Peña Nieto public security policy is mainly seen as a continuation of the PAN security policy of militarization of public security and counternarcotic operations. In 2013–2014, Peña Nieto created federal gendarmerie, under the control of the Federal Police (formerly called the National Police of Colombia, or PFP). This force was initially envisioned by the Peña Nieto administration as a rural militarized police whose goal was to provide public security to small municipalities without police. However, since its inception, the role of the federal gendarmerie has changed. It is now being oriented toward border missions and protecting industries threatened by organized crime, such as mining and agriculture. Specifically, this organization protects the transportation routes and supply chains for these industries. For instance, one of the sources of revenue for the Zetas cartel in the Gulf Coast is illegal oil tapping of the state-run petroleum company's pipeline. This oil is then sold on the black market. Under Peña Nieto's administration, the policy of centralizing police at the state level cleared major hurdles and achieved the support of most state governors in Mexico. Nevertheless, it was never seriously taken up by the Mexican Chamber of Deputies and faced stiff resistance from the Association of Municipal Governments of Mexico, representing the most significant 200 of Mexico's 2,440 municipalities (Castillo 2010).

Mired in scandals, Peña Nieto abandoned further reform attempts. The subsequent president of Mexico, Andrés Manuel López Obrador (AMLO), has intimated that he plans to implement a type of *mando único*. Although the details are not yet precise, AMLO has noted that his proposal "will unify all the forces: The Navy, the Army, the Federal Police, the state and municipal police, there will be coordination because now all the corporations act for your account" (Forbes 2018).

Reviewing Police Development in Mexico

The pattern linking all five presidential administrations from 1994 to 2024 is that each was or is attempting to centralize and professionalize police by building federal preventative police and bringing the municipal police under state control. Despite each administration's reform attempts, little has changed regarding policing at the municipal level. As such, citizen trust in police has been historically low. As Figure 4.1 illustrates, Mexican respondents do not trust their police. The highest level of confidence was found during the Zedillo administration after he implemented the National System for Public Security, but the trust level never went above 44 percent. The average level of trust for this period is 23 percent, indicating that a supermajority of citizens in Mexico are wary of their police forces precisely because of their penchant for misconduct.

However, Figure 4.1 obfuscates significant variation among local, state, and federal preventative police. And there are differences in trust among these three types of police: municipal police have the lowest level, state police have higher levels, and federal police generally have the highest level of trust of the people. What explains this variation among the three levels of police forces? In what follows, I demonstrate that the degree of centralization and professionalization correlates with the differing levels of misconduct.

Figure 4.1   Respondents with Some or a Lot of Trust in Mexican Police

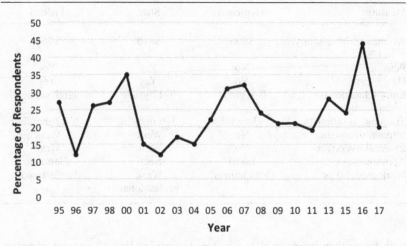

Source: Latinobarómetro Survey 1995–2017.

Specifically, the next section provides a nuanced comparison of municipal, state, and federal police in Mexico from 2004 to 2014. It highlights that moving from decentralized and occupational models (municipal police) to more centralized and professional models (state and federal police) decreases police misconduct. This is expected even though police at all three levels face the same security problems.

A Comparison of Police Forces in Mexico

Whereas the previous section discusses the historical development of police in Mexico, this section presents a comparative analysis of municipal, state, and federal police, which addresses police welfare, development, and oversight. There are two purposes to this analysis. The first is to show that municipal police best approximate occupational models, while state and federal police approximate professional standards. The second objective is to show that the municipal police are trapped in occupational modes of policing because they are decentralized, and state and federal police are more professional because they are more centralized. Table 4.2 summarizes the key distinctions.

Municipal Law Enforcement

Most municipal police in Mexico are from poor cities and are part of small departments. According to Moloeznik (2010), there are 1,100 municipalities

Table 4.2   Comparing Municipal, State, and Federal Police Indicators

Measures	Municipal	State	Federal
Average starting salary, in USD	$500	$810	$964
Pension	No	Yes	Yes
Health care	No	Yes	Yes
Entry educational requirement	0–9 grade	9–12 grade	High school
Training, in months	1–3 months	3–6 months	6–12 months
Internal oversight	No	Weak	Weak
External oversight	No	Weak	Weak
Administration	Local	Semi	National
Work model type	Occupational	Weak professional	Professional

with fewer than twenty police personnel, meaning that 52 percent of police in Mexico are from small police departments. Furthermore, 530 districts had between twenty-one and fifty police. Meanwhile, 210 towns count on 51–100 police officers. Only 250 cities have more than 100 police (Moloeznik 2010). In Mexico, 400 cities have gone ten years without a police force ("400 Municipios del Pais Llevan" 2010). These statistics directly correlate to the decentralized nature of the police system in Mexico.

As Pablo Monsalvo, professor at the Ibero-American University in Mexico City, correctly points out, "The problem is that Article 115 of the Constitution establishes that municipalities are the ones in charge of public security. But what if the municipalities are poor? How are they going to pay their own police?" (CNN 2010). Monsalvo notes that "40 of the 2,500 municipalities produce half of the country's wealth; the other ones are weak" (CNN 2010). However, the solution is not merely a matter of throwing money at these police because the decentralized system perpetuates the local patrimonial relationships with police. During this democratic era, political competition at the local level is a fundamental problem for decentralizing control over the police to local authorities.

In other words, resources are available, but they are wasted by corrupt mayors. One public security expert I worked with offers an example of how mayoral control is so problematic: Mayors provide salaries to police who do not work. If there are 100 police positions, 30 are given to officers who work. But there can be up to 70 posts filled by "shadow officers," where people are still paid, but they do no police work (Antia Mendoza, interview with author, September 23, 2014).

Indeed, these shadow officers are friends and allies of the local mayor. The officers who do actual police work are also loyal to the mayor's needs.

This blending of the private and public roles illustrates how local mayors mismanage police resources, which is made possible by the decentralized nature of the police. Another problem with municipal police is the lack of political motivation to create a professional police force.

Municipal police welfare benefits: salary, benefits, and pensions. I conceptualize professionalism as the outgrowth of police benefits, development, and oversight structures. By advancing salary, pensions, and other benefits, police forces can recruit better candidates. These candidates, in turn, have more incentive to commit to more arduous and longer training regiments. There should be robust internal and external control mechanisms to make sure police are not engaged in misconduct. This section focuses on the key benefit: salaries.

Ambar Varela, director of public policy evaluations for Contraloría Ciudadana, notes that the "the majority of police [in Mexico] are not given any benefits: they do not have pensions, housing," and they are poorly paid (Varela, interview with author, September 3, 2014). According to the Organisation for Economic Co-operation and Development (OECD) Better Life Index, the average monthly salary is roughly US$1,100 (OECD 2015). In Mexico, 85 percent of municipal police officers earn less than US$500 per month (Seventh National Survey on Insecurity 2011). Most of the small police departments, such as those in Candela in the state of Coahuila, can afford to pay their police only an average of US$230 per month (Instituto Nacional de Estadística y Geografía 2011b). Other municipalities, such as those in the impoverished state of Chiapas, have police who are paid "120 USD per month, and only work part-time" (Mendoza, interview with author, September 23, 2014). What is not surprising, given the decentralized nature of policing in Mexico, is that even the best-paid police do not reach the salary level of an average Mexican worker, and most police earn US$500 less than the national average. This is a major obstacle in the way of developing professional police, but it is not the only one. Merilee Serrill Grindle's (2007, 109) study of Mexican decentralization revealed that municipal police in Mexico "are paid poorly, and often had little or no education," and have to supplement "their pay by demanding bribes." Some municipalities are so weak that when police "collect fines, they were allowed to keep them as part of their pay" (Grindle's 2007, 109).

Beyond having a weak salary, municipal police in Mexico do not have a pension for their officers (García Ramírez 2013). A primary reason municipalities hesitate to provide these resources is because these cities do not have enough funds to maintain payment of higher salaries and benefits for police. In places where some pension benefits are provided for police, those benefits are doled out at the discretion of the municipal mayors, who use these advantages in a patrimonial manner. In the city of Ramos Arizpe in the state of Coahuila, a new pension law was geared toward removing this discretion. Mario Gómez, president of the Committee for Public Security, stated the goal of the reform was to take "away from the mayoral discretion in deciding who to provide pensions too. We cannot keep doing this. It is not a question of discretion, but a question of equity, and we are going to incorporate ourselves into the Pension Law proposed by the governor" (Gutiérrez 2015). Eventually, the law was passed. The point, however, is that few municipal police receive pensions, and when they do, these benefits are used as tools by politicians rather than as mechanisms of improving recruitment.

As Luis De la Barreda and colleagues (2013) explain, most "municipalities completely lack any social benefits for their police. As is the case with salaries, other police benefits are much greater in the Federal Police, who offer life insurance, medical insurance, and retirement benefits." The dangerous nature of police work necessitates an active protection system for injuries or disabilities. Because municipal police lack these advantages and are poorly paid, municipal police cannot set high recruitment standards, which is the topic of the next section.

Municipal police recruitment and training. As a result of small salaries and nonexistent benefits, average Mexican municipal police departments are not able to recruit selectively. Many police forces have minimal selection standards in terms of primary or secondary education. For instance, 64 percent of all municipal police in Mexico require candidates to have completed secondary school or less (zero to nine years of education). Only 30 percent of candidates are required to have a high school diploma, and only 3 percent are required to have a college or advanced degree (Instituto Nacional de Estadística y Geografía 2013).

The reason municipal Mexican police departments do not make completion of high school a mandatory requirement is twofold: the low salary and the small talent pool. First, if the minimum level of education was high school completion, not enough qualified candidates would apply for such a poor-paying job. With a high school degree, average citizens can earn more money in less risky occupations than they could by becoming a police officer. In short, without increasing remuneration, police departments cannot feasibly recruit higher-caliber applicants. A clear example of how increasing the education requirement without increasing pay can fail occurred in the 2015 case of the Gómez Palacio municipal police in the state of Durango. This municipality implemented completion of a twelfth-grade education as a requirement to enter the municipal police force; however, shortly thereafter, José Miguel Campillo, the mayor, was obliged to lower the standard to a tenth-grade education because there were not enough qualified applicants under the more stringent education requirement (El Siglo de Torreon 2015). Second, there is the problem that most municipalities and municipal police recruit from within their cities. However, as mentioned earlier, most cities in Mexico are miserably poor and cannot afford to pay higher wages and benefits for police. An academic expert shared with me that the smaller, poorer police departments have a pool of less-qualified personnel to draw from because not many people graduate high school in these more impoverished communities (Juan Salgado, interview with author, September 23, 2014).

Another issue for municipal police systems is that they do not vet their candidates thoroughly. For instance, most municipal police departments in Mexico do not conduct background checks on their officers as a result of lack of capacity or willingness. Municipalities that do perform background checks do not have access to criminal information from other cities or states, and therefore they do not know for sure whether their applicants are former criminals from other jurisdictions, only that they were not tried for crimes in their courts. In any event, incoming mayors value loyalty over a clean criminal record.

The municipal system in Mexico makes it difficult for police departments to recruit quality candidates and also impacts the training of recruits. Although some wealthier municipalities train recruits in academies for four to six months, they represent a minority. Most municipal police in Mexico can expect to receive one to three months of training. A police reform expert I spoke with noted that municipal police are not provided professional training. If they are lucky, they may receive one to three months of training, which is insufficient for teaching recruits how to use a gun, how to arrest, how to detain, how to use policing tactics, and how to deal with people (Antia Mendoza, interview with author, September 23, 2014).

The municipal police's poor recruitment and inadequate training allow criminal elements to enter the police force unchecked. For instance, in September 2018, several police officers in the city of Acapulco's municipal police, including the chief and several high-ranking officers, were arrested (Gibbs 2018). Subsequently, the entire police force was disarmed, and policing duties were taken over by federal police and military units because this police force of an important city was thoroughly infiltrated by the local cartels. Furthermore, as a result of inadequate training, the police who operate on the streets lack the necessary skills to provide basic security. Misconduct persists because municipal police continue to be under the influence of local politicians, who use the police for their own political and illicit ends. One way to reduce this undue influence is to remove local control over the police by centralization. Even this is not enough, because police may engage in misconduct of their own accord, independent of political influence. Hence, oversight mechanisms are critical to stopping police from abusing their power. Unfortunately, at the municipal level in Mexico, the standard monitoring mechanisms of hierarchy and internal affairs are weak or nonexistent.

Municipal police oversight. The first and most important factor in police oversight is a reliable hierarchical system. Theoretically, the commander of the police should have direct control over the lower ranks through a hierarchy. However, the nature of the municipal police system places all the power of police activities under the control of local authorities, such as the mayor or council members. The literature argues that this is theoretically a good thing, providing civilian input into police activities. However, in Mexico, the decentralized system makes implementation of this oversight mechanism more difficult. Local mayors are elected every three years, and they cannot be reelected. This is significant because each new municipal administration often shuffles the police commands. For example, commanders are demoted back to regular officers, patrol officers are made leaders, and new police chiefs are brought in from the outside. This is the best-case scenario. In municipalities with fewer than fifty police officers, mayors often wholly change the police staff, carrying over few officers from the old administration. This practice thoroughly undermines the development of a hierarchical system. Furthermore, the arbitrary nature of promotion threatens the meritocratic advancement typical of a professional bureaucratic system. Hierarchical ranks are not determined by seniority, training, education, or expertise (as a modern bureaucracy requires) but by the degree of loyalty to and favor of the new mayor.

More problematic are the weak internal oversight mechanisms that work in parallel to this feeble hierarchy. Although some of the bigger city police departments have a commission of honor, justice, and promotion in charge of internal affairs investigations, most do not. However, as Ernesto López Portillo, director of the Institute for Security and Democracy in Mexico, notes, where they exist, they "are chronically weak" and ineffective. Although citizens could report malfeasant police to the commission of honor and justice, appeal to the commission of human rights or to the police itself, or go to the public ministry, these oversight institutions rarely work (Ernesto López Portillo, interview with author, September 10, 2014).

Part of the reason internal affairs and oversight of municipal police remain weak is because local mayors do not benefit from their development. When mayors want to use the police for illicit purposes and to repress political and social movements, they must hide these activities. Hence, the creation of police oversight mechanisms is not in the interest of local mayors. This local influence over the operation of public security couples with the extreme poverty to perpetuate police misconduct. The municipality of Alcozauca de Guerrero represents a typical case of what afflicts municipal police.

Alcozauca de Guerrero is a poor city with a population of about 18,971 (Guzmán Sanchez and Suárez de Garay 2012, 3). The mountainous region where this municipality is located is "categorized as one of the most marginalized and poverty-stricken areas of Mexico, where 14 of the 19 cities are defined as very highly marginalized, and the other five are highly marginalized" (Instituto Para la Seguridad y la Democracia 2012, 3). This town has thirty-three police officers, all men, and their starting salary in 2014 was US$375 per month. The police officers have an average of 5.5 years of education, and many of the police have difficulty reading (Instituto Para la Seguridad y la Democracia 2012, 47). In her work on Mexican decentralization, Grindle (2007, 152) provides an example of the dearth of recruitment standards in these Lilliputian police forces throughout Mexico: In San Fernando, Tamaulipas, "when the director of public security took up his responsibilities after an election, he was shocked to discover that many police were illiterate or semiliterate, or had dropped out of school before finishing primary or secondary education."

There are no recruitment standards—that is, other than loyalty to the mayor. About 90 percent of the police have declared they were not provided any medical benefits from their work (Instituto Para la Seguridad y la Democracia 2012, 49). Additionally, there is no life insurance for these police (73). Because of labor insecurity and the poor conditions of work, there are high levels of job desertion (74). Substantial turnover is also correlated with changes in mayoral administrations because, as with other Mexican municipalities, in Alcozauca a new mayor comes to power every three years and completely changes the police force, filling police posts with loyal supporters (51–52). The municipal police of Alcozauca, like most police in Mexico, are occupational, are used by mayors to dole out rewards to loyal supporters and to repress opposition, and are susceptible to misconduct.

Municipal police misconduct. The previous sections on police welfare, development, and oversight reveal that there is a significant weakness in these institutions, which is rooted in local control over the police. When I asked one security expert why we do not see municipal police reform in Mexico, she noted that local politicians use the police for political ends, not for the function police were created for: to enforce laws, to stop crime, to ensure peace and order. Here, municipal police are used as an extension of the politicians. The security expert further noted that this is a primary reason why citizens do not trust the municipal police. Local elected officials seek to maintain the status quo by having a private army to suppress political dissent in their locality (Antia Mendoza, interview with author, September 23, 2014). As Grindle (2007, 152) notes, when "mayors assumed office, there were few formal limits on their ability to appoint officials. . . . [These] new administrations paid scant attention to [the policies] of their predecessors . . . even when they represented the same political party." In short, it is impossible to establish long-term public security policies and effective regulations because every three years a new mayor turns up and changes policies and staff. Often, the mayor also promotes officers of his liking, fires those he does not see as loyal, and appoints new ones who are his followers. Hence, decentralization of control over police at the local level continues the tradition of "extensive patronage opportunities offered by police work, and the consequent turnover of officers every three years," and it stifles any innovation or continuity of operation required for building institutional memory and capacity (Grindle 2007, 152).

Therefore, it makes little sense for local authorities to reform the police. This relationship, built around the logic of the PRI hegemonic period, persists to this day not only because of the political culture and the environment of insecurity but also because it is sustained by the decentralized nature of policing. The police must be centralized in their administrative capacity and control. Municipal police in Mexico are not professional, are widely occupational (discussed later), and are more malfeasant than their state and federal counterparts.

Semicentralized Police at the State Level

The state preventative police is a new concept in Mexico. States have had judicial police in charge of assisting state prosecutors in the investigation of crimes, and state highway patrol in charge of helping stranded motorists and policing traffic offenses. However, until recently, states have not had police with traditional roles of patrolling and preventing crime at the state level of jurisdiction. During Calderón's administration, national police forces proliferated across Mexico, and their sizes and functions increased around this time. The states of Sonora (2004), Nayarit (2006), and Durango (2006) all created state police to help coordinate the war on drugs in their regions, but they were not the only ones. All states now have state preventative police. Initially, the state police were tasked with securing buildings and property and protecting state officeholders. However, because of the relative weakness of the municipal police, some governors have been using the state police to enhance security in larger cities and in rural areas lacking police forces. Since 2004, the number of state police in Mexico has increased from a few hundred to thousands of police officers. This increase is correlated with increased budgets and increased policing duties. For instance, in 2011, Nayarit had only 346 state police officers, but the number has tripled, and in 2014, Nayarit had 1,100 state police officers (Rogelio Paaris López de la Vega, pers. comm., February 28, 2014). Similarly, the state police in Veracruz have grown from a few hundred in 2006 to 9,485 in 2014 (Teresa Parada Cortes, pers. comm., February 11, 2014).

One factor explaining this state-level police growth is that municipal police are historically weak, under the patrimonial control of local mayors, and are not a useful tool for state governors to implement public security policies. The municipal police are loyal to local mayors, not to the governor's office, and could, therefore, ignore state directives. Also, some municipalities completely lacked a police presence, leaving no one to carry out state directives. Thus, the growth is the result of the state government's desire to build institutions that it can use to support local municipalities and to implement their security plans.

A second factor explaining the growth of state preventative police is that Felipe Calderón (president of Mexico from 2006 to 2012) sought to establish a national police force but fell short. The first phase of Calderón's long-term federal preventative police reform proposal was to unify all municipal police into a state police agency and ultimately place them under the direct control of the governor. The proposal's purpose was to disrupt the patrimonial relationships that had developed among municipal police, mayors, and drug traffickers. The second phase was to unify municipal police into thirty-two state police forces. As discussed earlier, political and constitutional difficulties made this second phase too involved to achieve.

Nevertheless, as of 2012, the first phase was being implemented in most Mexican states. In the small state of Aguascalientes, for instance, all the police have come under the control of the governor and the state police force. Other larger states, like Veracruz, are slowly taking over municipal police organizations that fail to meet minimum policing requirements. These two initiatives have led to the growth of the state police forces across Mexico. Because of the more centralized nature of the state police, governors have been able to build more professional police forces, which are superior to their local counterparts concerning benefits, training, and oversight.

State police welfare benefits: salary, benefits, and pensions. In 2011, the average pay for state police officers was US$711 per month (Instituto Nacional de Estadística y Geografía 2011a). Additionally, about 55.5 percent of state police officers earned a salary of US$877 or more per month in 2011 (Instituto Nacional de Estadística y Geografía 2011a). Since 2011, many salaries have been increased. The latest data that I have collected through various transparency requests from states indicates that in 2014, police earned, on average, US$810 per month. Note that the average state police salary is US$310 per month *above* the average monthly wage of their local police counterparts.

Other benefits that municipal police do not receive are pensions and health care; however, state preventative police do receive these benefits. Most states offer retirement for agents between the ages of fifty-five and sixty years with twenty-five to thirty years of service. Upon meeting these requirements, the police officer receives a monthly pension equal to 100 percent of their last monthly salary. Officers who have served fifteen to twenty years receive 50 percent of their final salary for life.

Regarding healthcare coverage, all state police organizations cited in my transparency requests provide medical coverage to their agents and their families. Many also provide life insurance, such as the state of Morelos, which offers 80 months of pay to family members if an agent dies outside of work and 300 months of salary to relatives of officers who die in the line of service (Jorge Xavier Guevara Ramírez, pers. comm., October 15, 2014). Other states offer retirement or pension for injuries on the job if the person becomes disabled. Some states, but not all, such as the state of Durango, provide housing access to their state police (Martha Hurtado Hernández, pers. comm., February 14, 2014).

State police recruitment and training. For most Mexican state police candidates, the education requirement varies between secondary (middle school) and preparatory (high school) education; the latter is becoming the new norm. My investigation, based on Freedom of Information requests, reveals that police at the state level must go through a necessary background check, be clear of any criminal record and any drug use, and have no family connections to organized crime.

The training period for state police varies from three to six months, but all state police receive training. The states of Coahuila, Durango, and Morelos provide three months of training, and the rest of the responding states provide training that lasts six months (Jorge Xavier Guevara Ramírez, pers. comm., October 15, 2014; Erika Chaires González, pers. comm., February 17, 2014; Alonso Ulises Mendez Manuel-Gómez, pers. comm., August 31, 2014; María Teresa Parada Cortes, pers. comm., February 11, 2014; Oscar Agustín Rodríguez García, pers. comm., March 12, 2014; Raymundo Alfredo Bonilla Ibarra, pers. comm., January 30, 2014). Training consists of militarized physical training, technical classroom education, and one to two months of on-the-job training in the field.

State police oversight. Unlike their municipal counterparts, all the state police that I investigated do have an internal review board. For instance, the state of Sonora has the commission of honor, justice, and promotion (Manuel-Gómez, pers. comm., August 31, 2014). Citizens can submit complaints about police conduct to these boards for review. Nevertheless, the evidence indicates that few people make reports against police, and those few statements lead to only a few officers being removed from the institution.

Another mechanism of control of police at the state level is the control and confidence commissions. These boards conduct regular random drug tests and polygraphs on police officers to test their loyalty to the state, whether they are consuming drugs, and whether they have connections to criminal groups. This practice has been effective in removing many corrupt officers from these institutions. For instance, in 2010, 600 police officers were removed from the state police of Veracruz for failing these control tests.

Externally, the Ministerios de Fuero Comun (public prosecutor's offices) operate as external agencies in charge of investigating complaints against any state officer, whether in the bureaucracy, health department, or public security (Bonilla Ibarra, pers. comm., January 30, 2014). Theoretically, the other external oversight body is the state commission for human rights, which oversees investigating human rights violations. Although these internal and external monitoring mechanisms exist, they are relatively weak.

Centralized Policing: Federales Then and Now

At the federal level, the primary police force is called the Policía Federal Preventiva (PFP), or Federal Preventative Police. This, like the state police, is a relatively new institution, having its origins in the 1997 Ley de Policía Federal Preventiva (Federal Preventative Police Law). In 2012, the PFP absorbed the Federal Investigations Agency (AFI). The bolstered PFP was then placed under the control of the National Security Commission, a new agency under the control of the secretary of the interior. The PFP then merely became known as the Policía Federal (PF). The PF's jurisdiction encompasses all the national territory, and it is tasked with enforcing federal law (Vargas 2005). Its primary mission is to prevent crimes and administrative offenses against federal legislation, including anti-drug-trafficking laws (Secretaria de Seguridad Publica Mexico 2011). One of the PF's central goals is to participate in aid of national, state, and local authorities in the investigation and prosecution of crimes and the arrest of individuals (Juan Salgado, interview with author, March 14, 2014; María Eugenia Suárez de Garay, interview with author, September 10, 2014). They can also collaborate, when requested, with local governments. The PF became one of the federal government's most essential tools in addressing the shortcomings of its broken police system. As such, the federal government increased the size of the PF from 9,036 in the year 2000 to 39,711 in 2014 (Eldia Barbara Lugo Delgado, pers. comm., February 28, 2014).

Federal police welfare: salary, benefits, and pension. The entry ranks of federal police receive US$964 as their monthly base salary, but with bonuses factored in, the police can earn up to US$1,461 per month, which is above the national average wage. The federal police are paid twice as much as an average municipal police officer. Beyond the higher pay, these police also enjoy many benefits that most municipal police do not. After thirty years of service, federal police have a right to a pension of 100 percent of their last salary. For themselves and their families, the police are also provided life insurance, disability insurance, and the ability to pay into a matched retirement fund of up to 2 pesos for every 6.5 pesos contributed by the officer. The police agents also have access to medical coverage for themselves and their families. Another key benefit that the federal police have that municipal and state police do not have is access to low-interest loans to purchase or build a home or to make a home improvement (Lugo Delgado, pers. comm., February 28, 2014). These great benefits and salaries allow the PF to be more selective in recruitment, as discussed in the next section.

Federal Police Development: Recruitment and Training

Candidates must have a minimum high school education to enter the federal police force; for forensic positions, a college degree is required (Lugo Delgado, pers. comm., February 28, 2014). The PF conduct a thorough background check on each candidate and can access national information regarding criminal history, financial status, and family links to organized crime. Applicants also go through mental health exams, medical exams, and toxicological exams. The police at the federal level also receive more training than the average municipal and state police officer. The period of training varies depending on the role that the police agent will play. Patrol officers receive a minimum of six months of academy training along with one to two months of field training, and detectives and forensic officers receive one year of training. The welfare benefits, recruitment, and training allow the federal police to be more professional. However, this would be incomplete in deterring malfeasance without a dominant mechanism of oversight.

Federal police oversight. Concerning oversight, the PF has more reliable internal mechanisms rooted in its history and culture. The first is that the PF is more militarized, which has to do with the way the institution was created. Many of the operational/patrol agents transferred from the 3rd Military Police Battalion from the Mexican army to the federal police. The training also emphasizes military discipline and obedience to higher ranks. This allows the federal police to have a healthy system of vertical oversight within the institution. Ranks are not subjectively awarded; rather, promotion is based on meritocratic advancement, tenure in office, and education level. This is possible because of the centralized nature of the police force.

Even so, vertical oversight is not enough; another mechanism of monitoring is needed to control malfeasant practices. On this count, the federal police remains relatively weak when compared to the Carabineros de Chile and the National Police of Colombia. Remember that those institutions have high internal affairs divisions with added layers of military penal courts, and external oversight from other governmental agencies, charged with investigating crimes. Such redundancy provides more vigorous oversight of police and necessarily explains the degree of professionalism and, hence, lower levels of police misconduct in Chile and Colombia. However, the Mexican federal police lack such a reliable system. Whereas most municipal police forces lack an internal affairs division, the federal police does have such an institution. It is a relatively new institution, but it has been able to investigate some officers for infractions and illegal activity. But the evidence indicates that few officers have been convicted of charges. This evinces the relative weakness of this institution. As Table 4.3 shows, police are rarely investigated or found guilty.

Some external oversight is provided by the National Human Rights Commission (CNDH). However, this organization lacks disciplinary power over the police themselves. The CNDH's sole authority is to make recommendations for improved practices of public security institutions. Despite the superior salary, benefits, recruitment, and training offered, the PF needs stronger internal and external oversight to make the force even more professional.

Although PF officers have professional salaries and selection and training standards, they are considered weak as professional police because the institution requires a more robust system of internal and external oversight. Despite this weakness in control mechanisms, the other benefits render the federal police more professional than both its state and municipal counterparts. This also partly explains why the federal police is the least corrupt of the three Mexican police institutions.

Comparing Municipal Police, State Police, and Federal Police

Police corruption is common in Mexico, but it is most prevalent in the municipal police. Corruption is so common that municipal police themselves acknowledge its existence within their institutions. For instance, 83.4 percent of police officers in the Tijuana city police recognized that there was at least some corruption within their ranks (Justiciabarómetro 2015). In a survey of the Ciudad Juárez municipal police officers, 65 percent indicated that there was some corruption in their institution. In the metropolitan region of Guadalajara, 49 percent of respondents recognized that there were high levels of corruption in their department (ZMP Guadalajara; Justiciabarómetro 2009). The problem of corruption is not just found in these more massive municipal police forces but also becomes magnified at the

Table 4.3 **Mexican Federal Police Investigated and Convicted of Crimes**

	2006	2007	2008	2009	2010	2011	2012	2013	2014
Number investigated	4	3	20	11	46	42	57	53	23
Number condemned	0	2	1	2	7	8	4	26	5
Percentage condemned	0	66	.05	18	15	19	07	49	21

Source: Ana Patricia Amaro López, pers. comm., January 30, 2014.

local level. Figure 4.2 indicates that the public views the municipal police as the most corrupt type of police in Mexico. The state police are trusted at higher levels except in two states (Tlaxcala and Oaxaca). Similarly, the federal police gains the most citizen trust except in Tlaxcala and Oaxaca.

This data is not surprising when we compare the levels of professionalism in each type of system. Table 4.2 earlier in the chapter illustrates the key differences among the three levels of police organization.

Municipal police earn the lowest wages, far below the national average. Most do not enjoy any pensions or healthcare coverage. Recruitment standards are weak, ranging from no education to a secondary school requirement to join a local police force (Sanchez and Suárez de Garay 2014). Municipal police receive little training, at most one to three months, but it is common that many do not even know how to use their gun (Ernesto López Portillo, interview with author, September 10, 2014). Municipal police operate within a weak hierarchy that lacks internal oversight mechanisms, let alone external ones.

Figure 4.2   Mexican Respondents Who Perceive Police Institutions as Corrupt

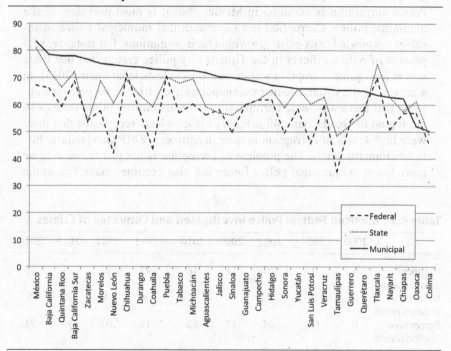

Source: Instituto Nacional de Estadística y Geografía 2011a.

Conversely, the state police force has higher salaries of about US$810 per month. It also offers a more substantial benefits package, and police enjoy a pension equivalent to 100 percent of their last salary for life after thirty years of service. They are also provide healthcare, life, and disability insurance coverage. State police entry requirements are stronger than those of municipal police, ranging from a ninth-grade to high school education. Training for state police is a minimum of three months in most states, which, although not ideal, is more training than most municipal police receive. Furthermore, every state police organization in this study had an internal affairs division that, although less efficient than it should be, provides a mechanism for some oversight.

The PF is the most professional institution offering the highest average wages of the three levels of police. It also provides the most robust benefits. For this reason, it can recruit at a higher level and establish a minimum educational level of high school completion as a requirement for entering the police force. Training ranges from six months to a year, depending on function. The PF includes an internal affairs division, though it is weaker than it should be. For this reason, the federal police is not entirely professional when compared to its Chilean and Colombian counterparts. Nevertheless, compared to the two other types of Mexican police, the federal police is by far the most centralized and professional force. These differences explain the variation in levels of corruption.

Human rights abuses occur at all levels of police. However, the municipal police engage in daily violence against citizens. When municipal police detain someone, this person is not taken to the public ministry to be processed. Mexico does not have police stations or precincts, as in the American context. Hence, the police drive suspects through the streets and mistreat them in their patrol cars (Francisco Hoyos, interview with author, September 3, 2014). Other times, they take suspects to "security houses" in order to extort money from them and their families or to get information, and all this happens because there is no accountability.

In her 2006 study of local misconduct in Mexico City, Claire Naval notes that police "continue to abuse their power, fail to treat individuals with due compliance with the law, and thus regularly violate civil as well as other rights. As the study confirms, resorting to abuse and ill-treatment is still a rather common behavior amongst law enforcement officers" (Naval 2006, 28). Citing data she obtained from the federal district police, the largest municipal police force in Mexico, she reveals that 43 percent of citizens who had some contact with police reported also being verbally or physically abused. Of these citizens, 88 percent indicated their communication experiences were verbally abusive, and 12 percent were physically abused, which totals to an estimated 280,000 police–citizen contacts in which abuse took place in a city of 9 million. But it is not just Mexico City—municipal police throughout the country engage in abuse as well. In an interview with Ernesto López Portillo, he noted that police use of "torture is generalized. Torture victims are usually the most vulnerable people that cannot defend themselves, without lawyers, without family" (López Portillo, interview with author, September 10, 2014). The next section discusses these findings.

Abrazos, No Balazos: AMLO's Reforms, 2018–2021

Leading up to the 2018 presidential election, the leading candidate, Andrés Manuel López Obrador (AMLO), campaigned on various leftist proposals. AMLO had a rough, although nebulous, public security policy sketched out that can be described by one of his famous refrains: *abrazos, no balazos* (hugs, not bullets). Though catchy, the phrase encodes a set of central tenets in public security scholarship. In this sociological view, crime and drug use are functions of anomie, or alienation from community, physically and economically. To be sure, the neoliberal policy implemented in Mexico had the effect of not just restructuring the economy but also displacing many farmers, workers, and family units as people migrated to the cities, northern regions, or the United States to look for work. The Mexican government had been increasing spending on public safety, but citizens saw little in terms of actual security (Kuritzkes 2017).

In July 2018, AMLO won the presidency with 53.19 percent of the votes, and thus began yet a new round of public security reforms to address the continued criminal threat of drug cartels. Currently, the military is legally authorized to act as an auxiliary of the National Guard, a militarized body of soldiers and sailors that has replaced Mexico's largest national police force, the federal police. New legally enshrined duties for the military include an ability to arrest people, to present them before a judge, and to collect evidence/preserve crime scenes. Oddly enough, the new laws do not authorize the military to conduct criminal investigations.

To address the alienation that drives people into crime, AMLO planned to get to the sociological roots of crime. By removing many of the requirements for the conditional cash transfer program and replacing them with the Benito Juárez scholarships, he guaranteed young people a certain basic income for attending school. This theoretically drives potential cartel recruits into school and provides them with enough income to cover basic needs. Other examples of this "softer" policy approach are AMLO's push for a higher minimum wage and the nationalization of health care, opening it up to everyone in Mexico.

However, in terms of police reforms, AMLO was less clear. There was some vague sense that AMLO would continue the same policies as his predecessors. However, upon taking office he struck out in his own direction. As is typical of his administration so far, AMLO has jettisoned any attempt to deepen the institutionalization of his predecessors' policies and has sought to reinvent the public security wheel in an extreme fashion.

Mando único was a policy of partial centralization at the state level, and while he was a candidate, AMLO announced that he would instead move toward a truer "nationalization" of public security forces. Paradoxically, AMLO also emphasized that he sought to demilitarize public security by replacing the military with a civilian national unit. To this end, AMLO dismantled the Federal Preventive Police force and EPN's Gendarmería Nacional and replaced them both with a National Guard. The National Guard itself is largely staffed by military units from the army and the navy. As such, the demilitarization of policing has not touched the institution. The goal is for these military officers and enlisted soldiers to be gradually replaced by civilians.

AMLO, like his predecessors, is already stepping back from the policy of full centralization as he had previously envisioned with a nationalization of public security under the National Guard. Now he envisions the National Guard as first among equals in coordinating with state and municipal police commanders as well as military counterparts to promote public security. Although this policy is, in my view, a step in the right direction, it is likely to end up like the rest of the police reforms: only partially implemented, and hence it is likely to fail in achieving the necessary institutionalization of professionalism required to truly reform policing in the long term. In the meantime, Mexicans continue to suffer at the hands of unprofessional, corrupt, and abusive police. In May 2020, a series of protests calling for further reform took place across Mexico after a video circulated on social media of Giovanni López Ramírez, who was beaten and arrested for violating the Covid-19 mask mandates. He later died in police custody. The protesters themselves were beaten by the police.

The prospects for deep police reform are likely to go nowhere, as in the case of Colombia, for the following two reasons. First, the midterm elections of 2021 are going to prove a difficult challenge for AMLO's party, MORENA. The slow economic growth, problems with energy distribution, and lack of access to medical supplies and vaccines have created a crisis of confidence in Mexico. If AMLO does not win support in Congress, his agenda is likely dead in the water. Furthermore, the Covid-19 pandemic itself will likely divert the precious little money spent on public services in addressing health reforms. This leaves few resources to continue to expand the National Guard as would be required by my model, let alone to professionalize it to the necessary levels to enact this reform. As it stands, the National Guard has 40,000 personnel. However, it would require something closer to 300,000–400,000 personnel to provide adequate coverage and to create a truly nationalized police force. Absent the full-scale implementation of centralization and professionalization seen in

Colombia and Chile, Mexico's prospects for a good quality police force
are not good.

Conclusion

This chapter has empirically assessed the way that structure and institutional configuration influence how police operate and how society views
them. I argued in Chapter 1 that if police are centralized, they will have
lower levels of mischief. If police are decentralized (locally controlled),
then they will have higher levels of misconduct. The Mexican federal
police is the least corrupt and most reliable because it is a national force,
and the decentralized municipal police are the least trusted as well as the
most malfeasant because patrimonial control continues to promote misconduct. Furthermore, my second argument is that if police are highly professionalized, they will have lower police wrongdoing. But if police are weakly
professionalized, they will have higher levels of misconduct. Evidence from
examining the police in Mexico confirms this argument. As police institutions
become more professional, they become less corrupt and garner higher levels
of trust. The federal police is the most professional and exhibits the least misconduct of the levels of police in Mexico. Municipal police are the least professional and the most likely to engage in wrongdoing.

Mexican municipal police have historically engaged in human rights
abuses but are rarely prosecuted. This has given rise to a "culture of impunity
[that] fatally undermines suspects' rights and continues to facilitate the use
of torture and ill-treatment as part of the routine practices of the police and
military" (Amnesty International 2014, 27). In Mexico, "Torture and other
cruel, inhuman or degrading treatment or punishment play a central role in
policing and public security operations by military and police forces across
Mexico" (Amnesty International 2014, 21). Beyond perpetrating human
rights abuses, Mexican police are notoriously corrupt. In a 2011 survey of
Mexicans, 90 percent of respondents believed that the Mexican police were
engaged in corruption (Instituto Nacional de Estadística y Geografía 2011a).
As Figure 4.3 illustrates, citizens view the police in Mexico as the most
corrupt institution in the country.

What is wrong with the Mexican police system? Why is it so corrupt and
morally broken? I have made the case that the system is dominated by municipal police who are ineffective, corrupt, and abusive. To this day, municipal
police are controlled by political actors who perceive the office as a predatory
mechanism by which to make money (Carlos Flores, interview with author,
September 9, 2014). As Antia Mendoza asserts, the police are one of the
institutions that have changed the least amount in the transition to democracy. Corruption and abuse remain part of the standard behavior of the
municipal police system despite other changes such as the political regime.

Figure 4.3 Institutional Corruption in Mexico

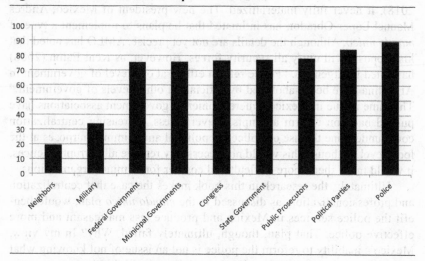

Source: Instituto Nacional de Estadística y Geografía 2011a.

As Grindle (2007, 109) notes, the municipal police are "the most frequently cited for small capacity and corruption" and "citizens regularly accused them of abusive behavior." The realization of the perceived weakness and misconduct of local authorities led to reform attempts from 1994 to 2014 that sought to both centralize and professionalize municipal police in Mexico. In early October 2010, President Felipe Calderón sent a bill to the Mexican Congress to unify all municipal police with state police forces to form a cohesive system of thirty-two police forces, one police force for each state. Calderón said that this legislation was "one of the most significant reforms in the fight for Mexican security" (Gould 2010).

Furthermore, Calderón claimed that municipal police forces are "vulnerable, weak and do not have the faculties, infrastructure, systems, protection, mobility or stability that would guarantee security for Mexicans" (Gould 2010). My argument contradicts much of the literature on decentralization as a mechanism of creating a more responsive government. In regards to policing, when "decentralization destroys the ability of the state to act coherently in ways reflecting general goals and diagnoses, then the unique character of its contribution is lost" (Evans, Rueschmeyer, and Skocpol 1985, 56).

One of the tendencies of the Mexican federal government is to attempt police centralization only to have this policy approach fall by the wayside. Part of the problem is the issues of federalism, lack of political will at the presidential level, and protests of municipal politicians. Although this policy initiative was born during the presidency of Felipe Calderón (2006–2012) and was at one point a campaign promise from Enrique Peña Nieto (2012–2018), it never fully materialized. The new president of Mexico, Andrés Manuel López Obrador, has intimated that he plans to implement a type of *mando único*. Although the details are not yet precise, AMLO has noted that his proposal will unify all security forces. However, as Kent Eaton (2008) has noted in Argentina, "Police reform efforts at one level of government in Argentina have been sabotaged by officials at other levels of government." The same is true in Mexico, where municipal government associations have pushed back on reform attempts. Nevertheless, increasing centralization could undermine the use of police for political and criminal purposes at the local level. Although this would not necessarily remove all corrupt practices, it would make them more difficult and costlier for criminal organizations.

Ultimately, the research in this book makes the case that centralization and professionalization, as discussed in the *mando único* plan, would benefit the police services in Mexico and produce less malfeasant and more effective police. That plan, though, ultimately failed. Why? In my view, Mexico's inability to reform the police is not an issue of not knowing what to do but simply a political problem revolving around the single-term presidential administrations coupled with alternation of parties in office. In essence, Mexico's various plans of creating federal police, then *mando único*, then the gendarmería, and now the National Guard could all have been blueprints for a more nationalized system of policing that would have implemented components of what this book has highlighted as improving policing overall. The problem comes from the fact that each presidential administration, Calderón, Peña Nieto, and now AMLO, has abandoned previous reforms and started from scratch.

This brings to the fore an additional component that I think is important, but that I leave undertheorized: time. Paul Pierson writes on the importance of time in political development. But here time matters in terms of continuity. What I found in Chile and Colombia is not just that they implemented the correct reforms but also that subsequent political leaders built upon these reforms and expanded them. In Mexico, the Sisyphean attempt at police reform is a self-inflicted parable. If a single administration simply carried through on the vision of a previous administration and continued to build some form of cohesive and centralized or semicentralized and professional policing, Mexico would be much better off. But the polarization of the party system and the personalization of the Mexican presidency are institutional barricades to meaningful police reforms. In the concluding chapter, I build on these insights to provide a set of policy prescriptions that would achieve the virtues of a centralized policing model while respecting federalism and local rights, which would fit into the Mexico political system quite well.

5

Overcoming the Sheep-Wolf-Dog Narrative

One curious thing about all police forces is that the men and women in uniform tend to have a similar worldview, one I call the Sheep-Wolf-Dog narrative. That narrative is as follows. First, the world is made up of good and bad people. Most people, 98 percent, are trying to do well for themselves, and the police consider them sheep. But there are a few out there, about 1 percent, who want to take advantage of police—these are the wolves. Lastly, the police consider themselves "sheepdogs" who protect the sheep from the wolves. One thing that the narrative misses entirely is the capacity for the protector also to become the victimizer: sheepdogs that eat sheep. Thus, in developing countries, the real question is not "How do you stop the wolves?" but "How do you keep the sheepdogs from attacking the flock?" I found that centralizing police and professionalizing their labor shift incentives away from a police logic of predation to a logic of protection. The question remains about how this argument could translate into broad policy initiatives to reform the police. In this chapter, I offer a few proposals that could be applied to improve police service in various contexts.

Much of Latin American politics has been about the struggle that states face when digging themselves out of their Spanish colonial legacies. Patrimonialism and police misconduct are some symptoms of state weakness inherited from the Iberian Peninsula. As such, what Max Weber referred to as "administrative modernization of state" is still an ongoing project in Latin America. I argue that police centralization and professionalization can achieve this Weberian ideal. I found that these two steps are vital to breaking patrimonialism. There can be no professional standards without first eliminating patrimonialism because elite actors at the local level have entrenched

125

interests in maintaining the status quo. As such, these patrimonial actors will work to stall, stop, or otherwise derail reform attempts that take control out of their hands and place it in a seminational or national authority. Only then can professionalization take place throughout a country.

However, professionalization of police in a few cities is not good enough. A police system must be able to work for small or big, rich or poor, rural or urban communities. This is what democratic governance is about: providing equal protection to all citizens. Without such guarantees of quality policing throughout a territory, a police system fails in its primary purpose: to protect the democratic rights of citizens. Centralization and professionalization of the police are appropriate and powerful approaches to accomplishing this democratic imperative.

In this book, I have focused on two issues of police misconduct. First, how do we shift the police's loyalty from political actors to the real principals of society? Second, once society becomes the principal, how do we ensure that the police do not violate their duty as agents of society? The significant contributions of the book rest on the assessment of the structural and institutional makeup of police and how these factors shape police behavior. I found that solving the problem is a matter of changing structures and institutions in the police to eliminate the incentive structure that leads to misconduct. When a country's police are locally controlled, there will be more misconduct. Locally controlled police forces are highly susceptible to being used for political purposes because of control by lower-level politicians.

Furthermore, locally controlled police are generally locally funded; hence, there will be an inherent inequality in police services across a nation. Wealthier cities have more resources to professionalize their police than poorer ones. As such, developing countries, where most cities are poor, will always have weak local police interested in stealing and abusing citizens to earn a livable wage commensurate with the risk they take. Conversely, when police are controlled not by cities but by national authorities, misconduct and corruption are reduced. Systems in which national-level politicians control the police can avoid controversies and the illicit use of police forces for politicized purposes. Moreover, national governments tend to have stronger coercive and taxation capacities, and hence more available resources to develop high-quality police forces.

Second, in this book, I claim that the way a country structures its police labor has pronounced effects on how the police behave. Countries that treat police labor as if it's an occupation/trade employ their police like construction workers, factory workers, and farmers: they are not well rewarded and have poor recruitment, meager training, and inadequate oversight. In this context, occupational-model police officers have an incentive to rob because they are not well paid. Corruptible officers are not weeded out during training and they don't fear being caught because of weak oversight. When a country structures its police labor as occupational, there will be more police abuse of authority.

Conversely, when a nation treats its police labor as a profession, such as the professionalized fields of architects or lawyers, with adequate pay and intense training and oversight, then police misconduct will decrease. I ultimately find that police with lower levels of misconduct also work in nationally organized and professionalized police systems. Decentralized systems have inferior resources to create professional models of police, and thus have higher levels of police abuse of authority.

The case studies of Chile and Colombia reveal that, historically, the process of decentralization was linked to politicized and abusive policing. Further, as police were centralized, politicization was controlled, and police were improved. In the chapter on Mexico, the more-centralized state and federal police forces are trusted at higher levels than their municipal counterparts. This fits with some of the growing literature on policing. In his analysis of the deteriorating Mexican security situation, Daniel Sabet (2010, 266) notes that local "executive power and police dependence on the executive appears to be one of the biggest obstacles to reform." The problem with decentralized systems is that subnational "executive appointment of police chiefs should make the police more accountable to citizens and executive discretion should facilitate rapid reform, but in practice, this power has led to window dressing reform patronage appointments, poor policies, and a lack of continuity in reform efforts."

John Bailey and Lucía Dammert (2006) have noted that Brazil's and Argentina's federal structure impedes reform. Mark Ungar (2011, 40) indicates that a decentralized system "accentuates executive and legislative imbalances." As Cardona (2008, 23) suggests, decentralized control of police into civilian hands can breed a corruption: "one in which police are not loyal to the system but an individual or an office. Such police are contingently attached to this individual or office." The literature hints that there are problematic differences between centralization and decentralization of police. This book confirms these insights.

In Chapters 2 and 3, it became clear that centralization often followed in lockstep with professionalization. Specifically, salaries, pensions, training, and oversight were built on the structure of centralized police forces. Although the literature hints at the importance of professionalizing the police, this book exhaustively details which reforms matter most for achieving this goal. Some scholars have linked rules and policies that circumscribe police compensation as necessary for reducing misconduct (Botella and Rivera 2000). Rachel Neild (2001, 27) recognizes that compensation "should be adequate to attract appropriately qualified candidates, provide a decent standard of living, and to reduce incentives for corruption." To reduce misconduct, Gary S. Becker and George J. Stigler (1974) used a game-theory model to illustrate that pensions, salary, and other benefit streams must, over a lifetime, outweigh the benefits gained from engaging in malfeasant practices. Second, policing scholars have found that training duration and content are valuable in advancing the professionalization of police (Celador 2005; Marenin 2004; Wiatrowski and Goldstone 2010). These authors profess that police who are poorly trained can undermine the legitimacy of a new democratic government. Therefore, the desire for security should not be met with more police, but with better police. Scholars also focus on recruitment of police personnel to increase diversity and representation and decrease the abuse of police powers by one group over others (Slater and Reiser 1988; Nield 2001). Police recruitment is also vital for democratic policing because it "can play a substantial role in the attitudinal development and shifts that may be experienced by those beginning their professional police services" (Garner 2005).

Finally, a large body of works focuses on police accountability and oversight. The idea is that police need to be accountable "for how they perform their duties" (Bayley 2006, 53). As such, there should be horizontal civilian oversight institutions outside the police institution and strong vertical oversight within the police institution to increase police accountability (Bayley 1990; Goldsmith 1999). When scholars study remuneration, supervision, and recruitment in isolation they end up missing the fact that these pieces must work together to produce better policing. In this book, I find through a historical analysis of Chile and Colombia that police must first create an extensive police welfare structure. Only then can they recruit more effectively and provide more significant training for officers. The oversight structure should also be capable of punishing and removing benefits should police engage in malfeasant behavior. The chapter on Mexico discusses how the federal and state police, having more robust compensation and better training, generally behave differently from their municipal counterparts. However, both still lack robust oversight structures.

In terms of misconduct, the Chilean police have comparatively low levels versus police in other Latin American. According to José Miguel Cruz (2009), only about 4 percent of citizens reported being physically or verbally abused by the Carabineros in 2009 as compared to 9 percent in Argentina, which was the highest rate in the region. In terms of corruption, a member of a citizen oversight NGO shared with me that "we have militarized police that does have problems, but a much more efficient control over corruption. Corruption is not systemic, and it's not a part of our culture." A former subsecretary of defense I interviewed confirmed that "on the theme of corruption, happily, we in Chile have a great pride [in] comparatively low levels of corruption" (Luciano Fouilloux, interview with author, November 7, 2012).

Figure 5.1 illustrates the differences in police forces along the dimension of susceptibility to bribery in Latin America.

The variations in outcome can be measured in two ways that illustrate the virtues of centralization and professionalism. In the Latin American Public Opinion Project Surveys for 2010, 2012, 2014, 2016, and 2018, respondents were asked whether they had been asked to pay a bribe by their police. In each year, the Carabineros had the lowest level of bribery. While the Colombians had higher levels of bribery, it was significantly lower than the number of respondents from Mexico who had to pay their police a bribe. Figure 5.2 illustrates the general findings across these five datasets.

Beyond corruption, there is a marked difference in trust of the police in Chile, Colombia, and Mexico, as exhibited in Figure 5.3. Notice in the figure how quickly Colombia's police force regained community trust following the period of reform in the early 1990s. Yet Mexican police trust remains mostly unchanged over the past twenty-five years. The Carabineros had established strong professionalized policing and have thus retained a high level of average trust during this period. Colombia improved its professionalism and increased its level of citizen trust, appearing closer to the Chilean standard level of confidence. This change correlates perfectly with the professionalization reforms that began to be implemented in 1993.

Figure 5.1 Percentage of Respondents Who Think Bribing Police Is Difficult

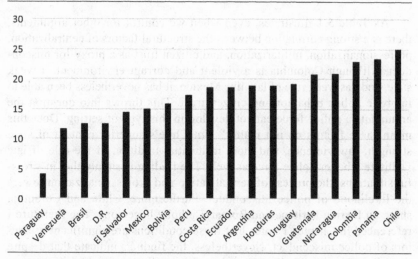

Source: Latinobarómetro 2017. The survey question asked, "What would a person in that country advise a foreign friend in how to approach police? Should they try to bribe them?"

Figure 5.2   Respondents Who Say Police Asked for a Bribe in Chile, Colombia, and Mexico

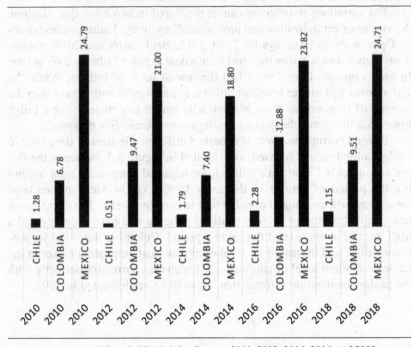

Source: Latin American Public Opinion Surveys 2010, 2012, 2014, 2016, and 2018.

As Table 5.1 illustrates, even when we control for other arguments, there is a strong correlation between the structural factors of centralization, professionalization, militarization, and citizen trust as a proxy for misconduct. Although Colombia is a violent and corrupt environment, a weak state, and has weak rule of law like Mexico, it has nevertheless been able to improve police behavior and citizen trust. This throws into question the arguments a police force cannot develop in this type of setting. Does this mean these factors do not matter? No. Chile's superior context of state strength, low violence, and more influential tradition of the rule of law facilitate a better police force as well. The finding is simply that in stressful situations, the process of centralization and professionalization lowers the likelihood of police misconduct. Furthermore, Chile and Colombia share an Iberian heritage and Roman Catholic hegemony. The literature I referenced in Chapter 1 notes that these conditions are significant predictors of police misconduct. Nevertheless, the findings indicate that despite these limitations, centralization and professionalization might drive a country toward less-malfeasant policing.

Figure 5.3   Variation in Public Trust Across Chile, Colombia, and Mexico, 1990–2017

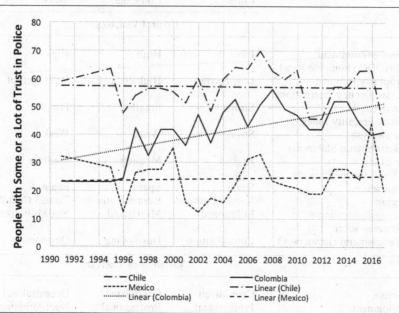

Sources: 1991 data from CIMA's Iberobarómetro Survey; 1995–2017 data from Latino-barómetro Survey.

There is also the conventional notion that militarized police are inherently anti-democratic and that quality will lead to the abuse of authority. For instance, George Berkeley (1970, 36) claimed that the "more the police resemble or take on the features and functions of the military, the more likely they are to cause problems for democratic societies." As Arthur Costa and Mateus Medeiros (2006) argue, "The more militarized a police force, the less the chance that a civilian authority will be able to use it, at least for the purposes of upholding the rule of law and protecting individual liberties." Hill, Beger, and Zanetti (2007) conclude that "unchecked growth of [militarized police] may have seriously detrimental effects on the provision of community-based policing . . . and undermine the development of democratic community-based police forces abroad."

This book illustrates that the Chilean and Colombian police, which are militarized, perform much better than their civilian counterpart in Mexico. At this point in the book, this issue merits further theorization. I argue that there are two forms of police militarization: "militarization of police institutions" and "militarization of police doctrine." The militarization of police

Table 5.1   The Findings Relative to Other Arguments

	Chile	Colombia	Mexico
	Control Variables		
Violent environment (UNODC Homicide Rate)	Low	High	High
Corrupt environment (Transparency International)	Low corrupt	High corrupt	High corrupt
State strength (State Fragility Index)	Strong	Fragile	Fragile
State strength (Bertelsmann Stateness)	Strong	Weak	Weak
Rule of law (World Justice Project)	High	Medium	Medium
Colonization	Spain	Spain	Spain
Religion	Roman Catholic	Roman Catholic	Roman Catholic
Police militarization	Militarized	Militarized	Not Militarized
Democracy score (Bertelsmann Democracy)	Consolidating	Developing	Developing
	Variables of Interest		
Structure	Centralized	Centralized	Decentralized
Development	Professional	Professional	Nonprofessional
Training	Professional	Professional	Nonprofessional
Oversight	Professional	Professional	Nonprofessional
	Outcome Variables		
Citizen trust in police	High	High	Low
Police misconduct	Low	Low	High

Sources: United Nations Office on Drugs and Crime 2010–2013; Transparency International 2013; Bertelsmann Stiftung 2018a, b, and c; World Justice Project 2019; Fund for Peace 2019.

institutions turns the police into a more militaristic entity that appropriates the organizational methods, discipline, uniforms, weaponry, and ranks of the military, but not necessarily the doctrine. The militarization of police doctrine does not necessarily apply the training, uniforms, weaponry, ranks, and organizational schemes of the military, but it does involve a tradition of militarized strategy that emphasizes social control, friend-enemy dichotomies, and militarized tactics to suppress threats.

Of the two, the militarization of police doctrine is by far the more dangerous. A militarized police doctrine emphasizes what is called "mano dura" doctrine and deemphasizes approaches to deescalating conflict, community-oriented policing, and less-than-lethal tools. Instead, a militarized police doctrine emphasizes the use of violence to stop violence, a strict separation from society, and the use of deadly weapons and military weapons as weapons of first resort to manage social conflicts. In this sense, police can be a militarized police institution but still apply civilian-oriented doctrines, strategies, and tactics to their police work. Nonmilitarized police organizations, conversely, can emphasize militarized principles, procedures, and tactics that are far more dangerous than a police force that uses military ranks. In short, what poses dangers is not the militarization of the uniform or the weapons but the intellectual and ideational militarization that takes place in the minds of officers. This reality needs to become a part of the public discourse, which is currently overly focused on what is in the hands of the police rather than what is in the heads of the police.

The militarization of police institutions appears to improve police performance. It was with the militarization of policing in the nineteenth and early twentieth centuries that police in Chile began to perform better than their more civilian counterparts. In Colombia, the replacement of local civilian police with a national and militarized one under the 1953 dictatorship of General Rojas Pinilla also led to improvements in policing. Meanwhile, the civilian police system in Mexico lacks the same type of military uniforms, training, weapons, and discipline, and results in poorer police performance. Militarization, in this sense, is a valid mechanism for the centralization, professionalization, and subsequent reduction of police misconduct. Although this project proposes that militarization brings about ripe conditions for centralization and professionalization, the reality is that there are other paths to this same end. But this finding does challenge the literature, which sees militarization as inherently antithetical to policing in a democracy.

Another interesting finding is the influence of the type of governing regime on policing. Other scholars have argued that authoritarianism drives police misconduct. For instance, Andrew John Goldsmith (2003) found that police in nondemocracies are used to repress ideological, racial, and ethnic minorities. These societies have legacies of misconduct, legacies that continue into the democratic present (Caldeira 2002; Thomassen 2013). One might be left with the notion that democratization automatically changes police behavior, as well. My contribution here is that I found democracy lowers police misconduct, and authoritarianism increases police abuse of authority. This means that wherever authoritarianism appears, so too will police misconduct.

During the PRI regime in Mexico, all police were utilized for partisan purposes of repression, while at the same time they used their power for self-enrichment and the enrichment of their party patrons. Once Mexico became a democracy, that behavior persisted. Thus, democracy is not a panacea for police corruption. At least in Mexico, the democratic era brought with it increased drug trafficking, which undoubtedly has resulted in continued corruption. In Colombia, a country with a long democratic tradition, police misconduct was rampant for much of its history. The police became less malfeasant only during a period of centralization, which correlated more with the degree of professional institutionalization. In Chile, the Carabineros were undoubtedly abusive and engaged in corrupt activity during the Pinochet era. The return to democracy might have meant nothing to improving police service if it was not coupled with presidential administrations that actively increased the budget for the Carabineros and helped to reinvigorate the professional institutions of the National Police.

The three cases, taken together, give us a mixed picture. Authoritarianism is linked to corrupt and abusive police practices—that much is clear. But sometimes democracy produces good police, and sometimes it produces terrible police. The key finding that dictates the variation is not regime type but robustness of professionalized institutions, which is contingent on the degree of centralization.

Using Latin America to Rethink US Policing

The critical reader might proclaim that the theoretical model does not fit well with the glaring case that comes to mind: the police system in the United States (Moule 2020). Indeed, the US police system is, at first glance, a much more professionalized and, at the same time, heavily decentralized police system. And the system appears to work well, with little misconduct.

However, a clarification needs to be made. For an advanced industrialized country, the United States has much more police misconduct than it should compared to other developed industrialized nations that have centralized police systems, such as Japan, Sweden, and the United Kingdom. The US police model was partially built around a network of patrolling for escaped slaves from 1700 to the mid-1800s, which is hardly a good foundation on which to create a new police force. Still, it is the political reality in the United States. The evolution from these traditions into the era of political influence in the late 1800s further entrenched a culture of misconduct in the police force. This was complemented by corruption during Prohibition in the early twentieth century. Throughout the 1950s and 1960s, police harassed Mexican-Americans in postwar Los Angeles; enforced Jim Crow in the South; and engaged in extensive extortion, as displayed by the Serpico investigation into the New York Police Department of the 1970s, the corruption scandals of the 1980s in big cities, the Rodney King beating in the 1990s, and the Rampart division corruption in Los Angeles in early twentieth century. Two common threads link these problems: local control and weak professionalization.

Furthermore, for most of US history, the police system has been in a precarious position—a perpetual state of crisis. The tension between police serving the public and serving their own interests has always been a part of the US policing landscape. To argue that cases of misconduct in the United States are isolated incidents ignores a historical pathology rooted in the structuring and institutionalization of police services. Cases of police misconduct are not isolated; they are symptoms of a chronic condition. My analysis of the Cato Institute data on police misconduct shows that, in 2010, 6,613 law enforcement officers were implicated in cases of police misconduct. These incidents involved lower-ranking officers, but also, in 2010, 354 police chiefs and sheriffs were implicated in cases of misconduct. In 2010, police misconduct lawsuits cost taxpayers $346 million, money that would have been better spent on improved benefits for and development and oversight of police (Cato Institute 2009). In data I compiled from the Cato Institute from January 2016 to January 2017, I found more than 2,500 cases of new or ongoing investigations into one or more officers engaged in police misconduct, including sexual assault, robbery, corruption, and drug use.

In 2017, Transparency International reported that 20 percent of respondents in the United States thought most police were engaged in corruption. Only 6 percent of Japanese, 6 percent of UK respondents, and 1 percent of Swedish respondents thought most police were corrupt (Transparency International 2017). The significance of these comparisons rests on the notion that Japan, the United Kingdom, and Sweden are advanced industrialized nations with more centralized police systems, yet they experience lower levels of police corruption. The continued problems of misconduct across the United States have undermined confidence in the police. Gallup published poll data that shows citizen trust in police in 2015 was at a twenty-two-year low, with only 52 percent of respondents having a great deal or a lot of trust in police (Jones 2015). By 2020, only 48 percent of respondents had a great deal or a lot of trust in police (Brenan 2020). In short, it is a myth to think that police in the United States do not exhibit significant levels of misconduct. When we place it in the context of advanced industrialized nations, the United States has a police that is less trusted and perceived as more corrupt than it should be given its status as an advanced industrialized democracy. My argument is that these numbers would be worse if it were not for the growing degree of centralization and professionalization that has already taken place and continues to take place in the system.

In terms of police professionalization, most US police officers receive adequate benefits from municipal governments, including pay that equals an average of $60,000 a year in salary, medical insurance, retirement pension, and vacation periods of two to three weeks per year (Bureau of Labor Statistics 2014). Furthermore, police work eight- to ten-hour shifts, four to five shifts per week, maintaining two to three days off. The federal government has centralized some of these benefits for killed or disabled officers through the Public Safety Officers' Benefits Program (Bureau of Justice Assistance 2015). In general, police remuneration has been professionalized.

Because of these persistent problems in municipal police, many states convened state-level commissions that would promulgate and enforce training and selection standards. From the 1930s through the 1970s, a slow process of state-level standardization of training and recruitment practices took place. The state of New York, by Chapter 446 of the Laws of 1959, became one of the first states "in the nation to establish basic training for newly appointed police officers" (New York State 2015). Although these types of boards do not personally conduct the training, they do ensure through monitoring that required police training standards are met (New York State 2015). California, almost simultaneously in 1959, also set up a similar state oversight body called the Commission on Peace Officer Standards and Training. The purpose of this agency was to "develop and administer selection and training standards for the betterment of California law enforcement."

Since New York and California set up these centralized state commissions on standards and training for police officers, every other state has done the same. Arkansas House Bill 577 of 1975 created the Executive Commission on Law Enforcement Standards, which was empowered "to establish reasonable minimum standards for selection and training of law enforcement officers in Arkansas, to certify officers as being qualified by training and education, to examine and evaluate instructors and courses of instruction and certify extent of qualification respectively" (State of Arkansas 2021). Hence, the standards for training and selection became centralized. Still, the final decisions for recruitment remain in the hands of local authorities, and oversight remains an internal function of the police. According to the State and Law Enforcement Training Academies survey for 2013, basic training programs of US police last an average of about 840 hours, or twenty-one weeks (Bureau of Justice Statistics 2013). This seems like a lot of training until you stack it up against training for other professions, such as cosmetology, which requires 1,405 hours of training (McClellan and Gustafson 2012, 107). Nevertheless, the increased state-level control over defining the legal standards for training and recruitment go a long way toward improving the professionalization of police forces in the United States. Absent this intervention, I argue, police in the United States would never have progressed and would resemble the Mexican police in terms of structure and behavior to this day.

In the United States, a process of federal centralization over criminal procedure controls police behavior through the Department of Justice and the Supreme Court, which provide more central oversight over police behavior. Since the 1994 Violent Crime Control and Law Enforcement Act, the Department of Justice can investigate police misconduct in any police force. If these investigations reveal systematic embezzlement, then the Department of Justice would supervise the implementation of police reforms through consent decrees. This nationalized investigative capacity and oversight of reform implementation have been applied in New Orleans, Los Angeles, and Chicago.

The American police system has undergone a process of centralization and professionalization that is not readily recognized. This process is incomplete and helps explain the persistent challenges of policing the United States faces despite its size, wealth, and democratic regime. As former Seattle police chief Norm Stamper (2016) noted, "American Policing is in a State of Crisis. . . . We must establish a meaningful and muscular role for the federal government in local policing." In short, the American police system has been professionalized and centralized much more than is apparent. In generalizing findings in this book, we can reinterpret the problems that remain in American policing as partial outgrowths of the continued level of decentralization and stifled professionalization.

How Can Reformers Build Centralized Control?

There are at least three possible ways that the virtue of centralization and professionalization can be gleaned without nationalization of a police system, wherein all police are part of a national body. This is pertinent for federal systems in which states retain significant constitutional rights to determine the shape of policing. The first path to centralization without nationalization is to place political control of the police in the hands of state or provincial governors rather than local mayors. This is what I refer to as the state command model. Switzerland, Germany, and Canada have elements of policing that are handled by provincial police forces. In places like the United States and Mexico, this reform would imply that local police departments would be subsumed by a state-based police force system. The virtue of this semicentralization at the subnational level is that it maintains states' rights while allowing for regional variation in police service to meet localized needs and the benefits of a more centralized policing structure such as standard training practices, regular and equal funding, state-based oversight, and a broader recruitment pool.

The second model, which I refer to as the hybrid policing model, is allowing local police agencies to maintain the training, oversight, and development for local low-rank officers. In this sense, little changes in the context of federal cases. However, all police in positions of command (equivalent to commissioned officers in the military) would instead be recruited, trained, paid for, and overseen by a state agency. In this sense, police commanders would be a part of the statewide police force and assigned a local command over lower-rank officers who have been trained in regional academies.

The third method of centralization without nationalization does not eliminate local police departments at all. I call this the state commission model. In this model, local police departments are allowed to exist. Again, the centralization comes from standardization and through statutory law, salaries, benefits, training, recruitment, and oversight standards across a state. Legislatures could write new rules and create new agencies that regulate all police services in the states. Of course, most US states have some commissions for peace officer training that regulate training requirements at academies. However, I would further empower these commissions to set higher standards for entry into police academies, including higher education standards; to standardize remuneration packages; and to act as an external investigative body that complements internal investigations in police departments. Though this would be easily achieved in the United States, given the fact that some of the institutional apparatus is already set up, it would also help improve other federal policing systems with local police forces that want to reap the benefits of centralization while balancing local operational autonomy necessary for police work.

A fourth model of policing is what I call the national commission model. This type of policing is already implemented in Japan and England. In this model, a national commission subsidizes local police departments, sets recruitment and training standards, and conducts general oversight of police work. The virtue of this model is that it maintains a high level of local autonomy while reducing inequality in police service. Inequality is best understood when we consider that the Beverly Hills Police Department in California draws its funding from one of the wealthiest tax bases in the nation, and therefore it can afford to provide better police services for residents. In contrast, residents living in the neighboring jurisdiction of the Los Angeles Police Department have a police force that is perennially understaffed and overextended. In this sense, not every citizen is treated equally in terms of public security. A national commission, though, could improve the resources of local police departments through subsidies and training standards to put them on equal footing.

Each of these alternatives introduces some of the critical virtues of centralization into systems where nationalization is impossible. However, both the semicentralized models that I have proposed and completely centralized-nationalized police forces can be improved through sequencing reforms and applying minimum standards to professionalize police labor.

How Can Professionalization Be Implemented?

All police services could improve in three general areas: luring bigger fish, upgrading the factory, and investigating fallen angels. These initiatives need to be sequenced in that order. First, police services need to lure better candidates to policing. As such, it is critical to begin any policing reform by improving all facets of police remuneration. Having an excellent salary and benefits system in place is vital because it provides labor stability and a higher quality of life for agents and their families, and it can be held as "leverage." What I mean by *leverage* is that if a police officer engages in malfeasant practices and they are discovered, they will lose these quality-of-life benefits for them and their families. The opposite logic applies to police who work within systems with weak benefits. When they engage in misconduct, they have nothing to lose and more to gain. In the case of fraud, it is rational to shake down citizens to make up the difference between their salary and the middle-class life they desire.

Furthermore, a substantial wage tends to attract better candidates with higher educational achievements. Educated candidates will bear the burden of police work better and be less likely to react in desperation in the face of complicated situations. An analytical mind is required of emergency services personnel, as well as investigative services people. An adequate benefits package and salary are primary priorities because they draw high-quality applicants, which in turn can cause the police service to raise entrance standards because they are more likely to draw from a pool of candidates who can meet those high standards. This addresses one of the issues that I discovered in this research: When police are poorly paid, police forces can recruit only the dregs of society, and often these ill-suited recruits abandon police work in search of better-paying jobs. As such, salary and recruitment standards are intimately linked.

The second step is to improve the police factory. To this end, the recruitment and selection of high-quality candidates are of paramount importance, as is weeding out the bad ones. Setting high entry standards, such as a complete K–12 education or its equivalent, is vital in ensuring that a police force has intelligent and capable officers. Applications are then processed, and candidates who do not meet these basic requirements are disqualified. The selection process continues with thorough physical, mental, and background examinations. The resulting pool of candidates are people who want to do the job and are morally, mentally, and physically likely to do a good job. The next component of police development is the training process, where the moral, mental, and physical aptitudes of recruits are strengthened. At a minimum, police need to be trained for nine to twelve months in an academy with three to four months of field training for lower ranks and two to three years for command ranks. The research suggests that this differentiation between enlisted and command officers is crucial for a more professionalized police force. The distinction is essential to make to insulate command ranks from organized crime but also to guarantee turnout of well-trained professionals who can lead lower ranks effectively and objectively.

Once qualified candidates are enticed to join and adequately trained, the issue remains that they may abuse their power or take advantage of it to enrich themselves. That is why the last step is considered the lynchpin of a professional system: investigating and punishing fallen angels. The first area that needs to be reinforced in police oversight is the internal controls that prevent, investigate, and sanction police behavior. Prevention is geared toward studying and identifying characteristics of officers who engage in corruption and officers who show traits susceptible to bribery, and intervening early in their careers to dissuade malfeasant activity. Another component is fielding plainclothes undercover investigative units that attempt to bribe uniformed officers. Finally, having reliable and expedient sanctioning mechanisms is essential. Command officers must have the capacity to immediately remove officers suspected of corruption or other malfeasant activities. In many cases, due process allows corrupt officers to continue their activities while they remain in the institution, which shows other officers that corruption does not lead to severe consequences, hence promoting a culture of impunity. When there is no due process, corrupt police engage in bribery or observe corruption but do nothing about it. Therefore, the stronger the sanctioning mechanism, the lower the level of corruption. But sanctioning also gains "teeth" with a healthy benefits system that could be leveraged, as discussed earlier. The power of sanctioning rests not so much in the threat of being excommunicated from the brotherhood of police, but in the way it threatens their quality of life.

Internal oversight mechanisms alone are insufficient for control over the police. Although they provide an excellent first line of defense, in the absence of external oversight, internal affairs investigations tend to maintain the blue code of silence: police protect their own. The key to effective external monitoring is redundancy (Ernesto López Portillo, interview with author, September 10, 2000). This means that more than one external body is tasked with maintaining oversight of the police. From the cases that I studied, I see three general types of oversight bodies available: first, elected commissions, or citizen review boards; second, specific government institutions tasked with investigating all state agencies for misconduct; and third, comptroller offices tasked with ensuring government spending is done through the proper channels established by law. These formal oversight bodies can be augmented by civil society's capacity to engage in oversight through the media, human rights organizations, and the average citizen filming police activity. The redundancies augmenting the external oversight mechanism then put pressure on the internal oversight mechanism to do their job, which in turn leaves zero tolerance for police misconduct. With scrupulous oversight, the high likelihood of police losing their job over an infraction would endanger the long-term quality of life that they have earned with their service and though the intense training they underwent. External oversight is the catalyst that makes the other components of training and benefits work more efficiently toward their intended goals of reducing the rationale that once facilitated police abuse of power.

Advancing the Study of Policing

This book explores how structural and institutional factors help shape police behavior. To focus on one dimension of a phenomenon, I spent less time dealing with systemic, leadership, cultural, and constructivist approaches. I do not see my approach and findings as contradictory to these other approaches; in fact, I consider them complementary. Future research should work within the theoretical construct that I have provided and combine with other approaches to refine our wholistic theoretical knowledge of comparative policing.

The theory developed from this analysis has internal validity in explaining the variation in police misconduct in the cases of Chile, Colombia, and Mexico. The first critical problem with the research is that it has limited external validity. What is crucial about these findings is that if they are valid elsewhere, they could be used to help make better policy decisions in developing states in Eastern Europe, Africa, and Southeast Asia. At the other end of the spectrum, this study does not speak to policing in advanced industrialized countries. More research is needed to test these findings outside Latin America, which presents future research opportunities.

This research does not address the different ways of organizing police around the world. Neither the literature in international criminology nor this book lays out the conceptual basis by which to typologize these various forms of the police organization. By conceptualizing various types of police, future research will be better able to understand how organizational patterns influence the level of misconduct around the world. Furthermore, this book only broaches the issue of authoritarianism and policing. The relationship between regime type and police behavior is an important one that we lightly touch on in our analysis of each case, which had very different police systems and varying experiences with authoritarianism. This presents an additional avenue for continued research.

Additionally, my focus was on the way police generally behave, and I did not address situations in which violence arises in the context of national emergencies, such as riots and looting. Under those conditions, Latin America tends to utilize special enlisted ranks called Grupos Anti-Motines, or anti-riot police, that, by their nature, are trained and expected to use excessive force to gain control over chaotic situations. These forces and circumstances are unique situations that imply a different logic of protest policing, which has been written about extensively (Della Porta 1999; Earle and Soule 2006; Soule and Davenport 2009). By and large, police tend to use a preponderance of force in mass-mobilization situations where violence erupts. My claims are, therefore, limited to understanding the contextual behavior of beat officers. Protest policing should be a continued focus of study for other scholars.

Finally, this research does not provide a comprehensive theory of why, when, and how police reform comes about (Aparicio 2017). Reform attempts occurred in Chile and Mexico after the end of authoritarian regimes, but with varying results. In Colombia, the impetus for reform was not a regime transition but increased public pressure on the leadership of President César Gaviria and Minister of Defense Rafael Pardo to bring about improvements to the police.

Recognizing the aforementioned limitations, future research should focus on addressing some of these problems. There are four major projects that I leave to others. First, there should be a comparative analysis of police development in the United States, Japan, and the United Kingdom that tests this theory of police misconduct in the context of advanced industrialized countries. Second, it would be advisable for future scholars to engage in a within-case comparison of police within federal systems to see how they vary professionally and in terms of centralized control in producing different outcomes. For instance, police in California have higher professional qualifications and remuneration than police in Florida; does this change the prevalence of misconduct? Third, there should be more work done on developing a typology of police models so that we can better categorize the types of police organizations around the world and see which ones are ubiquitous and which are rarer. Last, further work should be done on how leadership ideology and regime type (military, personalistic, or party-authoritarian) impact police development.

Final Thoughts

When local authorities do not control the careers of their police officers, the incentives for patrimonialism diminish, and this represents an important step in advancing professionalization. The story of police reform is part of a longer historical evolution of public administration. Patrimonialism, at one point, was the most efficient means of governance for divine right rulers. The ruler would empower local authorities as their representatives in far-flung areas of their empire. The ruler did not pay these individuals a salary but instead granted them exclusive rights in certain areas from which they could derive their wealth.

Further, these local administrative positions were not awarded to the most competent agents but to the most loyal ones and, in many cases, those who could purchase the right to the office itself and pass it down to their progeny. A narrative has arisen in Western political discourse that claims the rule of law has usurped divine rule, sweeping patrimonialism and all its vagaries aside. The truth, however, is that for much of the world, patrimonialism continues to be the norm of political life. Patrimonialism is a living relic of our past, haunting our present. The frustrating part of this continued plague is that we have the means and knowledge of a more efficient and effective way to organize the administration of policy and politics: the rational bureaucracy.

When Max Weber spoke about the development of a rational bureaucracy, he was referring to the professionalization of public administration. This innovation provided for more efficient, desirable, and effective outcomes. In the modern era (1890–1940), the world witnessed the rise of professionalization in the fields of politics, warfare, medicine, education, and law. Judges were to be appointed and selected on the basis of merit and paid a state wage so that they would be impartial. The military would no longer be staffed by mercenaries, nor would officer ranks be given to elites devoid of qualifications. Professionalization requires formal employment with a salary and benefits and with specialized training as a requirement for a promotion. Furthermore, professionalization requires hierarchical relationships and oversight.

Northern Europe moved toward the professionalism ideal much earlier in its development, then southern Europe, which maintained patrimonial forms of government late into the modern era. Even so, where the rational-legal professionalism in public administration did spread, it paid high dividends. A more professional state apparatus reduced transaction costs, increased security, reinforced property rights, and promoted industry. The rise of the rational state bureaucracy also compelled states to war with one another, but what was different was that they did so with more advanced and logistically well-supported fighting forces.

The problem we see in many developing countries today is that, due to their histories of colonialism, neocolonialism, and the Cold War, the logic of patrimonialism has never been completely replaced. I would say that most developing countries are at war with themselves: the rationalized professionals are attempting to do away with the patrimonial dons, caudillos, caciques, and bosses who still retain much of the power. Thus, this book is about more than just the struggle to reform the police; it is about the cosmic battle for a more effective, efficient, and democratic world that is trying to break free of its medieval past. In this sense, police misconduct is a manifestation of the premodern world trying to survive alongside the modern one. When I discuss police reform, I am talking about the destruction of patrimonial policing and its replacement with rational-legal policing.

The argument I make is that local political control over the police combined with weak professionalism proves a noxious blend that gives rise to fertile conditions for police misconduct. Countries in which local officials control the police have lower levels of professionalism in policing because domestic political actors tend to utilize the police for civic and private services, thus undermining efforts to professionalize the police. Indeed, when police are fully professionalized, local authorities cannot easily manipulate them. This local pushback is often the reason for stymied professionalization. The other key idea is that decentralization of fiscal and administrative responsibilities for policing results in cities with responsibilities for public security but with limited resources to carry out such obligations. By removing direct local control in some regulatory areas and implementing decentralization, leaders can professionalize the police more easily. Police in these areas tend to provide better services because they can focus on their role as police rather than as protectors of partisan interest.

Perhaps the most significant policy prescription to be drawn from this research is to treat the police as professionals. Doctors, lawyers, architects, engineers are all treated as professionals and are paid very well because they must undergo extensive training. Additionally, professional associations and governmental bodies provide strong oversight over these professions. Why? Because of the one thing they have in common: their work involves the welfare of human life. We want to ensure that professionals who are responsible for our well-being are well trained and that someone is making sure that these professionals have our best interests at heart. Malpractice, by any of these professions, can lead to destructive consequences for human life. Police also have our security in their hands. Thus, it is surprising that many jurisdictions do not see the analogous need to make sure that police meet professional standards. To this end, police must be paid well and provided health care, life insurance, and disability insurance. They must also be trained extensively and selected from a qualified and well-educated pool of candidates, competitively and objectively. Furthermore, both internal and external institutions must oversee them to ensure compliance with professional ethical standards. On the basis of this empirical analysis, I advance three significant theoretical and practical debates on policing. First, this project provides a comparative analysis outside the well-studied context of the European and American cases by looking to Latin America. Second, whereas most of the existing research examines police in the late twentieth and early twenty-first centuries, my work provides a detailed historical analysis of the police in Chile and Colombia going back to the nineteenth century.

Last, most of the studies on police reform pay scant attention to the structure of a police system *and* the organization of police labor. While not a panacea, the changes outlined in this book would provide a better scaffolding for democratic policing. Convincing politicians to engage in these types of reforms and implementing them are topics for another project.

This work deals with a phenomenon that is at the heart of the paradox of stable democracies. For instance, in 2006, to make up for the weakness of police, the president of Mexico, Felipe Calderón, deployed the military against drug cartels that were ravaging the nation. This drug war had dire consequences, and by 2012 resulted in approximately 47,000 deaths from drug-related violence (Cave 2012). In Central America, 900 gangs are operating with an estimated 70,000 members. Honduras, Guatemala, and El Salvador are at the epicenter of the gang crisis, which has led to a massive wave of undocumented children traveling to the United States to flee the violence. In 2004, the estimated murder rate per 100,000 people was 45.9 in Honduras, 41.2 in El Salvador, and 34.7 in Guatemala (Ribando 2005). In South America, the Venezuelan murder rate in 2010 was 67 per 100,000 (BBC 2011). At the core of rampant criminality are issues of poverty, inequality, and a weak criminal justice system. It has become clear that problems of police misconduct extend beyond Latin America to many other places in the developing world. Violence and criminality, coupled with police misconduct, prove a volatile mix that undermines trust in the state, the rule of law, and democratic legitimacy.

Governments that cannot address crime lose legitimacy and limit citizens' ability to participate freely, openly, and entirely in politics and the political process. Police oversee public and citizen security, both of which are necessary for democratic governance. Despite the importance of police to democracy, social sciences outside of criminology do not study the impact of the police on society and politics writ large. Police, more than any other institution, embody the state itself. In Weberian terminology, it is the police who ought to apply and manage the legitimate use of force within a given territory. Although police are central to politics and the state, we do not know enough about them, how they change, persist, or evolve. We also know little about how structural and institutional changes impact the overall quality of police behavior. The puzzle for poor developing nations is how to build a better police force that is impervious to the social ills of patrimonialism, clientelism, and corruption. This book provides some tentative answers to the question of how best to structure a police system to serve and protect everyone equally.

References

Acero, Hugo. 2013. International police and public security adviser, Bogotá, Colombia. Interview with author, March 18, 2013.

Acevedo, Darío. 2000. "La Caricatura y la Violencia Liberal-Conservadora." *Revista Credencial de Historia*, no. 125, Bogotá.

Agboga, Victor. 2021. "Beyond Decentralising the Nigerian Police: How Lagos State Circumvented Debates on Police Reforms." *Journal of Contemporary African Studies* 39, no. 1: 135–150.

Agren, David. 2017. "Mexico City Has Mostly Been Spared from Grisly Drug Violence. Now That May be Changing." *Washington Post*. July 26, 2017.

Aguilera, Lautaro Contreras. 2012. Retired general and former director of personnel, Carabineros de Chile, Santiago, Chile. Interview with author, December 18, 2012.

Aguiló, Sergio. 2012. Elected parliamentarian from 37th District of Talca, 1990–present, Santiago, Chile. Interview with author, November 18, 2012.

Alessandri, Arturo. 1922. Presidential address to Congress. Santiago, Chile, Imprenta Fiscal de La Penitenciaria de Santiago.

Alvarez Llanos, Jaime. 2010. "¡Políticos de Guante Blanco!": La Variedad de las Transgresiones Electorales en el Caribe Colombiano a Principios el Siglo XX." *Memorias: Revista Digital de Historia y Arqueología Desde el Caribe*, no. 13: 87–109.

Amaro López, Ana Patricia. 2014. Head of the Transparency and Information Access Unit, Mexico City, Mexico. Personal correspondence with author, January 30, 2014.

Americas Barometer. 1990–2012. Latin American Public Opinion Project (LAPOP). https://www.vanderbilt.edu/lapop/.

Amnesty International. 2014. *Fuera de Control: Tortura y Otros Malos Tratos en México*. http://www.amnistia.org.

Amnesty International. 2017. "South Africa 2016/2017." https://www.amnesty.org.

Aparicio, Juan. 2017. "El Proceso de Amalgamación, Centralización y Unificación de los Cuerpos de Policía en America." PhD diss., Externado University of Colombia.

Aparicio, Juan. 2003. "La Ideología de la Policía Nacional de Colombia en las Decadas de Los '60s y '70s. Master's thesis, National University of Colombia.

Aparicio, Juan. 2013. Lieutenant in National Police of Colombia and editor of *Revista Criminalidad*, the PNC's professional journal, Bogotá, Colombia. Interview with author, February 26, 2013.

147

Aparicio, Juan. 2013. Retired sergeant (active 1971–1990), National Police of Colombia, Bogotá, Colombia. Interview with author, April 4, 2013.

Araya, José. 2012. Expert in human rights and protest policing, Observatorio Ciudadano: Human Rights NGO, Santiago, Chile. Interview with author, November 20, 2012.

Arias, Enrique Desmond, and Mark Ungar. 2009. "Community Policing and Latin America's Citizen Security Crisis." *Comparative Politics* 41, no. 4: 409–429.

Arrigo, Bruce A., and Natalie Claussen. 2003. "Police Corruption and Psychological Testing: A Strategy for Preemployment Screening." *International Journal of Offender Therapy and Comparative Criminology* 47, no. 3: 272–290.

Arteaga Botello, Nelson, and Adrian López Rivera. 2000. "Everything in This Job Is Money." *World Policy Journal* 17, no. 3: 61–69.

Aylwin, Patricio. 1990. President Patricio Aylwin annual address to the 320th Legislature of Chile, Ordinary Plenary Session, Monday, May 21, 1990. http://historiapolitica .bcn.cl.

Aylwin, Patricio. 1991. President Patricio Aylwin annual address to the 322nd Legislature of Chile, Ordinary Plenary Session, Tuesday, May 21, 1991. http://historiapolitica .bcn.cl.

Aylwin, Patricio. 1992. President Patricio Aylwin annual address to the 324th Legislature of Chile, Ordinary Plenary Session, Thursday, May 21, 1992. http://historiapolitica .bcn.cl.

Bachelet, Michelle. 2007. President Michele Bachelet annual address to the 356th Legislature of Chile, Ordinary Plenary Session, May 21, 2007. http://historiapolitica .bcn.cl.

Baeza, Guillermo Felipe. 2010. "Legitimidad Ciudadana al Accionar de Carabineros de Chile: Una Aproximación a la Comprensión del Fenómeno." Tesis. Universidad de Chile. http://www.tesis.uchile.cl/tesis/uchile/2010/cs-ruz_g/pdfAmont/csruz_g.pdf.

Bailey, John, and Lucía Dammert, eds. 2006. *Public Security and Police Reform in the Americas*. Pittsburgh: University of Pittsburgh Press.

Banco de la República. 1916. "Colombia y El Mundo." http://www.banrepcultural.org.

Barnes, Tiffany D., Emily Beaulieu, and Gregory W. Saxton. 2016. "Restoring Trust in the Police: Why Female Officers Reduce Suspicions of Corruption." *Governance* 31: 143–161.

Bayley, David H. 1990. *Patterns of Policing: A Comparative International Analysis*. New Brunswick: Rutgers University Press.

Bayley, David H. 2005. *Changing the Guard: Developing Democratic Police Abroad*. Oxford: Oxford University Press.

Bayley, David H. 2006. "US Aid for Foreign Justice and Police." *Orbis* 50, no. 3 (2006): 469–479.

Bayley, David H., and Clifford D. Shearing. 2000. *New Structure of Policing: Description, Conceptualization, and Research Agendas—Final Report*. Washington, DC: National Institute of Justice.

Becerra, Dayanna. 2010. "Historia de la Policía y del Ejercicio del Control Social en Colombia." *Prolegómenos* 13(26): 143–162.

Becerra, Dayanna. 2011. "History of Police in Colombia: Factional, Political and Social Actors." *Dailogos de Saberes* 34:253–270.

Becker, Gary S. 1968. "Crime and Punishment: An Economic Approach." In *The Economic Dimensions of Crime*. London: Palgrave Macmillan.

Becker, Gary S., and George J. Stigler. 1974. "Law Enforcement, Misconduct, and Compensation of Enforcers." *Journal of Legal Studies* 3, no. 1.

Becker, Sascha O., Katrin Boeckh, Christa Hainz, and Luger Woessmann. 2014. "The Empire Is Dead, Long Live the Empire! Long-Run Persistence of Trust and Corruption in the Bureaucracy." *Economic Journal* 126:40–74.

Bedoya, Jineth. 2012. Journalist at El Tiempo News Agency, Bogotá, Colombia. Interview with author, April 12, 2013.

Beede, Benjamin R. 2008. "The Roles of Paramilitary and Militarized Police." *Journal of Political and Military Sociology*, 2008, vol. 36, no. 1 (Summer): 53–63.

Bender, Jeremy, and Armin Rosen. 2014. "Mexico's Drug War Is Entering a Dark Phase." *Business Insider*, October 24, 2014.

Berkley, George E. 1969. *The Democratic Policeman*. Boston: Beacon Press.

Berkley, George E. 1970. "Centralization, Democracy, and the Police." *Journal of Criminal Law, Criminology, and Police Science* 61, no. 2: 309–312.

Bertelsmann Stiftung. 2018a. "Colombia Country Report 2018." https://bti-project.org/fileadmin/api/content/en/downloads/reports/country_report_2018_COL.pdf.

Bertelsmann Stiftung. 2018b. "Mexico Country Report 2018." https://bti-project.org/fileadmin/api/content/en/downloads/reports/country_report_2018_MEX.pdf.

Bertelsmann Stiftung. 2018c. "Chile Country Report 2018." https://bti-project.org/fileadmin/api/content/en/downloads/reports/country_report_2018_CHL.pdf.

Bertelsman Stiftung. 2022. "BTI 2006-2022 Scores." https://bti-project.org/fileadmin/api/content/en/downloads/data/BTI_2006-2022_Scores.xlsx.

Biblioteca Nacional de Chile. 2014. "Ley de Comuna Autónoma: Elecciones, Sufragio y Democracia en Chile (1810–2012)." *Memoria Chilena*. http://www.memoriachilena.cl.

Blanchard, Emmanuel. 2014. "French Colonial Police." In *Encyclopedia of Criminology and Criminal Justice*, edited by G. Bruinsma and D. Weisburd, 1836–1846. New York: Springer.

Boateng, Francis D., and Isaac Nortey Darko. 2016. "Our Past: The Effect of Colonialism on Policing in Ghana." *International Journal of Police Science & Management* 18, no. 1: 13–20.

Bonilla Ibarra, Raymundo Alfredo. 2014. Secretariat of Public Security Department of Judicial Affairs, Sinaloa, Mexico. Personal correspondence with author, January 30, 2014.

Bonner, Michelle D. 2013. "The Politics of Police Image in Chile." *Journal of Latin American Studies* 45, no. 4: 669–694.

Bonner, Michelle D., Guillermina Seri, Mary Rose Kubal, and Michael Kempa. 2018. *Police Abuse in Contemporary Democracies*. London: Palgrave Macmillan.

Brenan, Megan. 2020. "Amid Pandemic, Confidence in Key U.S. Institutions Surges." Gallup News, August 12, 2020. https://news.gallup.com/poll/317135/amid-pandemic-confidence-key-institutions-surges.aspx.

Brinks, Daniel M. 2007. *The Judicial Response to Police Killings in Latin America: Inequality and the Rule of Law*. Cambridge: Cambridge University Press.

British Broadcasting Corporation. 2011. "Venezuela Sees 'Record Murder Rate' in 2011." https://www.bbc.com/news/world-latin-america-16349118.

Bullock, Allan, and Stephen Trombley. 1999. *The New Fontana Dictionary of Modern Thought*. London: HarperCollins.

Bureau of Justice Assistance. 2015. "Public Safety Officers' Benefits Program." Department of Justice. https://bja.ojp.gov/program/psob.

Bureau of Justice Statistics. 2013. "State and Local Law Enforcement Training Academies, 2013." Department of Justice. https://bjs.ojp.gov/library/publications/state-and-local-law-enforcement-training-academies-2013.

Bureau of Labor Statistics. 2014. "Police and Detectives." https://www.bls.gov.

Bustamante Bascunan, Francisco. 1918. Estudio sobre La Policía de Chile. *Memoria*. Concepción, Chile: Imprenta Litografía José V. Soulodre.

Buvinic, Mayra, Andrew Morrison, and Michael Shifter. 1999. "Violence in Latin America and the Caribbean: A Framework for Action." In *Sustainable Development Department*. Washington, DC: Inter-American Development Bank.

Cabildo, Miguel. 1984. "Durazo Obligaba a Su Personal a Entregarle el Producto de Sus Mordidas." *Proceso* 386:16–17.

Caldeira, Teresa P. R. 2002. "The Paradox of Police Violence in Democratic Brazil." *Ethnography* 3, no. 3: 235–263.

Camacho Leyva, Bernardo. n.d. "Conferencias de Historia de La Polica."

Candina, Azun. 2012. Professor of history and philosophy at the University of Chile and expert in public security matters, Santiago, Chile. Interview with author, December 20, 2012.

Cao, Liqun, Yung-Lien Lai, and Ruohui Zhao. 2012. "Shades of Blue: Confidence in the Police in the World." *Journal of Criminal Justice* 40, no. 1: 40–49.

Carabineros de Chile. 2009a. "Reglamento de Disciplina de Carabinero de Chile, No. 11." http://www.carabineros.cl.

Carabineros de Chile. 2009b. "Reglamento de Seleccion y Ascensos del Personal de Carabineros No. 8." http://www.carabineros.cl.

Carabineros de Chile. 2012. "Carabineros de Chile: Evolución de la Función Policial." Museo Histórico de Carabineros de Chile, Santiago.

Carabineros de Chile. 2013. *Manual de Doctrina*. Escuela de Formación de Carabineros. http://www.esfocar.cl.

Carabineros de Chile. 2014. "Prestamos." Mutualidad de Carabineros. http://www.mutucar.cl.

Cardia, Nancy. 1997. "The Fear from Police and the Gross Human Rights Violations." *Tempo Social* 9, no. 1: 249–265.

Cardona, Christopher Michael. 2008. "Politicians, Soldiers, and Cops: Colombia's la Violencia in Comparative Perspective." PhD diss., University of California, Berkeley.

Carothers, Thomas. 2011. *Aiding Democracy Abroad: The Learning Curve*. Washington, DC: Carnegie Endowment.

Castillo, Elly. 2010. "Municipios de Mexico Rechazan Policía Única." *El Universal*, October 7, 2010. http://www.eluniversal.com.

Cato Institute. 2009. National Police Misconduct Reporting Project. http://www.policemisconduct.net/.

Cave, Damien. 2012. "Mexico Updates Death Toll in Drug War to 47,515, but Critics Dispute the Data." *New York Times*, January 11, 2012.

Celador, Gemma Collantes. 2005. "Police Reform: Peacebuilding Through Democratic Policing?" *International Peacekeeping* 12, no. 3: 364–376.

Centro Nacional de Memoria Histórica. 2015a. "Asesinatos Selectivos 1981–2012." Base de Datos. http://www.centrodememoriahistorica.gov.co.

Centro Nacional de Memoria Histórica. 2015b. "Masacres 1980–2012." Base de Datos. http://www.centrodememoriahistorica.gov.co.

Chabat, Jorge. 2002. "Mexico's War on Drugs: No Margin for Maneuver." *Annals of the American Academy of Political and Social Science* 582:134–148.

Chaires González, Erika. 2014. Public Information Access Unit, Coahuila, Mexico. Personal correspondence with author, February 17, 2014.

Champion, Dean J. 2001. *Police Misconduct in America: A Reference Handbook*. Santa Barbara, CA: ABC-CLIOs

CNN. 2010. "400 Municipios del Pais Llevan al Menos una Decada Sin Policía Proira." Cable News Network Mexico, February 22, 2010. http://mexico.cnn.com.

Collier, Simon, and William F. Sater. 1996. *A History of Chile, 1808–1994* (Vol. 82). Cambridge: Cambridge University Press.

Consorcio Iberoamericano de Investigaciones de Mercados y Asesoramiento (CIMA). 1991–2012. "Barómetro Iberoamericano de Gobernabilidad." Accessed July 1, 2012 http://cimaiberoamerica.com/

Constitution of the United States of Mexico. Title V, Article 115, Sub-Section VII of the Mexican Constitution. www.diputados.gob.mx.

Costa, Arthur Trindade Maranhão. 2011. "Police Brutality in Brazil: Authoritarian Legacy or Institutional Weakness?" *Latin American Perspectives* 38, no. 5: 19–32.

Costa, Arthur, and Mateus Medeiros. 2006. "Police Demilitarisation: Cops, Soldiers and Democracy." *Conflict, Security & Development* 2, no. 2: 25–45.

Crank, John P. 1990. "Police: Professionals or Craftsmen? An Empirical Assessment of Professionalism and Craftsmanship Among Eight Municipal Agencies." *Journal of Criminal Justice* 18:333–349.

Cruz, José Miguel. 2009. "Maltrato Policial en América Latina." No. 11 in the Perspectivas desde el Barómetro de las Américas series, edited by Mitchell A. Seligson and Elizabeth Zechmeister. Nashville: Vanderbilt University. https://www.vanderbilt.edu/lapop/insights/I0811es.pdf.

Cruz, José Miguel. 2011. "Criminal Violence and Democratization in Central America: The Survival of the Violent State." *Latin American Politics and Society* 53, no. 4: 1–33.

Cruz, José Miguel. 2015. Police Misconduct and Political Legitimacy in Central America. *Journal of Latin American Studies* 47, no. 2: 251–283.

Cuerpo de Generales de Carabineros. 2016. "Origen de los Hospitales de Carabineros." https://generales.cl/.

Dammert, Lucía. 2012. Associate professor, Universidad de Santiago de Chile; expert on public security issues in Latin America; Global Fellow Latin American Program at the Wilson Center, Santiago, Chile. Interview with author, October 25, 2012.

Davis, Diane E. 2006. "Undermining the Rule of Law: Democratization and the Dark Side of Police Reform in Mexico." *Latin American Politics and Society* 48, no. 1: 55–86.

Deas, Malcom. 2002. "El Papel de la Iglesia, el Ejército y la Policía en las Elecciones Colombianas Entre 1850 y 1930." *Boletin Cultural y Bibliographico* 39, no. 60.

De la Barreda, Luis, Alejandra Velez, J. Antonio Aguilar, Cecilia Sayeg, and Begoña Ayuso. 2013. "Hacia una Nueva Policía Diagnóstico y Respuesta." *Perseo 13*. Universidad Nacional Autonoma de México. http://www.pudh.unam.mx/perseo/hacia-una-nueva-policia-1/.

De la Torre, Luis V. 2008. "Drug Trafficking and Police Corruption: A Comparison of Colombia and Mexico." Master's thesis, Naval Postgraduate School, Monterey, California.

Della Porta, Donatella. 1999. "Protest, Protesters, and Protest Policing: Public Discourses in Italy and Germany from the 1960s to the 1980s." In *How Social Movements Matter*, edited by Marco Giugni, Doug McAdam, and Charles Tilly, 66–96. Minneapolis: University of Minnesota Press.

Delpar, Helen. 1994. *Rojos Contra Azules: El Partido Liberal En La Política Colombiana 1863–1899*. Bogotá: Procultura SA.

Dinnen, Sinclair, Abby McLeod, and Gordon Peake. 2006. "Police-Building in Weak States: Australian Approaches in Papua New Guinea and Solomon Islands." *Civil Wars* 8, no. 2: 87–108.

"Drug Violence Blamed for Mexico's Record 29,168 Murders in 2017." 2018. *The Guardian* (Manchester), January 21, 2018.

Durán-Martínez, Angélica. 2015. "To Kill and Tell? State Power, Criminal Competition, and Drug Violence." *Journal of Conflict Resolution* 59, no. 8: 1377–1402.

Earl, Jennifer, and Sarah Soule. 2006. "Seeing Blue: A Police-Centered Explanation of Protest Policing." *Mobilization: An International Quarterly* 11, no. 2: 145–164.

Eaton, Kent. 2008. "Paradoxes of Police Reform: Federalism, Parties, and Civil Society in Argentina's Public Security Crisis." *Latin American Research Review* 43, no. 3: 5–32.

Eitle, David, Stewart J. D'Alessio, and Lisa Stolzenberg. 2014. "The Effect of Organizational and Environmental Factors on Police Misconduct." *Police Quarterly* 17, no. 2: 1–24.

Ellingwood, Ken. 2010. "Mexican President Wants To Do Away with Local Police." *Los Angeles Times*, October 6, 2010.

Esparza, Diego, and Thomas C. Bruneau. 2019. "Closing the Gap Between Law Enforcement and National Security Intelligence: Comparative Approaches." *International Journal of Intelligence and Counterintelligence* 32, no. 2: 322–353.

Esparza, Diego, and Antonio Ugues. 2020. "The Impact of Law Enforcement Centralisation and Professionalisation on Public Opinion of the Mexican Police." *Journal of Politics in Latin America* 12, no. 1: 104–120.

La Estrella de Valparaíso. 1922. Hemeroteca Biblioteca Nacional. 22 de Noviembre 1922.

Evans, Peter B., Dietrich Rueschemeyer, and Theda Skocpol, eds. 1985. *Bringing the State Back In*. Cambridge: Cambridge University Pres

Expansión. 2010. "En México Hay un Policía Local por Cada 960 Habitantes, Segun el INEGI." September 24, 2010.

Figueroa, Juan Pablo. 2012. Investigative journalist at Centro de Investigación Periodística (CIPER) covering crime and law enforcement topics, Santiago, Chile. Interview with author, November 15 2012.

Finocchiaro Castro, Massimo, and Calogero Guccio. 2020. "Birds of a Feather Flock Together: Trust in Government, Political Selection and Electoral Punishment." *Public Choice* 184:263–287.

Flisfisch, Ángel, and Marcos Robledo. 2012. "Gobernabilidad Democrática de la Defensa en Chile: Un Indice para el Periodo 1990–2010." United Nations Development Program. Santiago, Chile.

Flores, Carlos. 2014. Researcher, Center for Research and Superior Studies in Social Anthropology (CIESAS), Mexico, and expert in Mexican political-criminal networks, Mexico City. Interview with author, September 9, 2014.

Forbes Mexico. 2018. "AMLO Anuncia Coordinaciones de Seguridad con Mando Único." October 3, 2018.

Foreign Radio Broadcast. 1948a. "Civilians, Police Clash in El Carmen." *Daily Report*, FBIS-FRB-48-355. July 19, 1948.

Foreign Radio Broadcast. 1948b. "National Police Re-Organization Begun." *Daily Report*, FBIS-FRB-48-306. May 7, 1948.

Foreign Radio Broadcast. 1949a. "Police Charged with Hazing La Raya." *Daily Report*, FBIS-FRB-49-179. September 16, 1949.

Foreign Radio Broadcast. 1949b. "Violence in Caldas." *Daily Report*, FBIS-FRB-49-013. January 19, 1949.

Fornes, Victor Manuel. 2012. Retired corporal 1st class (1983–2010), 27-year veteran, Santiago, Chile. Interview with author, December 12, 2012.

Fouilloux, Luciano. Sub-secretary of Carabineros under President Frei (1994–2000), Santiago, Chile. Interview with author, November 7, 2012.

Frei, Eduardo. 1999. President Eduardo Frei annual address to the 340th Legislature of Chile, Ordinary Plenary Session, Friday, May 21, 1999. http://historiapolitica.bcn.cl.

Friesendorf, Cornelius, and Jörg Krempel. 2011."Militarized Versus Civilian Policing: Problems of Reforming the Afghan National Police." PRIF Report No. 102. Peace Research Institute Frankfurt/HSFK, Frankfurt.

Frühling, Hugo. 2009. "Recent Police Reform in Latin America." In *Policing Insecurity: Police Reforms, Security, and Human Rights in Latin America*, edited by Niels Uildriks, 21–45. Lanham, MD: Lexington Books.

Frühling, Hugo. 2012. Executive secretary of the Coordinating Council of Public Security for the Government of Chile (1992–1994) and special adviser to the Ministry of the Interior, Santiago, Chile. Interview with author, October 19, 2012.

Frühling, Hugo, Joseph S. Tulchin, and Heather A. Golding, eds. 2003. *Crime and Violence in Latin America: Citizen Security, Democracy, and the State*. Washington, DC: Woodrow Wilson Center Press.

Fuentes, Claudio. 2005. *Contesting the Iron Fist: Advocacy Networks and Police Violence in Democratic Argentina and Chile*. London: Routledge.

Fuentes, Claudio. 2012. Director of the Social Science Research Institute (ICSO) at Universidad Diego Portales in Santiago, Chile, and expert on human rights and public security policy, Santiago, Chile. Interview with author, December 12, 2012.

Fund for Peace. 2019. "Fragile State Index 2019." https://fragilestatesindex.org.

Gaitán, Fernado. 1997. "La Policia de Hoy y de Mañana: Lo Que Hace y Lo Que Debería Hacer." *Dikaion: Revista de Actualidad Jurídica*, no. 6: 111–260.

Gallup Colombia LTDA. 2007. "Tiene Usted una Opinion Favorable o Desfavorable Sobre la Policía." Ficha Technica PPT, note 79.

Galleguillos, Nibaldo H. 2004. "Re-Establishing Civilian Supremacy over Police Institutions: An Analysis of Recent Attempted Reforms of the Security Sector in Chile." *Journal of Third World Studies* 21, no.1: 57–77.

Gálvez, Juan Ignacio. 1912. "Conferencias." Bogotá: Casa Editorial de El Republicano.

Gálvez, Mario. 2012. Journalist at largest paper in Chile, *El Mercurio*, covering crime and policing issues, Santiago, Chile. Interview with author, November 8, 2012.

García, Gustavo Castillo. 2010. "Equivocado, Querer Crear en Mexico una Policía Única, Aseveran Especialistas." *La Jornada*, August 6, 2010.

García, Hector. 2013. National Police major and chief of legal and human rights affairs for DIPOL, National Police of Colombia, Bogotá, Colombia. Email correspondence with author, March 20, 2013.

García Ramírez, Lorena. 2013. "Buscan Darle a los Policías un Fondo de Retiro." *El Mexicano*, June 7, 2013.

Garner, Randy. 2005. "Police Attitudes: The Impact of Experience After Training." *Applied Psychology in Criminal Justice* 1, no. 1: 56–70.

Gatica, Jimmy Walter. 2013. Retired Carabinero (2008–2011), Santiago, Chile. Interview with author, January 4, 2013.

Getty, Ryan M., John L. Worrall, and Robert G. Morris. 2016. "How Far from the Tree Does the Apple Fall? Field Training Officers, Their Trainees, and Allegations of Misconduct." *Crime & Delinquency* 62, no. 6: 821–839.

Gerber, Theodore P., and Sarah E. Mendelson. 2008. "Public Experiences of Police Violence and Corruption in Contemporary Russia: A Case of Predatory Policing?" *Law & Society Review*, 42(1), pp. 1–44.

Gibbs, Stephen. 2018. "Mexican Army Replaces Acapulco's 'Infiltrated' Police." *The Times* (London). September 26, 2018.

Glebeek, Marie-Louise. 2009. "Police Reform in Latin America." In *Policing Insecurity: Police Reform, Security, and Human Rights in Latin America*, edited by Niels Uildriks. Lanham, MD: Lexington Books.

Gobierno de México. 2015. "Remuneracíon." Portal Transparencia. http://www.portaltransparencia.gob.mx.

Gobinet, Pierre. 2008. "The Gendarmerie Alternative: Is There a Case for the Existence of Police Organizations with Military Status in the Twenty-First Century European Security Apparatus?" *International Journal of Police Science and Management* 10, no. 4: 448–463.

Goldsmith, Andrew. 1999. "The Police We Need." *Alternative Law Journal* 24, no. 3.

Goldsmith, Andrew. 2003. "Policing Weak States: Citizen Safety and State Responsibility." *Policing and Society* 13:3–21.

Goldsmith, Andrew. 2010. "Policing's New Visibility." *British Journal of Criminology* 50, no. 5: 914–934.

Gómez, Miguel Antonio. 2009. "Busqueda de la Identidad a la Luz de la Ciencia de Policía: ¿Que Es la Policía?" Editorial Gente Nueva. *Memoirs of the First International Congress on Police Sciences*, Bogotá. http://www.cienciadepolicia.com.

Gómez Rojas, Claudia, and Estela Baracaldo. 2007. "Shared Responsibility: A Strategy for Coexistence and Citizen Security in the National Police of Colombia." *Revista Latinoamericana de Seguridad Ciudadana*. No. 2, Quito, September 2007, pp. 99–111.

González, Mónica. 2019. "Furia Sesatada en Carabineros: Fuéra de Control y Sin Piloto." CIPER. https://www.ciperchile.cl/2019/11/12/furia-desatada-en-carabineros-fuera-de-control-y-sin-piloto/.

González, Yanilda María. 2020. *Authoritarian Police in Democracy: Contested Security in Latin America*. Cambridge: Cambridge University Press.

González Camus, Ignacio. 1988. *El Día en Que Murió Allende*. Santiago: LOM Lta.

Gould, Jens Erik. 2010. "Calderon Seeks To Unify Mexico's Police Forces Amid Corruption, Killings." Bloomberg News, October 6, 2010.

Grayson, George. 2009. *Mexico: Narco-Violence and a Failed State?* Livingston, NJ: Transaction Publishers.

Grindle, Merilee Serrill. 2007. *Going Local: Decentralization, Democratization, and the Promise of Good Governance.* Princeton: Princeton University Press.

Guevara Ramírez, Jorge Xavier. 2014. Director general of administracion and head of the Public Information Unit under the secretary of the interior, Morelos, Mexico. Personal correspondence with author, October 15, 2014.

Guillermo, Felipe Ruz Baeza. 2010. "Legitimidad Ciudadana al Accionar de Carabineros de Chile: Una Aproximación a la Comprensión del Fenómeno." Master's thesis, Universidad de Chile. http://www.tesis.uchile.cl.

Gunson, Phil. 2000. "Obituary: Arturo Durazo—Mexico City's Crooked Cop Chief." *The Guardian* (Manchester), August 13, 2000.

Gutierrez, Rodolfo. 2015. "Ramos Arizipe Pensión." *El Zocalo Zaltillo*, January 2, 2015.

Gutiérrez, Rufino. 1920. "Monografías Tomo I and II." Biblioteca Virtual Luis Angel Arango. Bogotá: Imprenta Nacional.

Gutiérrez-Garcia, J. Octavio, and Luis-Felipe Rodríguez. 2016. "Social Determinants of Police Corruption: Toward Public Policies for the Prevention of Police Corruption." *Policy Studies* 37, no. 3: 216–235.

Guzmán, German, Orlando Fals, and Eduardo Umaña. 1962. "La Violencia en Colombia: Tomo I." Bogotá: Nomos Impresores.

Guzmán Sanchez, Ruben, and María Eugenia Suárez de Garay. 2014. "Alcozauca: Ser Policía Municipal en la Montaña de Guerrero." Instituto de Seguridad y Democracia. https://web.archive.org/web/20141204144428/http://insyde.org.mx/alcozauca-ser-policia-municipal-en-la-montana-de-guerrero/.

Greene, Jack R., and Stephen D. Mastrofski, eds. 1988. *Community Policing: Rhetoric or Reality.* New York: Praeger.

Haarr, Robin N. 2001. "The Making of a Community Policing Officer: The Impact of Basic Training and Occupational Socialization on Police Recruits." *Police Quarterly* 4, no. 4: 402–433.

Hadden, Sally E. 2001. *Slave Patrols: Law and Violence in Virginia and the Carolinas.* Cambridge, MA: Harvard University Press.

Hansen, John G. 2012. "Racialized Policing: Aboriginal People's Experiences with the Police." *Canadian Journal of Native Studies* 32, no. 2: 231.

Harboe, Felipe. 2012. Sub-secretary of Carabineros under President Lagos (2002–2004), former deputy minister of the interior under Bachelet (2006–2008), Congress deputy from the 22nd District in Santiago Centro (2009–2014), Santiago, Chile. Interview with author, December 13, 2012.

Hassell, Kimberly D. 2016. "Reducing Police Misconduct." In *Stress in Policing*, edited by Haus Toch. London: Routledge.

Henderson, James D. 1985. *When Colombia Bled: A History of the Violencia in Tolima.* Tuscaloosa: University of Alabama Press.

Heslop, Richard. 2011. "The British Police Service: Professionalisation or 'McDonaldization'?" *International Journal of Police Science & Management* 13, no. 4: 312–321.

Hilal, Susan, James Densley, and Ruohui Zhao. 2013. "Cops in College: Police Officers' Perceptions on Formal Education." *Journal of Criminal Justice Education* 24, no. 4: 461–477.

Hill, Stephen M., and Randall R. Beger. 2009. "A Paramilitary Policing Juggernaut." *Social Justice* 36, no. 1: 25–40.

Hill, Stephen M., Randall R. Beger, and John M. Zanetti. 2007. "Plugging the Security Gap or Springing a Leak: Questioning the Growth of Paramilitary Policing in US Domestic and Foreign Policy." *Democracy and Security* 3, no. 3: 301–321.

Hinton, Mercedes S. 2006. *The State on the Streets: Police and Politics in Argentina and Brazil.* Boulder: Lynne Rienner Publishers.

Honorato, Oscar C., and Waldo Urzua Alvarez. 1923. "Album Gráfico de la Policía de Santiago." *Memoria Chilena*. Santiago: Biblioteca Nacional de Chile. http://www .memoriachilena.cl.

Hoyos, Francisco. 2014. Public relations officer at Consejo Ciudadano, an NGO geared toward improving transparency and accountability, Mexico City, Mexico. Interview with author, September 3, 2014.

Hu, Rong, Ivan Y. Sun, and Yuning Wu. 2015. "Chinese Trust in the Police: The Impact of Political Efficacy and Participation." *Social Science Quarterly* 96, no. 4: 1012–1026.

Hudson, Rex. 2010. *Colombia: A Country Study*. Washington, DC: Federal Research Division, Library of Congress.

Huenumil Lezana, Gonzalo. 2012. Carabinero colonel, head of Department of Public Information, RSIP No 19204, Santiago, Chile. Personal correspondence with author, April 12, 2012.

Huerta, Helmuth. 2013. "Pensiones de Carabineros y PDI Superan en Mas de 6 Veces a la Población Común." Saturday, December 14, 2013. http://radio.uchile.cl.

Huggins, Martha K. 1987. "US-Supported State Terror: A History of Police Training in Latin America." *Crime and Social Justice*, nos. 27/28: 149–171.

Huggins, Martha K. 1998. *Political Policing: The United States and Latin America*. Durham: Duke University Press.

Human Rights Watch. 2009. "Lethal Force: Police Violence and Public Security in Rio de Janeiro and São Paulo." https://www.hrw.org/report/2009/12/08/lethal-force /police-violence-and-public-security-rio-de-janeiro-and-sao-paulo.

Human Rights Watch. 2014. "World Report 2014: Mexico." https://www.hrw.org/world -report/2014/country-chapters/mexico.

Hurtado Hernández, Martha. 2014. The State of Durango Unit of Engagement, Transparency Access and Public Information, Durango, Mexico. Personal correspondence with author, February 14, 2014.

Ibáñez, Voltaire Opazo. 2012. General and president of the Carabineros General Corps, professor at Escuela Superior de Carabineros, Santiago, Chile. Personal correspondence with author, December 12, 2012.

Inglehart, R., C. Haerpfer, A. Moreno, C. Welzel, K. Kizilova, J. Diez-Medrano, M. Lagos, P. Norris, E. Ponarin, and B. Puranen, eds. 2022. World Values Survey: All Rounds-Country-Pooled Datafile. Madrid, Spain, and Vienna: JD Systems Institute and WVSA Secretariat. Dataset Version 3.0.0. doi:10.14281/18241.17.

Instituto Nacional de Estadística y Geografía. 2011a. Encuesta Nacional de Victimización y Percepción Sobre Seguridad Pública (ENVIPE).

Instituto Nacional de Estadística y Geografía. 2011b. "Seventh National Survey on Insecurity." https://en.www.inegi.org.mx.

Instituto Nacional de Estadística y Geografía. 2013. Encuesta Nacional de Victimización y Percepción Sobre Seguridad Pública (ENVIPE). https://www.inegi.org.mx /programas/envipe/2013/.

Instituto Nacional de Estadística y Geografía. 2018. Encuesta Nacional de Victimización y Percepción Sobre Seguridad Pública (ENVIPE). https://www.inegi.org.mx /programas/envipe/2018/.

Instituto Para la Seguridad y la Democracia. 2010. "Cuantos Policías Hay en México?" http://www.insyde.org.mx.

International Law Enforcement Agency. 2021. "Training Schedule." San Salvador, El Salvador. https://sansalvador.ilea.state.gov.

Jenkins, Clinton D. 2021. "Effective Police Recruitment: Professional Misconduct Risk Regression Analysis for Law Enforcement Officers." PhD diss., Walden University, Minneapolis, Minnesota.

Jones, Jeffrey. 2015. "In U.S., Confidence in Police Lowest in 22 Years." Gallup News, June 19, 2015. https://news.gallup.com/poll/183704/confidence-police-lowest-years.aspx.

Jorquera, Jaime. 2012. Retired Carabinero (2002–2010) and lawyer specializing in topics of Carabineros and their disciplinary rules norms, and regulations, Santiago, Chile. Interview with author, December 3, 2012.

Justiciabarometro. 2009. "Result of the Survey of Municipal Preventative Police of the Metropolitan Zone of Guadalajara." University of San Diego. https://justiceinmexico .org/justicebarometer/.

Justiciabarometro. 2011. "A Comprehensive Assessment of the Municipal Police of Ciudad Juárez." University of San Diego. https://justiceinmexico.org/justicebarometer/.

Justiciabarometro. 2015. "A Wholistic Diagnostic of the Municipal Police of Tijuana." University of San Diego. https://justiceinmexico.org/justicebarometer/.

Kaariainen, Juha Tapio. 2007. "Trust in the Police in 16 European Countries." *European Journal of Criminology* 4, no. 4: 409–435.

Kakachia, Kornely, and Liam O'Shea. 2012. "Why Does Police Reform Appear to Have Been More Successful in Georgia Than in Kyrgyzstan or Russia?" *Journal of Power Institutions in Post-Soviet Societies*, no. 13. https://journals.openedition.org /pipss/3964.

Kane, Robert J. 2005. "Compromised Police Legitimacy as a Predictor of Violent Crime in Structurally Disadvantaged Communities." *Criminology* 43, no. 2: 469–498.

Karstedt, Susanne. 2012. "Comparing Justice and Crime Across Cultures." In *SAGE Handbook of Criminological Research Methods*. Thousand Oaks, CA: Sage.

Kimani, Mary. 2009. "Security for the Highest Bidder." *Africa Renewal* 23, no. 3. https://www.un.org.

Kirk, David S., and Mauri Matsuda. 2011. "Legal Cynicism, Collective Efficacy, and the Ecology of Arrest." *American Society of Criminology* 49, no. 2: 443–472.

Klinger, David A. 2004. "Environment and Organization: Reviving a Perspective on the Police." *ANNALS of the American Academy of Political and Social Science* 593:119–136.

Kuritzkes, Caroline. 2017. "Increased Mexico Security Spending Not Delivering Security Gains: Report." InSight Crime, August 14, 2017. https://insightcrime.org/news /brief/increased-mexico-security-spending-not-delivering-security-gains-report/.

Lagos, Ricardo. 2002. President Ricardo Lagos annual address to the 346th Legislature of Chile, Ordinary Plenary Session, May 21, 2002. http://historiapolitica.bcn.cl.

Larraín Donoso, Ramiro F. 2012. Carabinero colonel, chief of the Department of Information, Complaints, and Suggestions, Santiago, Chile. Personal correspondence with author, November 23, 2012.

Latin American Weekly Report. 1974. "5 April 1974, Chile." https://www.latinnews.com /search/80.html?archive=32449&sea.

LaSusa, Mike. 2016. "Cop's Killing, Drug Dispute Spotlight Argentina Police Corruption." InSight Crime, October 29, 2016. https://insightcrime.org/news/brief/cops -killing-drug-dispute-spotlight-argentina-police-corruption/.

Latinobarómetro Survey. 1995–2017. "Online Data Analysis." Santiago de Chile: Latinobarómetro Corporation. https://www.latinobarometro.org/latOnline.jsp.

Lauchs, Mark, Robyn Keast, and Nina Yousefpour. 2011. "Corrupt Police Networks: Uncovering Hidden Relationship Patterns, Functions and Roles." *Policing & Society* 21, no. 1: 110–127.

Leal Buitrago, Francisco. 2013. Expert on political history of Colombia, professor at National University of Colombia, Bogotá, Colombia. Interview with author, March 21 2013.

Liebertz, Scott. 2020. "Political Elites, Crime, and Trust in the Police in Latin America." *International Criminal Justice Review* 30, no. 2: 175–196.

Ligthart, Jenny E., and Peter van Oudheusden. 2015. "In Government We Trust: The Role of Fiscal Decentralization." *European Journal of Political Economy* 37:116–128.

Ljubetic, Yerko. 2012. Principal investigator at the National Institute for Human Rights and former minister of labor and welfare under President Lagos, Santiago, Chile. Interview with author, October 19, 2012.

Llorente, Maria Victoria. 1997. "Perfil de la Policía Colombiana." Documento de Trabajo No. 9. Programa de Estudios de Seguridad, Justicia y Violencia. Universidad de Los Andes, Bogotá.

Llorente, Maria Victoria. 2013. Executive director for Ideas para la Paz, a public security NGO, Bogotá, Colombia. Interview with author, March 11, 2013.

Londoño Cardenas, Fabian A. 2013. Retired brigadier general of the National Police of Colombia and former police officer and professor at Police Postgraduate School, Bogotá, Colombia. Interview with author, March 4, 2013.

Londoño Orozco, Jaime Ivan. 2013. National Police major and chief of network services for the Directorate of Health of the National Police Colombia, Bogotá, Colombia. Personal correspondence with author, March 20, 2013.

López Cabarcas, Jose. 2013. Lieutenant colonel in National Police of Colombia, judge for Military Penal Court for Police in Medellín, Colombia. Interview with author, May 9, 2013.

López de la Vega, Rogelio Paaris. Operative director, Nayarit, Mexico. Personal correspondence with author, February 28, 2014

López Portillo Vargas, Ernesto. 2000. "La Policía en México: Función Politica y Reforma." *Inseguridad Publica y Gobernabilidad Democrática: Retos Para México y Estados Unidos*. Smith Richardson Foundation, Febrero 2000, Mexico.http://pdba.georgetown.edu.

López Portillo Vargas, Ernesto. 2014. Director and founder of Institute for Security and Democracy, Mexico City, Mexico. Interview with author, September 10, 2014.

López Riaño, Yed M. 2013. Lieutenant colonel in National Police of Colombia (22-year veteran) and head of community policing in Medellín (2013), Medellín, Colombia. Interviews with author, May 7 through May 15, 2013.

Lowatcharin, Grichawat, and Judith I. Stallmann. 2017. "Developing a Cross-National Index of Police Decentralization." *Social Science Asia* 3, no. 4: 29–53.

Lowatcharin, Grichawat, and Judith I. Stallmann. 2019. "Decentralization and Citizen Trust: An Empirical Study of Policing in More and Less Developed Countries." *Journal of Public Affairs* 20, no. 1: e1974.

Luengas Diaz, Diana. 2013. National Police lieutenant colonel and chief of discounted housing for police, National Police of Colombia, Bogotá, Colombia. Personal correspondence with author, March 10, 2013.

Lugo Delgado, Eldia Barbara. 2014. General inspector, Office of General Commissioner, Federal Police, Mexico City, Mexico. Personal correspondence with author, February 28, 2014.

Lutterbeck, Derek. 2005. "Blurring the Dividing Line: The Convergence of Internal and External Security in Western Europe." *European Security* 14, no. 2: 231–253.

MacVean, Allyson, and Carol Cox. 2012. "Police Education in a University Setting: Emerging Cultures and Attitudes." *Policing: A Journal of Policy and Practice* 6, no. 1: 16–25.

Maguire, Edward R. 2003. *Organizational Structure in American Police Agencies: Context, Complexity, and Control*. Albany: State University of New York Press.

Mahecha, Yesenia. 2013. Major in National Police of Colombia and chief of research, Police Postgraduate School, Bogotá, Colombia. Interview with author, March 18, 2013.

Manuel-Gómez, Alonso Ulises Mendez. 2014. Director general of state public security, Sonora, Mexico. Personal correspondence with author, August 31, 2014.

Marcella, Gabriel, Orlando J. Pérez, and Brian Fonseca, eds. 2021. *Democracy and Security in Latin America: State Capacity and Governance Under Stress*. London: Routledge.

Marenin, Otwin. 2004. "Police Training for Democracy." *Police Practice and Research* 5, no. 2: 107–123.

Mario, Roberto. 1917. *La Corrupción de la Policía Secreta de Santiago*. Imprenta America. Santiago, Chile.

Martin, Gerard. 2012. "Medellín Trafedia y Resurrección: Mafia, Ciudad y Estado 1975–2012." *Planeta*, Bogotá.

Martinez, Frédéric. 2001. *El Nacionalismo Cosmopolita. La Referencia Europea en la Construcción Nacional en Colombia, 1845–1900*. Bogotá: Banco de la Republica e Instituto Frances de Estudios Andinos.

Mastrofski, Stephen D., R. Richard Ritti, and Debra Hoffmaster. 1987. "Organizational Determinants of Police Discretion: The Case of Drinking–Driving." *Journal of Criminal Justice* 15:387–402.

Matus-González, Mario. 2009. "Precios y Salarios Reales en Chile Durante el Ciclo Salitrero, 1880–1930." Departamento de Historia y Instituciones Economicas. Universidad de Barcelona. http://www.tdx.cat.

Mawby, Rob C., and Alan Wright. 2012. "The Police Organisation." *Handbook of Policing*, 252–280. London: Willan Publishing.

Mazzuca, Sebastian, and James A. Robinson. 2009. "Political Conflict and Power Sharing in the Origins of Modern Colombia." *Hispanic American Historical Review* 89:2.

McClellan, Sara E., and Bryon G. Gustafson. 2012. "Communicating Law Enforcement Professionalization: Social Construction of Standards." *Policing: An International Journal of Police Strategies & Management* 35, no. 1: 104–123.

McFadyen, Alistair, and Melanie Prideaux. 2014. "The Placing of Religion in Policing and Policing Studies." *Policing and Society* 24, no. 5: 602–619.

McNamara, Robert P., and Maria Tempenis. 1999. "The Role of Religion in Policing." In *Police and Policing: Contemporary Issues*. Westport, CT: Praeger.

Medicina Legal. 2012. "Homicidios." Instituto Nacional de Medicina Legal y Ciencias Forenses. https://www.medicinalegal.gov.co/.

Memoria de la Granja. 1914. "Memoria de la Alcaldía Municipal de la Granja Correspondiente a Los Años 1912 y 1913." Santiago de Chile. Imprenta y Encuadernacion El Globo San Isidro 59. http://www.bcn.cl.

Memoria Nortina. 1907. "La Lenta Decadencia Nacional." https://web.archive.org/web/20180303091611/http://memorianortina.cl/1907-la-lenta-decadencia-nacional/.

Mendez, Estela Baracaldo. 2013. Adviser to Project of Training and Citizen Security, Government of Bogotá, Colombia (1995–2003), Bogotá, Colombia. Interview with author, February 11, 2013.

Mendoza, Antia. 2014. Independent consultant for security and citizen peace, consultant in police reform in Chihuahua, and employee of the Secretariat of Governance for Mexican Federal Government, Mexico City, Mexico. Interview with author, September 23, 2014.

El Mercurio de Santiago. 1922. "El Día de Carabineros." Hemeroteca Biblioteca Nacional, Santiago de Chile, 22 de Noviembre de 1922.

El Mercurio. 2003. "Minute by Minute 1973 to 2003." September 11, 2003. http://www.emol.com/noticias/nacional/2003/09/11/122757/minuto-a-minuto-de1973-y-2003.html.

Michel, Victor Hugo. 2011. "Recomienda Colombia Mando de Policía Única en México." *El Millennia*, September 23, 2015.

Miranda Beccera, Diego. 1997. "Un Siglo de Evolución Policiales de Portales a Ibáñez." Departamento de Estudios Históricos Instituto Superior de Ciencias Policiales Carabineros de Chile. www.memoriachilena.cl.

Mohor, Alejandra. 2012. Researcher at the University of Chile Institute for Public Policy, Santiago, Chile. Interview with author, October 17, 2012.

Moloeznik, Marcos Pablo. 2010. "An Approach to the Mexican Municipal Preventive Police: The Municipality of Tlajomulco de Zuniga, Jalisco." *Revista del CESLA*, no. 13: 595–609.

Moncada, Eduardo. 2009. "Toward Democratic Policing in Colombia? Institutional Accountability Through Lateral Reform." *Comparative Politics* 41, no. 4: 431–449.

Montero, Alfred P., and David J. Samuels. 2004. *Decentralization and Democracy in Latin America*. South Bend, IN: University of Notre Dame Press.

Morales Aguirre, Patricio. 2012. Sub-secretary of Carabineros in the Ministry of Defense under President Lagos (2000–2002) and lawyer at Pérez Donozo Legal Study, Santiago, Chile. Interview with author, November 22, 2012.

Morris, Camie S. 2011. "A Cross-National Study on Public Confidence in the Police." PhD diss., Northeastern University, Boston.

Morris, Stephen D., and Joseph L. Klesner. 2010. "Corruption and Trust: Theoretical Considerations and Evidence from Mexico." *Comparative Political Studies* 43, no. 10: 1258–1285.

Mosquera, Clara Cecilia. 2013. Major in National Police of Colombia and head of the Executive Directorate of Military Penal Justice, National Police of Colombia, Bogotá, Colombia. Personal correspondence with author, April 1, 2013.

Mosquera, Lorena. 2013. Civilian staff in National Police of Colombia and thesis coordinator, Police Postgraduate School, Bogotá, Colombia. Interview with author, March 18, 2013.

Moule, Richard K., Jr. 2020. "Under Siege? Assessing Public Perceptions of the 'War on Police.'" *Journal of Criminal Justice* 66:1–12.

Müller, Markus-Michael. 2012. *Public Security in the Negotiated State: Policing in Latin America and Beyond*. New York and Basingstoke: Palgrave Macmillan.

Müller, Markus-Michael. 2018. "Policing as Pacification: Postcolonial Legacies, Transnational Connections, and the Militarization of Urban Security in Democratic Brazil." In *Police Abuse in Contemporary Democracies*, edited by Michelle D. Bonner, Guillermina Seri, Mary Rose Kubal, and Michael Kempa. New York and London: Palgrave Macmillan.

Muñoz Silva, Ramón. 1916. "Escándalos Policiales, o Lo Que Ocurre en la Policía de Santiago: La Desorganización de Nuestras Policías y Su Desmoralización." Santiago, Chile. Biblioteca Nacional Digital.

Murray, John. 2005. "Policing Terrorism: A Threat to Community Policing or Justice Shift in Priorities?" *Police Practice and Research: An International Journal* 6, no. 4: 347–361.

Museo Histórico de Carabineros de Chile. 2012. "Carabineros de Chile: Evolución de la Función Policial." https://www.museocarabineros.cl/web/storage/books/1626713395_Libro-verde-2020-web-full.pdf.

Mutualidad de Carabineros. 2014. "Prestamos." http://www.mutucar.cl/Portal.Base/Web/VerContenido.aspx?GUID=e677e4fd-8e9b-4c20-9660-79fa161e2036&ID=37.

Mwangi, Oscar Gakuo. 2017. "Statelessness, Ungoverned Spaces and Security in Kenya." In *Understanding Statelessness*. London: Routledge.

National Commission for Truth and Reconciliation. 1990. "The National Commission for Truth and Reconciliation Report" (Rettig Report). United States Institute of Peace. https://www.usip.org/publications/1990/05/truth-commission-chile-90.

National Police of Colombia. 2013a. "Caja de Sueldos y Retiro de la Policía Nacional de Colombia." http://www.casur.gov.co/.

National Police of Colombia. 2013b. "Caja de Vivienda. Dirección de Bienestar Social de la Policía Nacional." https://www.policia.gov.co/.

National Police of Colombia. 2013c. Centro Estratégico de Direccionamiento Institutional Histórico Virtual. Located inside of the Miguel Antonio Lleras Pizzaro National Police Postgraduate School. Information accessed in person April 19, 2013. Access not available to public.

National Police of Colombia. 2019. "Missión y Reseña Histórica." Directorate of Police Intelligence. https://www.policia.gov.co.

Naval, Claire. 2006. *Irregularities, Abuses of Power, and Ill-Treatment in the Federal District: The Relation Between Police Officers and Ministerio Público Agents, and the Population*. Mexico City: Centro de Análisis e Investigación.

Navarrete, F. 2000. *Represión Política a los Movimientos Sociales, Santiago 1890–1910.* Tesis para Optar al Grado de Licenciado en Historia, Pontificia Universidad Católica de Chile. Biblioteca Nacional de Chile.

Neild, Rachel. 2001. "Democratic Police Reforms in War-Torn Societies." *Conflict, Security & Development* 1, no. 1: 21–43.

New York State. 2015. *History of the Basic Course for Police Officers.* Criminal Justice New York State. https://www.criminaljustice.ny.gov.

Nino Marin, Naryi. 2013. Major in National Police of Colombia and chief of human development, National Police of Colombia, Bogotá, Colombia. Personal correspondence with author, April 1, 2013.

Oates, Wallace E. 2011. *Fiscal Federalism.* Cheltenham, UK: Edward Elgar Publishing.

O'Donnell, Guillermo. 2004. "The Quality of Democracy: Why the Rule of Law Matters." *Journal of Democracy* 15, no. 4: 32–46.

Olivares Ferreto, Edith. 2010. "Condiciones Sociolaborales de los Cuerpos Policiales y Seguridad Pública." *Análisis Político*, December 1, 2010. http://library.fes.de.

Organisation for Economic Co-operation and Development. 2015. "Real Minimum Wages." https://stats.oecd.org/Index.aspx?DataSetCode=RMW.

Ortiz, Francisco. 2013. Retired Carabineros sergeant major (active 1992–2002), Santiago, Chile. Interview with author, January 1, 2013.

Palma Alvarado, Daniel. 2011. *Ladrones. Historia Social y Cultural del Robo en Chile, 1870–1920.* Santiago: LOM.

Paoline, Eugene A., III, William Terrill, and Michael T. Rossler. 2015. "Higher Education, College Degree Major, and Police Occupational Attitudes." *Journal of Criminal Justice Education* 26, no. 1: 49–73.

Parada Cortes, Teresa. 2014. Chief of Transparency Unit, Veracruz, Mexico. Personal correspondence with author, February 11, 2014.

Pardo, Rafael. 2013. Former minister of labor and former minister of defense (1990–1994), Bogotá, Colombia. Interview with author, May 17, 2013.

Paredes, Carlos Sixirei. 2011. *La Violencia en Colombia (1990–2002): Antecedentes y Desarrollo Histórico.* Servizo de Publicacions da Universidade de Vigo.

Pérez Ricart, Carlos A. 2020. "Taking the War on Drugs Down South: The Drug Enforcement Administration in Mexico (1973–1980)." *Social History of Alcohol and Drugs* 34, no. 1: 82–113.

Peruzzotti, Enrique, and Catalina Smulovitz, eds. 2006. *Enforcing the Rule of Law: Social Accountability in the New Latin American Democracies.* Pittsburgh: University of Pittsburgh Press.

Piñeda, Roberto. 1950. *La Policía, Doctrinea, Historia, Legislación.* Bogotá: Consejo de Bogotá.

Pion-Berlin, David. 2010. "Neither Military nor Police: Facing Heterodox Security Challengers and Filling the Security Gap in Democratic Latin America." *Democracy and Security* 6, no. 2: 109–127.

Pion-Berlin, David, and Harold Trinkunas. 2011. "Latin America's Growing Security Gap." *Journal of Democracy* 22, no. 1: 39–53.

Pogarsky, Greg, and Alex R. Piquero. 2004. "Studying the Reach of Deterrence: Can Deterrence Theory Help Explain Police Misconduct?" *Journal of Criminal Justice* 32, no. 4: 371–386.

Pollitt, Christopher. 2005. "Decentralization." In *The Oxford Handbook of Public Management*, edited by Ewan Ferlie, Laurence E. Lynn Jr., and Christopher Pollitt. Oxford: Oxford University Press.

Potts, Lee W. 1982. "Police Professionalization: Elusive or Illusory?" *Criminal Justice Review* 7, no. 2: 51–57.

Poveda Montes, José. 2013. Colonel in National Police of Colombia and head of criminal investigation in Medellín (2001–2003), Bogotá, Colombia. Interview with author, March 3, 2013.

Prenzler, Tim, and Carol Ronken. 2001. "Models of Police Oversight: A Critique." *Policing and Society: An International Journal* 11, no. 2: 151–180.
Presidencia de la Republica. 2012. "Sexto Informe de Gobierno." *Gobierno de Los Estados Unidos Mexicanos.* http://calderon.presidencia.gob.mx.
Price, Barbara R. 1979. "Integrated Professionalism: A Model for Controlling Police Practices." *Journal of Police Science and Administration* 7: 93–97.
Prieto, Carlos M. 1996. "Orden Publico en el Chile del Siglo XX: Trayectoria de una Policía Militarizada." In *Justicia en la Calle. Ensayos Sobre la Policía en América Latina,* edited by Peter Waldmann. Augsburg, Germany: ISLA Universitat Augsburg.
Procuraduría General de la República. 2006. "La Segunda Guerra Mundial Prefigura el Escenario que Nos Ocupa." Informe Histórico de la Sociedad Mexicana. http://nsarchive.gwu.edu/NSAEBB/NSAEBB209/informe/tema02.pdf.
Puentes, Mauricio. 2013. "Policía y Control Social en Bogotá: Fundando la Autoridad y el Orden Como Política Nacional (1885–1899)." *Historia, Archivista y Redes de Investigación.*
Pulido, Claudia. 2013. Lieutenant colonel in National Police of Colombia and chief of Observatory for Integrity, Work, Police Ethics, and Human Rights, Bogotá, Colombia. Interview with author, March 18, 2013.
Punch, Maurice. 1989. "Researching Police Deviance: A Personal Encounter with the Limitations and Liabilities of Field-Work." *British Journal of Sociology* 40, no. 2: 177–204.
Quah, Jon S. T. 2006. "Preventing Police Corruption in Singapore: The Role of Recruitment, Training and Socialisation." *Asia Pacific Journal of Public Administration* 28, no. 1: 59–75.
Ramírez, Juan Lozano. 2011. "Situación salarial y prestacional de los miembros de la Fuerza Pública." http://leyes.senado.gov.co/proyectos/images/documentos/Textos%20Radicados/Ponencias/2011/gaceta_467.pdf.
Ramos, Jorge, and María de la Luz Gonzales. 2010. "Calderon Firma Propuesta de Policía Unica." *El Universal,* October 6, 2010. http://www.eluniversal.com.mx/notas/714143.html.
La Razon. 2019. "667 Negocios Saqueados y Quemados en Protestas."
La Reforma. 2012. "Exhiben Corrupcíon en Caso Moreira." October 18, 2012.
La Reforma. 2013. "Tienen Autodefensas en 68 Municipios." March 12, 2013
Renda, Mary A. 2001. *Taking Haiti: Military Occupation and the Culture of US Imperialism, 1915–1940.* Durham: University of North Carolina Press.
Republic of Chile. 1891. "Ley de Comuna Autónoma." http://www.leychile.cl.
Republic of Chile. 1904. Supreme Decree N. 3901 of 1904. http://www.leychile.cl.
Republic of Chile. 1906. *Recopilación de Leyes por Orden Numérico.* El Consejo de Chile.
Republic of Chile. 1919. "Ley 3547." September 10, 1919. http://www.leychile.cl.
Republic of Chile. 1924. "Decreto Supremo: Reglamento Orgánico de la Ley 4052." http://www.leychile.
Republic of Chile. 1925. "Decreto Ley 283." http://www.leychile.cl.
Republic of Chile. 1927. "Decreto Fuerza Ley 2484." http://www.leychile.cl.
Republic of Chile. 1974. "Decreto Ley 444." http://www.divdecar.interior.gob.cl.
Republic of Chile. 2011. "Gobierno promulgó ley que crea el nuevo Ministerio del Interior y Seguridad Pública." https://www.interior.gob.cl/sitio-2010-2014/n2196_10-02-2011.html.
Republic of Colombia. 1885. "Decreto 819 de 1885." http://oasportal.policia.gov.co.
Republic of Colombia. 1930. "Ley 72 de 1930." http://oasportal.policia.gov.co.
Republic of Colombia. 1953. "Decreto 1814 de 1953." http://oasportal.policia.gov.co.
Republic of Colombia. 1990. "Decreto 1213 de 1990." http://oasportal.policia.gov.co.
Republic of Colombia. 1993. "Decreto 62 de 1993." http://www.alcaldiabogota.gov.
Republic of Colombia. 1994. "Decreto 353 de 1994." http://www.secretariasenado.gov.co.

Republic of Colombia. 2012. "Decreto 0842 de 2012." https://www.funcionpublica.gov
   .co/eva/gestornormativo/norma.php?i=64631.
Reyes, José Juan. 2012. "Policía Nacional Tendrá Disciplina Militar: Vazquez Mota." *El
   Economista*, April 13, 2012.
Ribando Seelke, Clare. 2005. *Gangs in Central America: CRS Report for Congress*.
   Washington, DC: Library of Congress.
Riccucci, Norma M., Gregg G. Van Ryzi, and Cecilia F. Lavena. 2014. "Representative
   Bureaucracy in Policing: Does It Increase Perceived Legitimacy?" *Journal of Pub-
   lic Administration Research and Theory* 24, no. 3): 537–551.
Rincón, Victor M. 2003. "La Violencia Política en Colombia y la Policía Nacional." In *His-
   torical Academy of Colombian Police*. Historical Book No. 9. https://oas.policia.gov
   .co/sites/default/files/publicaciones-institucionales/cuaderno-historico-edicion-9.pdf.
Ríos, Juan A. M. 1914. *Orijen y Desarollo de la Policía en Chile*. Concepción: Jose V.
   Soulodre Press.
Ripetti, Carlos. 2012. Retired sergeant major in Carabineros (active 1985–2011), Santiago, Chile. Interview with author, December 1, 2012.
Robledo, Marcos. 2012. Special foreign policy adviser to President Michelle Bachelet
   (2006–2010), adviser to the minister of defense (1998–2005), and sub-secretary of
   defense in Ministry of Defense, Santiago, Chile. Interview with author, October 26,
   2012.
Rodríguez García, Oscar Agustín. 2014. Head of the Unit of Public Engagement, Zacate-
   cas, Mexico. Personal correspondence with author, March 12, 2014.
Rodríguez Zapata, Amadeo. 1971. *Bosquejo Historiopolicial de Colombia*. Bogotá:
   Grupo Editorial Ibáñez.
Roich, Cynthia Fernandez. 2017. "Beyond the Police Reform (1999–2003)." In *Media
   and Crime in Argentina*, 159–181. London: Palgrave Macmillan.
Rubio, Mauricio. 1997. "Los Costos de la Violencia en Colombia." *Programa de Estu-
   dios Sobre Seguridad, Justicia y Violencia*. Universidad de Los Andes. Documento
   de Trabajo Nº 11. http://pdba.georgetown.edu.
Rueda Zacipa, Angel Horacio. 2013. Lieutenant colonel in National Police of Colombia
   and vice rector of education and distance learning, National Police of Colombia,
   Bogotá, Colombia. Personal correspondence with author, March 14, 2013.
Ruiz, Juan Carlos. 2009. "El Cambio en la Policía Colombiana: Una Vision Neo-Institu-
   cional." *Memoirs of the First International Congress on Police Sciences*. Bogotá,
   Colombia, October 28–30, 2009. Editorial Gente Nueva, Colombia.
Ruiz, Juan Carlos. 2013. Expert in public security and policing and professor at Rosario
   University, Bogotá, Colombia. Interview with author, March 14, 2013.
Sabet, Daniel. 2010. "Police Reform in Mexico: Advances and Persistent Obstacles." In
   *Shared Responsibility: US–Mexico Policy Options for Confronting Organized
   Crime*, edited by Eric L. Olson, David A. Shirk, and Andrew Selee. Washington,
   DC: Wilson Center.
Salgado, Juan. 2014. Professor of economics at Center for Research and Teaching
   (CIDE), Mexico City, Mexico. Interview with author, September 23, 2014.
Sanchez, Ruben, and Maria Eugenia Suarez de Garay. 2014. *Alcozauca: Ser Policía
   Municipal en la Montana de Guerrero*. Mexico City: Instituto de Segurdad y
   Democracia.
Secretaria de Seguridad Pública. 2011. "Policía Federal." http://ssp.mx.
Secretaria de Seguridad Pública Municipal de Tijuana. 2015. "Incorporate." http://
   policia.azurewebsites.net.
Sellbom, Martin, Gary L. Fischler, and Yossef S. Ben-Porath. 2007. "Identifying MMPI-
   2 Predictors of Police Officer Integrity and Misconduct." *Criminal Justice and
   Behavior* 34, no. 8: 985–1004.
Serrano, José. 1994. *Policía Nacional: Una Nueva Era*. Bogotá: Prolibros Ltda.
Sherman, Lawrence W. 1978. *Controlling Police Corruption: The Effects of Reform Poli-
   cies*. Summary Report. Washington, DC : US Department of Justice.

El Siglo de Torreon. 2015. "Bajan Requisitos para Ingresar a Policía Municipal." February 16, 2015.

Silva, Andrea, and Diego Esparza. 2021. "Explaining the American Crisis of Policing: Media, Malfeasance, and Racial Prejudice." *Social Science Quarterly.* Published online September 3, 2021. https://doi.org/10.1111/ssqu.13061.

Silva, Andrea, Diego Esparza, Valerie Martinez-Ebers, and Regina Branton. 2020. "Perceived Police Performance, Racial Experiences, and Trust in Local Government." *Politics, Groups, and Identities.* Published online October 28, 2020. https://doi.org/10.1080/21565503.2020.1824122.

Sinclair, G., and C. A. Williams. 2007. "'Home and Away': The Cross-Fertilisation Between 'Colonial' and 'British' Policing, 1921–85." *Journal of Imperial and Commonwealth History* 35, no. 2: 221–238.

Sklansky, David A. 2011. "The Persistent Pull of Police Professionalism." Paper from Harvard Kennedy School Program in Criminal Justice Policy and Management. National Institute of Justice, March 1, 2011. https://nij.ojp.gov/library/publications/persistent-pull-police-professionalism.

Sklansky, David A. 2013. *The Promise and the Perils of Police Professionalism.* London: Routledge.

Skogan, Wesley G. 2006. "The Promise of Community Policing." In *Police Innovation: Contrasting Perspectives,* edited by David Weisburd and Anthony A. Braga. New York: Cambridge University Press.

Skogan, Wesley G., Maarten Van Craen, and Cari Hennessy. 2015. "Training Police for Procedural Justice." *Journal of Experimental Criminology* 11, no. 3: 319–334.

Skolnick, Jerome H., and David H. Bayley. 1988. *The New Blue Line: Police Innovation in Six American Cities.* New York: Simon & Schuster.

Slater, Harold R., and Martin Reiser. 1988. "A Comparative Study of Factors Influencing Police Recruitment." *Journal of Police Science and Administration* 16, no. 3: 168–176.

Soares, Rodrigo R., and Joana Naritomi. 2007. "Confronting Crime and Violence in Latin America: Crafting a Public Policy Agenda." In *Understanding High Crime Rates in Latin America: The Role of Social and Policy Factors.* Cambridge, MA: Instituto Fernando Henrique Cardoso, Harvard University.

Soto, Daniel. 2012. Major in Carabineros and lawyer in the Carabinero Department of Human Rights, Santiago, Chile. Interview with author, December 5, 2012.

Soule, Sarah, and Christian Davenport. 2009. "Velvet Glove, Iron Fist, or Even Hand? Protest Policing in the United States, 1960–1990." *Mobilization: An International Quarterly* 14, no. 1: 1–22.

Stamper, Norm. 2016. *To Protect and Serve: How to Fix America's Police.* New York: Bold Type Books.

State of Arkansas. 2021. "History: Commission on Law Enforcement Standards and Training." https://www.dps.arkansas.gov/law-enforcement/clest/about-clest/history/.

Steinmetz, Kevin F., Brian P. Schaefer, and Howard Henderson. 2017. "Wicked Overseers: American Policing and Colonialism." *Sociology of Race and Ethnicity* 3, no. 1: 68–81.

Suárez de Garay, María Eugenia. 2010. "Mexican Law Enforcement Culture: Testimonies from Police Behind Bars." In *Police and Public Security in Mexico,* edited by Robert A. Donnelly and David A. Shirk, 147–168. San Diego: University Readers.

Suárez de Garay, María Eugenia. 2014. Lead investigator, Institute for Security and Democracy, Mexico City, Mexico. Interview with author, September 10, 2014.

Sun, Ivan Y., Rong Hu, and Yuning Wu. 2012. "Social Capital, Political Participation, and Trust in the Police in Urban China." *Australian and New Zealand Journal of Criminology* 45, no. 1: 87–105.

Tamayo Cabello, Jorge. 2012. "The Modernization of the Police During Ibáñez's Dictatorship: Functions and Tasks Assigned to the Police at the Beginnings of the Twentieth Century." *Revista Divergencia,* no. 2: 125–134.

Tankebe, Justice. 2009. "Public Cooperation with the Police in Ghana: Does Procedural Fairness Matter?" *Criminology* 47, no. 4: 1265–1293.

Tankebe, Justice. 2010. "Public Confidence in the Police: Testing the Effects of Public Experiences of Police Corruption in Ghana." *British Journal of Criminology* 50, no. 2: 296–319.

Tankebe, Justice. 2013. "Viewing Things Differently: The Dimensions of Public Perceptions of Police Legitimacy." *Criminology* 51, no. 1: 103–135.

Taylor, Brian D. 2011. *State Building in Putin's Russia: Policing and Coercion After Communism*. New York: Cambridge University Press.

Theobald, Nick A., and Donald P. Haider-Markel. 2009. "Race, Bureaucracy, and Symbolic Representation: Interactions Between Citizens and Police." *Journal of Public Administration Research and Theory* 19, no. 2: 409–426.

Thomassen, Gunnar. 2013. "Corruption and Trust in the Police: A Cross-Country Study." *European Journal of Policing Studies* 1, no. 2: 152–168.

Tiebout, Charles M. 1956. "A Pure Theory of Local Expenditures." *Journal of Political Economy* 64, no. 5: 416–424.

El Tiempo. 1994. "Reajustan Sueldos de las Fuerzas Armadas." January 13, 1994.

Transparency International. 2017. "Corruption Perceptions Index." https://www.transparency .org/en/gcb/global/global-corruption-barometer-2017/press-and-downloads.

Transparency Request RSIP No. 18433. 2012. Republic of Chile. Correspondence received by author, November 20, 2012.

Treisman, Daniel. 2000. "The Causes of Corruption: A Cross-National Study." *Journal of Public Economics* 76:399–457.

Tuozzo, Celina. 1999. *El Estado Policial en Chile: 1924–1931*. Buenos Aires: Ed. La Crujia.

Tyler, Tom R. 2003. "Procedural Justice, Legitimacy, and the Effective Rule of Law." *Crime and Justice* 30:283–357.

Tyler, Tom R., and Yuen J. Huo. 2002. *Trust in the Law: Encouraging Public Cooperation with the Police and Courts*. New York: Russell Sage Foundation.

Uildriks, Niels. 2010. *Mexico's Unrule of Law: Implementing Human Rights in Police and Judicial Reform Under Democratization*. Lanham, MD: Lexington Books.

Ungar, Mark. 2011. *Policing Democracy: Overcoming Obstacles to Citizen Security in Latin America*. Washington, DC: Woodrow Wilson Center Press.

United Nations Office on Drugs and Crime. 2006. "Colombia 2006." http://www .unodc.org.

United Nations Office on Drugs and Crime. 2010–2013. "Homicide Rates." https:// data.unodc.org.

United Nations. 2019. "Los Carabineros y Militares en Chile Cometieron Graves Violaciones de Derechos Humanos." https://news.un.org.

El Universal. 2013. "Pablo Escobar Mato a 400 Policías en Enero del 90." *El Universal*, December 2, 2013.

Unnamed reporter 3. 2012. Reporter at a major newspaper in Chile (requested anonymity due to professional relationship with Carabineros), Santiago, Chile. Interview with author, November 20, 2012.

Urquieta, Claudia. 2019. "Carabineros Informa 947 Efectivos Heridos Sin Entregar Detalles de las Lesiones de 786." CIPER, October 31, 2019. https://ciperchile.cl.

US Department of State. 2015. Overseas Security Advisory Council. https://www.osac.gov.

Vanderwood, Paul J. 1970. "*Rurales*: Mexico's Rural Police Force, 1861–1914." PhD diss., University of Texas, Austin.

Van de Ven, Andrew H. 2007. *Engaged Scholarship: A Guide for Organizational and Social Research*. New York: Oxford University Press.

Varela, Ambar. 2014. Director of public policy evaluations, Contraloria Ciudadana, consultant on reviewing implementation of federal grants for public security in various municipal police forces in Mexico, Mexico City, Mexico. Interview with author, September 3, 2014.

Vargas, Alejo. 2013. Expert in civil-military relations and security studies, professor at National University of Colombia, Bogotá, Colombia. Interview with author, February 20, 2013.

Vargas, Ernesto López Portillo. 2005. "Mexico." In *World Police Encyclopedia*, edited by Dilip K. Das and Michael J. Palmiotto, 555. New York: Routledge.

Vargas Ramírez, Emiliana. 2013. Lieutenant colonel in National Police of Colombia and vice rector for academic affairs, National Police of Colombia, Bogotá, Colombia. Personal correspondence with author, March 20, 2013.

Vásquez, María Del Rosario. 2014. "Anticlericalismo y Primera Violencia en la Diocesis de Nueva Pamplona, Colombia (1930–1934): Clero, Políticos, Jueces y Policía." *Hispania Sacra, LXVI*, 133 (Enero–Junio): 263–285.

Vera, Robustiano. 1899. *Estudios Sobre Policía*. Santiago de Chile: Mejia Press.

Vicuña Mackenna, Benjamin. 1875. *La Policía de Seguridad en las Grandes Ciudades Modernas: Londres, Paris, Nueva York, Santiago*. Santiago: Imprenta de La Republica.

Vidal, Ximena. 2012. Parliamentary deputy from District 25, Santiago, Chile. Interview with author, December 13, 2012.

Villaveces, Andrés. 2001. "A Comparative Statistical Note on Homicide Rates in Colombia." In *Violence in Colombia 1990–2000: Waging War and Negotiating Peace*, edited by Charles W. Bergquist, Ricardo Peñaranda, and Gonzalo Sánchez G. Wilmington, DE: Scholarly Resources.

Vinasco Rendón, Diana C. 2013. Second lieutenant in National Police of Colombia and chief of the Educative Service Group, National Police of Colombia, Bogotá, Colombia. Personal correspondence with author, April 13, 2013.

Weber, Max. 2019. *Economy and Society*. Cambridge, MA: Harvard University Press.

Weber, Max, and Stephen Kalberg. 2013. *The Protestant Ethic and the Spirit of Capitalism*. London: Routledge.

White, Michael D., and Gipsy Escobar. 2008. "Making Good Cops in the Twenty-First Century: Emerging Issues for the Effective Recruitment, Selection and Training of Police in the United States and Abroad." *International Review of Law, Computers & Technology* 22, no. 1–2: 119–134.

Wiatrowski, Michael D., and Jack A. Goldstone. 2010. "The Ballot and the Badge: Democratic Policing." *Journal of Democracy* 21, no. 2: 79–92.

Williams Hubert. 2002. "Core Factors of Police Corruption Across the World." *Forum on Crime and Society* 2, no. 1: 85–99.

Wolf, Sonja. 2009. "Subverting Democracy: Elite Rule and the Limits to Political Participation in Post-War El Salvador." *Journal of Latin American Studies* 41, no. 3: 429–465.

Wolfe, Scott E., and Alex R. Piquero. 2011. "Organizational Justice and Police Misconduct." *Criminal Justice and Behavior* 38, no. 4: 332–353.

World Justice Project. 2019. "Rule of Law Index 2019." https://worldjusticeproject.org.

Zalaquett, Jorge. 2012. Professor of law at the University of Chile, expert on human rights, commissioner of the Truth and Reconciliation Commission, Santiago, Chile. Interview with author, December 23, 2012.

Zaverucha, Jorge. 2000. "Fragile Democracy and the Militarization of Public Safety in Brazil." *Latin American Perspectives* 27, no. 3: 8–31.

Zuñiga, Liza. 2012. Civilian staff in Department of Criminal Analysis, Carabineros de Chile, and political scientist with expertise in public security, Santiago, Chile. Interview with author, November 23, 2012.

Index

abuse, 88–91
Acapulco, Mexico, 109
accountability, 128; in democracy, 3–4; reduction in, 7–8
AGI. *See* Federal Investigation Agency
Aguascalientes, Mexico, 113
Allende, Salvador: coup against, 45–46; Pinochet, Carabineros de Chile, and, 44–48
AMLO. *See* López Obrador
Argentina, 13, 23, 124
Arkansas House Bill 577 (United States, 1975), 136
assassinations, 88*fig*
authoritarianism, 2
autonomous centralized body, 3
Avenida Chile (Bogotá), 58

Bachelet, Michelle, 50–51
background check, 6, 9, 109
BACRIMS. *See* Bandas Criminales
Bandas Criminales (BACRIMS), 19
banditry, 62; in Chile, 19, 28, 30–31, 33, 37–38, 41; in Colombia, 68
benefits: expanded for Carabinero Regiment, 40; of federal police in Mexico, 115; improvement of, 139; militarization providing, 41; for municipal police, 107–108; of PNC, 85; reform of police, 80–83; Section of Social Welfare for the Police Forces of Colombia, 75; state police welfare in Mexico, 113–114; for US police, 135–136
Benito Juárez scholarships, 120
Beverly Hills, California, 138
Biden, Joe, 91

the bite. *See la mordida*
Blanco, Griselda, 70–71
Bogotá, Colombia, 63–64, 73; car bombing in, 92; military club of, 75; violence in, 71; withdrawal of military police in, 72
Bogotazo (disaster), 71–72
Bolivia, 13–14
Brazil, 15
bribery, 98, 129, 129*fig*, 130*fig*, 140
Brigada de Policía d Santiago, 26
budgets, 32–33; municipal tax bases linked to, 31; 1983 increase in Chilean, 47
bureaucracy: hierarchy in, 110; Weber theory of, 12

cabeceras, 33, 36–37
cabinet ministry, 3
Calderón, Felipe, 102–103, 113, 121, 123–124, 144–145
Cali, Colombia, 16, 63, 73, 78–79
Calles, Plutarco Elías, 97–98
Carabineros Credit Union. *See* Mutualidad de Carabineros 2014
Carabineros de Chile, 19, 21, 23–24, 25; bribery in, 129; corruption in, 56–57; discharge of members of, 57; fusion of Policía Fiscal, communal police, and, 41; hierarchy of, 54–56; history of, 42–44; Pinochet, Allende, and, 44–48; police misconduct and, 60–61, 134; professionalism of, 44–45; protest and, 57–61; recruitment in, 53; repression by, 47; salary of, 43–44; training and oversight of the, 42, 56; 21st century in, 51–57; welfare of, 51–53

167

Rapid Deployment Special Forces, 45
recruitment, 6, 8, 27, 31–32; in Carabineros de
   Chile, 53; in Colombia, 85; within
   democracy, 128; higher standards for, 139;
   Mexican state police training and, 114; in
   Mexico, 111; partisanship motivating, 67–
   68; in SPOR, 33–34; training and, in
   Mexican municipal police, 108–109
reform: of AMLO, 120–122; centralization
   and, 137–138; inequality *vs.*, 94; of police
   welfare regimes, 80–83
regime, 12; anti-regime mobilizations in
   Chile, 46–47; change of, in Chile, 25;
   police misconduct linked to, 13
religion, 12, 13
remuneration, 6, 8, 128
Renovación Nacional, 60
repression, 41, 44–45, 68; by Carabineros de
   Chile, 47; of PRI, 98
Republic of Colombia, 65. *See also* Colombia
Revolution in Liberty, 45
Revolutionary Armed Forces of Colombia
   (FARC), 16, 76, 91–94
Revolutionary Democratic Party (PRD), 101
Rio de Janeiro, Brazil, 15
Roman Catholicism, 13, 65, 130
rural police. *See* police, rural
Rurales period, in Mexico, 18

salary: of Carabineros de Chile, 43–44; of
   Mexican federal police, 115; of Mexican
   municipal police, 107–108; Mexican state
   police welfare benefits, 113–114; of PNC,
   80–83
Salinas de Gortari, Carlos, 100
Santander, 70–71
Santiago, Chile, 26, 29, 52, 57–61
Santiago Fiscal Police, 34, 35, 37
Santiago Police Department (SPD), 32–37
Santiago Police Organization Regulation
   (SPOR), 33–34
São Paolo, Brazil, 15
secret police, 47
Section of Social Welfare for the Police
   Forces of Colombia (1953), 75
Serenos 25–26, 64–65
Serpico investigation, 134
Serrano-Vigilante system, 24
shadow officers, 106–107
Sheep-Wolf-Dog narrative, 125–145
El Siglo (newspaper), 72
Social Security and Welfare of the Police
   (INSSPONAL), 82–83
SPD. *See* Santiago Police Department
SPOR. *See* Santiago Police Organization
   Regulation
State Command model, 137

State Commission model, 138
state police. *See* police, state
State Preventative Police, 103, 113–114
strongman. *See* caudillo
Superior Commissioned Personnel (PNS), 53–
   54
Supreme Decree 255 (Chile, 1907), 38
Supreme Decree 3901 (Chile, 1904), 35
Supreme Decree 4540 (Chile, 1932), 42

Tarapacá, Chile, 30
El Tarapaca (newspaper), 30
El Tiempo (newspaper), 73
training, 6, 8; extension of training process,
   139–140; improvements in, 85; oversight
   and, of the Carabineros de Chile, 42, 56;
   recruitment and, in Mexican municipal
   police, 108–109; in United States, 136
Travels with Charley (Steinbeck), 1
Trujillo, Colombia, 72

UNIPEP. *See* Police Unit for the Construction
   of Peace
United Fruit Company, 68
United States, 7; benefits for US police, 135–
   136; citizen trust in, 135; corruption in,
   135; Latin America as model for US
   policing, 134–137; police misconduct in,
   134–135; professionalism in, 135–136;
   training in, 136
Uribe, Álvaro, 16, 91
Uruguay, 13–14
US Mission for Police Reform in Colombia
   (1963), 76

Venezuela, 13
Vigilantes, 25–26
La Violencia, 76–77
violence, 21; in Bogotá, 71; criminality and,
   145; Mexico history of, 17–18; police
   misconduct influenced by, 14–15, 16
Violent Crime Control and Law Enforcement
   Act (United States, 1994), 136–137
voter fraud, 68

wages, 39–40
war, dirty, 98–99
Weber, Max, 12, 125, 143, 145
welfare, 6, 8; of Carabineros de Chile, 51–53;
   improvement of police, 48–49, 95; for
   Mexican municipal police, 107–108;
   reform of police, regimes, 80–83; reforms
   in development, oversight, and, 78–87;
   Section of Social Welfare for the Police
   Forces of Colombia, 75; underfunding of
   oversight, development, and, 77

About the Book

Though police are supposed to serve and protect, they all too often rob and abuse. Why? And what can be done about it? That is the central puzzle addressed in this book.

Drawing on the disparate cases of Chile, Colombia, and Mexico, Diego Esparza analyzes why some countries' police forces are more corrupt than others and considers what policy initiatives can turn an abusive police force into one that works for its citizens. His findings, perhaps most notably, fundamentally challenge assumptions about the virtues of local control.

Diego Esparza is assistant professor of political science at the University of North Texas.